012 ICD-10-CM and ICD-10-PCS
'orkbook

ary Jo Bowie MS, BS, AAS, RHIA, RHIT
ail I. Smith MA, RHIA, CCS-P

DELMAR
CENGAGE Learning

2012 ICD-10-CM and ICD-10-PCS Workbook
Mary Jo Bowie and Gail I. Smith

Vice President, Careers & Computing: Dave Garza

Director of Learning Solutions: Matthew Kane

Acquisitions Editor: Rhonda Dearborn

Managing Editor: Marah Bellegarde

Product Manager: Lauren Whalen

Vice President, Marketing: Jennifer Baker

Marketing Director: Wendy E. Mapstone

Marketing Manager: Nancy Bradshaw

Marketing Coordinator: Piper Huntington

Production Manager: Andrew Crouth

Senior Art Director: Jack Pendleton

Content Project Management: PreMediaGlobal

Library of Congress Control Number: 2012937666

ISBN-13: 978-1-133-59193-1

ISBN-10: 1-133-59193-0

Delmar
5 Maxwell Drive
Clifton Park, NY 12065-2919
USA

Cengage Learning is a leading provider of customized learning solutions with office locations around the globe, including Singapore, the United Kingdom, Australia, Mexico, Brazil, and Japan. Locate your local office at: **international.cengage.com/region**

Cengage Learning products are represented in Canada by Nelson Education, Ltd.

To learn more about Delmar, visit **www.cengage.com/delmar**

Purchase any of our products at your local college store or at our preferred online store **www.cengagebrain.com**

Printed in the United States of America
1 2 3 4 5 6 7 16 15 14 13 12

Table of Contents

Appendices

Preface

The transition from ICD-9-CM to ICD-10-CM/PCS will require extensive education and training for thousands of coding/billing professionals in the United States. This workbook is structured to provide hands-on application exercises for all specialty content areas of ICD-10-CM and a comprehensive, unique step-by-step approach for building a code in ICD-10-PCS.

The workbook has been written for both the novice and experienced coder in any work setting. The new coder can use additional practice exercises to enhance his or her knowledge and skill in a variety of coding specialties. An experienced coder will be able to perform a self-assessment in the individual specialty areas of coding (ICD-10-CM or ICD-10-PCS) in order to continue to explore the characteristics of the classification systems. Many of the exercises have been selected to emphasize key elements of ICD-10-CM/PCS and/or application of coding guidelines.

Assessment Methods

The variety of assessment techniques provides coders with methods to further identify their strengths and weaknesses in medical terminology, clinical concepts, and anatomy and physiology. With over 400 coding exercises/case studies and 50+ supplemental learning components, this workbook provides a wide-ranging tool for any coding training program. In addition to coding exercises, the supplemental assessment methods include:

- Matching Exercises
- Check Your Clinical Knowledge Completion Questions
- Identification of Disease Process
- Identification of Anatomical Structures
- Applying Clinical Knowledge to Case Studies

Many of the distinctive characteristics of the workbook are outlined below.

Exercises

Each chapter has a variety of exercises that allow for a focused application of coding guidelines for that particular section. This chapter-by-chapter approach paves the way for "chunking" of content that can be easily referenced at a later date. The exercises highlight some of the most common diagnoses encountered in hospitals, physician offices, and alternative health care facilities.

New to This Edition

The workbook has been updated to include the latest ICD-10-CM and ICD-10-PCS code sets and guidelines. To allow users even more practice, each chapter now includes further coding assignments. In addition, the workbook contains more Operative Reports and decision tree examples for applying definitions of Root Operations.

Chapter 20, "Coding with ICD-10-PCS," has also been expanded with exercises focusing on each individual character. To aid users in their understanding of ICD-10-PCS, Appendix E, containing the ICD-10-PCS Guidelines, has been added to the workbook.

Transition from ICD-9-CM to ICD-10-CM

Students in education programs and experienced coders will be able to analyze the coding characteristics of ICD-9-CM compared to ICD-10-CM using a side-by-side approach in a chapter devoted to a compare-and-contrast activity. After implementation of ICD-10-CM/PCS, coders will still need to retrieve and analyze data from legacy systems that used ICD-9-CM. A total of 50 coding exercises allow for detailed examination of both systems.

Coding with ICD-10-PCS

The procedure coding system (PCS) chapter contains exercises highlighting several of the key elements for "building a code" using the new classification system. Emphasis will be placed on differentiating between root operations, body parts, approaches, devices, and qualifiers. Appendix C of the workbook provides a comprehensive list of the root operations and their definitions.

Application of Official Coding Guidelines

A key component before final selection of any code assignment is application of coding guidelines. Chapter 21 is dedicated to using case studies to emphasize the new ICD-10-CM/PCS *Official Guidelines for Coding and Reporting*.

Coding Case Studies

Chapter 22 permits coding professionals to integrate and apply all of their skills and knowledge to real-world case studies. The abstracts from health record documentation provide the entire story and permit a comprehensive review of the link between documentation and coding.

Computer-Assisted Coding

As technological systems become more advanced, computer-assisted coding will become a reality in the near future. Chapter 23 addresses the changes to workflow and abstracting key elements of documentation to support coding decisions. This last chapter permits coders to put all the pieces together to justify ICD-10-CM/PCS coding decisions in a simulated computer-assisted coding environment.

Detailed Answer Keys

All of the answers to the support questions (e.g., Check Your Clinical Knowledge) are provided in Appendix A of the workbook. In addition, half of the answers to the coding exercises are contained in Appendix A. At the request of faculty from training and education programs, the other half of the answers is only released to educators through online access to resources.

The majority of the chapters in the workbook provide detailed answer keys to assist coders with the methodology of using the Alphabetic Index, Table of Neoplasms, Table of Drugs and Chemicals, and the Tabular List.

Instructor Resources at the Instructor Companion Site

All instructor resources can be accessed at www.cengagebrain.com to create a unique user login. Contact your sales representative for more information. Online instructor resources at the Instructor Companion site are password-protected and include the following:

- Complete answer key.
- Revisions to workbook due to coding changes as they become available.

ICD-10-CM/PCS Implementation Timeline

As we go to press the timeline for implementation of ICD-10-CM/PCS is under review with a possible delay until October 1, 2014. ICD-10-CM, including the *ICD-10-CM Official Guidelines for Coding and Reporting,* will replace the ICD-9-CM for all health care settings for diagnosis reporting with dates of service, or dates of discharge for inpatients, that occur on or after October 1, 2014. The Centers for Medicare & Medicaid Services (CMS) has stated that there will be no grace periods or delays.

ICD-10-PCS procedure codes will be required for hospital claims for inpatient hospital procedures only; however, facilities may elect to capture the codes for internal data analysis. ICD-10-PCS will not be used on physician claims, even those for inpatient visits. CPT and HCPCS will continue to be used for physician and ambulatory services including physician visits to inpatients. The following provides a visual snapshot of implementation dates by types of services:

October 1, 2014, Implementation Plan for Reporting Services

Physicians	• ICD-10-CM for diagnoses • CPT/HCPCS for procedures and services
Ambulatory	• ICD-10-CM for diagnoses • CPT/HCPCS for procedures and services
Inpatients	• ICD-10-CM for diagnoses • ICD-10-PCS for inpatient procedures

Bowman S, Brooks P. Preparing for ICD-10 Implementation in 2011 National Provider Teleconference

Annual updates for each system (ICD-10-CM and ICD-10-PCS) are posted on the CMS website.

Partial Code Freeze

The annual updates to the coding systems make transition planning difficult for vendors, system administrators, third-party payers, and educators who must prepare in advance of the October 1, 2014, implementation date. For that reason, CMS has published the following schedule for freezing the code sets:

Date	Freeze Initiative
October 1, 2011	Last regular annual updates to both ICD-9-CM and ICD-10-CM
October 1, 2012	Limited code updates to both ICD-9-CM and ICD-10-CM code sets. Updates will be focused only on new technology and new diseases
October 1, 2013	Limited code updates to ICD-10-CM to capture new technology and new diseases
October 1, 2013–October 1, 2014	No updates for ICD-9-CM
October 1, 2015	Regular updates to ICD-10-CM will begin

Transition Timeline

The planning and assessment phase of the transition to ICD-10-CM/PCS has begun for many organizations. The following is an overview of implementation guidelines that have been suggested by CMS with the understanding that the phases may vary depending on the type, size, and complexity of the organization:

Phase 1
Implementation plan
Present–June 2011

- Establish committee, goals, project plan
- Assess impact
- Workflow analysis
- Conduct gap analysis for coding professionals
- Assess training needs
- Assess quality of documentation
- ***Education: Familiar with structure and features***

Bowman S, Brooks P. Preparing for ICD-10 Implementation in 2011 National Provider Teleconference

Phase 2
Implementation preparation
January 2011–June 2013

- Complete tasks identified in impact assessment
- Refine project plan, timeline, and budget if needed
- ***Begin education to users***

Bowman S, Brooks P. Preparing for ICD-10 Implementation in 2011 National Provider Teleconference

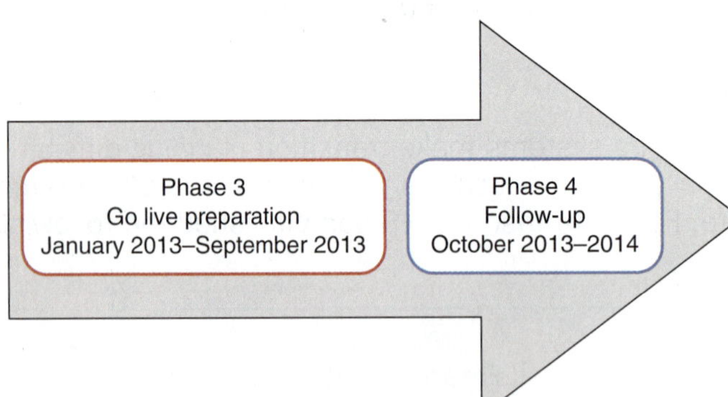

Bowman S, Brooks P. Preparing for ICD-10 Implementation in 2011 National Provider Teleconference

Education and Training

Although education to users should begin prior to 2012, experts suggest that *intensive* coder training should be conducted 6 to 9 months prior to implementation. For experienced coders, a 2-day training session will likely be sufficient.

About the Authors

Mary Jo Bowie, MS, BS, AAS, RHIA, RHIT

Mary Jo has worked in the health information field for over 30 years as a consultant, HIM director, and college instructor. She is owner of Health Information Professional Services in Binghamton, New York, and an instructor, in the health information technology program, at Broome Community College, Binghamton, New York. Mary Jo is an active member of the American Health Information Management Association. She has served the New York State Health Information Management Association as education director and on the board of directors, 1989–1991; Ambulatory Care Coding Guidelines (ACGC) Committee, 1995–2001; and chairperson, ACGC Committee, 1993–1995. She was the American Health Information Management Association nominee for New York State for National Award for Literary Contribution to Profession, 1993 and 1994. At the collegiate level, teaching both in the classroom and in an Internet-based format, she has taught numerous health information technology and coding and reimbursement classes. Mary Jo has conducted professional coding workshops for coders as well as for physicians and clinical staff. Mary Jo is a coding trainer for the Cengage TEAM UP program that offers professional workshops to college faculty. She has conducted numerous workshops on ICD-10-CM and ICD-10-PCS. Ms. Bowie has completed the AHIMA train the trainer program for ICD-10-CM/PCS from AHIMA.

Gail I. Smith, MA, RHIA, CCS-P

Gail I. Smith is president of Gail I. Smith Consulting, LLC in Cincinnati, Ohio. Prior to starting a consulting business in 2011, Gail was an associate professor and director of the Health Information Management (HIM) program at the University of Cincinnati. Previously, she served as the director of the HIM program at Cincinnati State Technical and Community College for 18 years. Before a career in education, Smith held management positions in two Cincinnati hospitals. On a part-time basis, Gail has served as a coding consultant for over 20 years. Her projects include developing content for courses/workshops, delivering seminars, performing coding reviews, and mapping ICD-10-CM/PCS for database conversions.

Ms. Smith has authored several coding textbooks and is a national speaker and content expert on e-Learning and instructional design.

Gail has served as president of the Ohio Health Information Management Association and received the Professional Achievement Award in 1996 and Distinguished Member Award in 2005. Gail also served on the Board of Directors of the American Health Information Management Association from 2003 through 2006.

Ms. Smith received her bachelor's degree in HIM from The Ohio State University and her master's degree in education from the College of Mt. St. Joseph in Cincinnati, Ohio.

Acknowledgments

To my husband, Bill, who always supports me in all of my writing projects and everything I have done for the last 30 years. To my daughters, Sarah and Bethannie, and my parents, who encourage me to keep on going.

To the Cengage family, especially Rhonda Dearborn and Lauren Whalen, who guided the creation of the book.

To my technical reviewer, Patricia Griffin for her attention to detail and commitment to the project. You are a joy to work with!

—Mary Jo Bowie

To my technical reviewer, Lynn Kuehn, for her attention to detail.

I wish to acknowledge my husband, Mark, and daughter, Kristin, for their endless support and encouraging words.

—Gail Smith

Technical Reviewers

Patricia Griffin, RHIT
Health Information Coordinator
United Methodist Homes
Binghamton, NY

Lynn Kuehn, MS, RHIA, CCS-P, FAHIMA
President
Kuehn Consulting, LLC
Waukesha, WI

Reviewers

Marie T. Conde, MPA, RHIA, CCS, FAHIMA
HIT Program Director and Instructor
City College of San Francisco
San Francisco, CA

Rhoda Cooper, CPC, RMC, NCICS
Director of HIM
Piedmont Virginia Community College
Charlottesville, VA

Robin Douglas, AHIMA Certified ICD-10-CM/PCS Trainer and Ambassador
Healthcare Data Technology Instructor
Holmes Community College
Grenada, MS

Rashmi Gaonkar, MS
Professor
ASA College
Brooklyn, NY

Carrie Heinz, RHIT
Director of HIM
Rolette Community Care Center
Rolette, ND

Pat King, MA, BS, RHIA
Program Coordinator, MIS and Coding and Adjunct Faculty
Baker College of Auburn Hills
Auburn Hills, MI

Barbara Marchelletta, CMA (AAMA), CPC
Allied Health Program Director
Beal College
Bangor, ME

Jennifer V. Muncy, CPC
Instructor/Consultant/Owner of A Plus Billing and Consultants
Daymar College- LVS
Louisville, KY

CHAPTER 1

Infectious and Parasitic Diseases

Many conditions are reclassified in this chapter if an infectious disease causes the illness (e.g., *Salmonella* arthritis or gonococcal pneumonia). Sequencing guidance is provided with the phrase "code first." In addition to "code first," notes appear to direct the coder to "use additional code" to support consistency within the classification system.

Check Your Knowledge of Infectious Diseases

Match Column A with the appropriate term in Column B. Answers are located in Appendix A.

Column A	Column B
1. _____ bacterial organism	**a.** histoplasmosis
2. _____ viral infection	**b.** *Staphylococcus*
3. _____ fungal infection	**c.** malaria
4. _____ protozoal disease	**d.** herpes zoster

Check Your Clinical Knowledge

Answers located in Appendix A.

1. ____________________ is the most common infectious disease complication of both measles and influenza. (Pneumococcal pneumonia, *Clostridium difficile*)
2. ____________________ is the most frequently transmitted tick-borne disease. (Chagas disease, Lyme disease)
3. The ____________________ causes infectious mononucleosis. (Epstein-Barr virus, human papillomavirus)
4. ____________________ is the most common pathogen for pneumonia. (*Escherichia coli*, *Staphylococcus aureus*)
5. ____________________ is most commonly associated with AIDS. (Kaposi's sarcoma, Merkel cell carcinoma)

Coding

Assign ICD-10-CM codes to the following. Answers to exercises 1–10 are located in Appendix A, and the remaining answers are only provided to educators through the instructor online companion.

1. Western equine encephalitis ____________
2. Cytomegaloviral mononucleosis ____________
3. Chickenpox ____________
4. Meningitis due to Lyme disease ____________
5. Gonococcal conjunctivitis of the left eye ____________
6. Acute viral hepatitis C ____________
7. Shingles of the eyelids ____________
8. Toxic shock syndrome (*Staphylococcus* identified as organism) ____________
9. Severe gastroenteritis due to *Salmonella* food poisoning ____________
10. Vulvovaginitis due to chlamydial infection ____________
11. Plantar warts, left foot ____________
12. AIDS ____________
13. Genital herpes type 2 (HSV-2) on scrotum of male patient ____________
14. Whooping cough caused by bacterium *Bordetella pertussis* ____________
15. Toxic shock syndrome, confirmed to be *Staphylococcus aureus* ____________
16. West Nile virus with encephalitis ____________
17. Meningococcal endocarditis ____________
18. Athlete's foot ____________
19. Echoviral enteritis ____________
20. Sepsis due to *E. coli* ____________

21. Legionnaires' disease __________

22. Early congenital syphilitic pneumonia __________

23. Ringworm of nails, right hand __________

24. Tuberculous pneumothorax __________

25. Mumps complicated by hepatitis __________

CHAPTER

2 Neoplasms

The chapter on neoplasms contains codes for most benign and malignant neoplasms; however, certain benign neoplasms may be found in the other chapters. Coders must identify the morphology (behavior) of the neoplasm to appropriately classify as benign, in situ, malignant, or of uncertain behavior. The ICD-10-CM Neoplasm Table is located after the Alphabetic Index. Codes that appear with a dash (–) at the end (e.g., Neoplasm, auditory canal C44.2–) require verification in the Tabular List to complete the code assignment.

Check Your Knowledge of Neoplasms

Identify the following neoplasms as "B" for benign, "M" for malignant, or "U" for uncertain behavior. Locating the morphological term in the Alphabetic Index will assist with this exercise. Answers are located in Appendix A.

_____ **1.** Adenoma of prostate

_____ **2.** Infiltrating duct carcinoma of the breast

_____ **3.** Osteofibroma of the femur

_____ **4.** Endometroid adenoma (pathology report states borderline malignancy)

_____ **5.** Hepatic mesenchymal sarcoma

Check Your Clinical Knowledge

Circle one of the selections provided in parentheses to complete the following sentences. Answers are located in Appendix A.

1. The pathology report states that the patient has carcinoma in situ of the cervix. This morphology indicates that the cancer cells have _________. (spread beyond the borders, not invaded the surrounding tissues)

2. _________ is most often identified as skin cancer. (Melanoma, Mesothelioma)

3. A uterine leiomyoma is commonly known as a _________. (fibroid, cystic lesion)

4. Condylomas are commonly known as _________. (plantar warts, genital warts)

5. An adenomatous polyp in the colon would be identified as a _________ tumor. (benign, malignant)

Coding

Assign ICD-10-CM codes to the following. Answers to exercises 1–10 are located in Appendix A, and the remaining answers are only provided to educators through the instructor online companion.

1. Myxofibrosarcoma of the neck ______________
2. Female patient was diagnosed with carcinoma of the lower-inner quadrant of the right breast ______________
3. Malignant melanoma of the skin of the cheek ______________
4. Carcinoma of the upper lobe of the right lung with metastasis to the bone (spinal column) ______________
5. Adenocarcinoma of the prostate ______________
6. Osteofibroma of the right femur ______________
7. Condyloma acuminatum of the penis ______________
8. Diffuse lymphoblastic lymphoma (of lymph nodes of left axilla and arm) ______________
9. Mixed glioma of the right optic nerve ______________
10. Malignant melanoma of forehead ______________
11. Benign adenomatous polyp of the descending colon ______________
12. Osteoblastoma of the left thumb ______________
13. Carcinoma of the anterior wall of the bladder ______________
14. Wilms tumor, left kidney ______________
15. Carcinoma of the colon with metastasis to the liver and lung (middle lobe) ______________
16. Merkel cell carcinoma of the nose ______________
17. Pleural mesothelioma, malignant ______________

18. Basal cell carcinoma of the left pinna ______________

19. Adenocarcinoma of the larynx (cancerous lesion overlapping several sites in the larynx) ______________

20. Transitional cell papilloma of the bladder ______________

21. Adenomatosis, pulmonary ______________

22. Granulocytic leukemia in remission ______________

23. Carcinoma in situ of colon ______________

24. Neoplasm of lingual tonsil, benign ______________

25. Melanocytic nevi of anal skin ______________

Diseases of the Blood and Blood-Forming Organs

CHAPTER

3

This short chapter includes blocks of codes for reporting anemia and other disorders of blood and blood-forming organs. Coders are cautioned to read notes that provide guidance for "code irst," "code also," and "use additional code" for this chapter.

> **Example: D61.82 Myelophthisis**
>
> Code also the underlying disorder, such as:
> malignant neoplasm of breast (C50.-)
> tuberculosis (A15.-)

Check Your Clinical Knowledge

Match the following clinical description with the diagnosis that would best support the findings. Answers are located in Appendix A.

Clinical Description	Diagnosis
1. _____ 34-year-old man experiences excessive bleeding after surgery, reports that he bruised easily.	**a.** sickle cell disease
2. _____ 5-year-old African American child reports abdominal pain and trouble breathing. Clinician notes delayed growth.	**b.** vitamin B deficiency
3. _____ 22-year-old woman, who is a vegetarian, reports chronic fatigue, generalized aching, and insomnia.	**c.** von Willebrand disease
4. _____ 5-year-old child is pale, tired, and irritable. Recently treated for digestive disorder. Reddish tint to urine.	**d.** Christmas disease (hemophilia B)
5. _____ Child experiences excessive bleeding following circumcision. Lab results reveal hereditary clotting disorder.	**e.** hemolytic uremic syndrome

Coding

Assign ICD-10-CM codes to the following. Answers to exercises 1–5 are located in Appendix A, and the remaining answers are only provided to educators through the instructor online companion.

1. Posttraumatic cyst of the spleen ______
2. Christmas disease (hemophilia B) ______
3. Normocytic chronic blood loss anemia ______
4. Vitamin B12 deficiency anemia—vegan anemia ______
5. Coagulation disorder, factor X ______
6. Alpha thalassemia trait ______
7. Congenital neutropenia with fever ______
8. Abnormal hemoglobin ______
9. Sickle cell anemia, Hb-SE with crisis and acute chest syndrome ______
10. von Willebrand disease ______
11. Iron deficiency anemia ______
12. G6PD deficiency anemia ______
13. Hemophilia A ______
14. Vascular purpura ______
15. Basophilic leukopenia ______

Endocrine, Nutritional, and Metabolic Diseases

CHAPTER 4

This chapter is dominated by codes for diseases associated with diabetes mellitus. The combination codes identify the type of diabetes, the body system affected, and the complications affecting that body system.

> Example: E10.331 Type 1 diabetes mellitus with moderate nonproliferative diabetic retinopathy with macular edema

Even though the combination codes thoroughly describe the conditions, occasionally a note will appear that instructs the coder to use an additional code (e.g., use *additional code to identify stage of chronic kidney disease*) or "code first" such as in the following example.

> Example: E66.1 Drug-induced obesity
> Code first (T36-T50) to identify the drug

Check Your Clinical Knowledge: Case Studies

Match the following clinical descriptions in the case studies with the diagnosis that would best support the findings. Answers are located in Appendix A.

Case Study #1

HISTORY: This 52-year-old man complains of polyuria and polydipsia. He reports that he has gained weight over the years but more recently has been losing weight even though his appetite is the same.

PHYSICAL EXAMINATION: Hypertensive male (BP 180/90) who is obese.

LABORATORY FINDINGS: Fasting plasma glucose 168 mg/dL. Urinalysis: protein and glucose present.

DISEASE MANAGEMENT: Nutritionist will discuss lifestyle changes and dietary modification program. Glucotrol prescribed.

This profile would best support which of the following diagnoses? ____________

a. Type 1 diabetes mellitus

b. Type 2 diabetes mellitus

c. Graves disease

d. Hypothyroidism

Case Study #2

HISTORY: A 35-year-old woman reports palpitations, frequent bouts of anxiety, profuse sweating, and the inability to concentrate for the past couple of months.

PHYSICAL EXAMINATION: Low-grade fever with tachycardia. Thyroid gland is enlarged without tenderness. Papules noted over the shins.

LABORATORY FINDINGS: Mild leukocytosis with normal glucose. TSH: High.

IMAGING: Nuclear thyroid scan revealed diffuse uptake throughout the thyroid gland.

DISEASE MANAGEMENT: Propranolol for treatment of rapid heart rate and anxiety. Tapazole prescribed, twice daily.

This profile would best support which of the following diagnoses? ____________

a. Type 1 diabetes mellitus

b. Type 2 diabetes mellitus

c. Graves disease

d. Hypothyroidism

Case Study #3

HISTORY: This 19-year-old woman reports that she has been feeling tired and has excessive thirst and recent weight loss over the past several weeks.

PHYSICAL EXAMINATION: Vital signs: No fever; normal blood pressure, elevated R/R. Thin, lethargic female with poor skin turgor and fruity smell on breath.

LABORATORY FINDINGS: Hyponatremia, decreased bicarbonate, elevated glucose and ketonuria.

DISEASE MANAGEMENT: IV insulin, hydration, and correction of electrolyte imbalance. Treatment will include dietary education and regular glucose monitoring and periodic glycosylated hemoglobin (HbA1c).

This profile would best support which of the following diagnoses? ____________

a. Type 1 diabetes mellitus

b. Type 2 diabetes mellitus

c. Graves disease

d. Hypothyroidism

Case Study #4

Patient is a 58-year-old woman with Type 1 diabetes and peripheral neuropathy disease. Over the past 20 months, she has developed a (diabetic) skin ulcer of the left ankle. This type of skin ulcer would be classified as a: ____________.

a. Decubitus

b. Pressure ulcer

c. Nonpressure ulcer

Coding

Assign ICD-10-CM codes to the following. Answers to exercises 1–5 are located in Appendix A, and the remaining answers are only provided to educators through the instructor online companion.

1. Graves disease ____________

2. Hyperkalemia ____________

3. Vitamin B12 deficiency ____________

4. Diabetic cataract, Type 1 diabetic patient ____________

5. Type 1 diabetes with diabetic chronic skin ulcer of the left heel and midfoot *(breakdown of skin only)* ____________

6. Idiopathic hypoparathyroidism ____________

7. Type 1 diabetes mellitus with chronic stage III kidney disease as a result of the diabetes ____________

8. Hypocalcemia ____________

9. Elevated triglycerides and cholesterol levels ____________

10. Type 2 diabetes mellitus with proliferative diabetic retinopathy with macular edema ____________

11. Infarction of thyroid ____________

12. Deficiency of Vitamin C ____________

13. Dysfunction of pineal gland ____________

14. Postirradiation hypopituitarism ____________

15. Respiratory acidosis ____________

CHAPTER 5

Mental, Behavioral and Neurodevelopmental Disorders

This section was developed alongside the American Psychiatric Association's *Diagnostic & Statistical Manual of Mental Disorders* (*DSM*) which provides a common language and standard criteria for the classification of mental disorders in the United States. Although the coding system in *DSM* is designed to correspond with ICD, there are some differences. The two publications are not revised on the same schedule. The fifth edition of *DSM* is scheduled for publication in May 2013.

Check Your Clinical Knowledge

Match the following clinical description with the diagnosis that would best support the findings. Answers are located in Appendix A.

Clinical Description	**Diagnosis**
1. _____ inattentive, impulsive, and hyperactive	**a.** panic disorder
2. _____ loss of interest, no pleasure in life	**b.** schizophrenia
3. _____ episodes of palpitations, diaphoresis, fear of losing control	**c.** depression
4. _____ flashbacks, nightmares, intrusive memories	**d.** attention-deficit disorder
5. _____ delusional, hallucinations, disorganized thinking	**e.** posttraumatic stress syndrome

Coding

Assign ICD-10-CM codes to the following. Answers to exercises 1–5 are located in Appendix A, and the remaining answers are only provided to educators through the instructor online companion.

1. Anorexia nervosa—patient alternates between binge eating and purging ____________

2. Posttraumatic stress disorder, acute ____________

3. Complete auditory hallucinations ____________

4. Bipolar disorder (current episode of depression), mild ______________

5. Schizotypal personality disorder ______________

6. Chronic alcoholism, dependence with intoxication ______________

7. Early onset of Alzheimer disease with aggressive, combative behavior ______________

8. Alcohol abuse, patient is intoxicated ______________

9. Cocaine dependence, cocaine-induced anxiety disorder ______________

10. Manic-depressive disorder, recurrent, mild ______________

11. Depressive neurosis ______________

12. Fear of blood ______________

13. Anxiety hysteria ______________

14. Dissociative convulsions ______________

15. Psychogenic teeth grinding ______________

CHAPTER

6 Diseases of Nervous System (Eyes and Ears)

This chapter focuses on coding diseases of the nervous system as well as the eye/adnexa and ear and mastoid process. Neurologic diseases are disorders of the brain, spinal cord, and nerves throughout the body. Referencing the Tabular List of ICD-10-CM, this chapter of this workbook encompasses Chapters 6, 7, and 8 of ICD-10-CM. Exercises in this chapter will include common diseases from the following categories of codes:

G codes – Diseases of Nervous System
H codes (H00-H59) – Disorders of the Eye and Adnexa
H codes (H60-H95) – Diseases of the Ear and Mastoid Process

Check Your Clinical Knowledge

Circle one of the selections provided in parentheses to complete the following sentences. Answers are located in Appendix A.

1. The physician documents that the patient's middle ear infection was producing pus. Producing pus would be classified as __________. (exostosis, purulent).
2. The elderly patient's eyelids were drooping and causing problems with vision. The physician scheduled the patient for surgery with the diagnosis of __________. (dermatochalasis, dermatitis)
3. The physician noted that the patient's __________ pain was severe, constant, and not curable. (chronic, intractable)
4. The documentation states that the patient's eye (iris and ciliary body) is swollen and inflamed. The physician concludes with the diagnosis of __________. (iridocyclitis, synechiae)
5. The pathology report describes the __________ as a noncancerous growth of the conjunctiva (presbyopia, pterygium)

Coding

Assign ICD-10-CM codes to the following. Answers to exercises 1–10 are located in Appendix A, and the remaining answers are only provided to educators through the instructor online companion.

1. Left ulnar nerve entrapment at the elbow ____________
2. Left tympanic membrane perforation ____________
3. Intracranial meningioma ____________
4. Retinal detachment, left eye ____________
5. Carpal tunnel compression, left, severe ____________
6. Patient seen in emergency department as a result of an injury at work. Diagnosis: Foreign body of left eye—sliver of metal located in cornea ____________
7. Dermatochalasis of bilateral upper eyelids ____________
8. Acute otitis media, left, producing pus ____________
9. Classic migraine, intractable with aura ____________
10. Spastic hemiplegia of right (dominant) side ____________
11. Recurrent, acute iridocyclitis of both eyes ____________
12. Meningoencephalitis ____________
13. Recurrent pterygium, right eye ____________
14. Intraspinal extradural abscess ____________
15. Nasolacrimal duct obstruction due to stenosis, right eye ____________
16. Multiple perforations of tympanic membrane of both left and right ears ____________
17. Conductive hearing loss, right ear ____________
18. Episodic, tension headaches ____________
19. Streptococcal group A meningitis ____________
20. Macular hole, right eye ____________

21. Bilateral, hyphema ______________

22. Retinal hemorrhage of the right eye ______________

23. Abscess of the left external ear ______________

24. Ototoxic hearing loss ______________

25. Acute mastoiditis of the left ear ______________

Diseases of the Circulatory System

CHAPTER 7

The chapter on diseases of the circulatory system can be challenging because of the anatomy, the complexity of the guidelines, and the detailed documentation necessary for an accurate code assignment. A significant change between ICD-9-CM and ICD-10-CM occurred with the definition of acute myocardial infarction (AMI). In ICD-10-CM guidelines, an acute AMI is described as being 4 weeks or less in contrast to 8 weeks in ICD-9-CM.

Check Your Knowledge of Anatomy

Label Figure 7-1 correctly by using the following terms. Answers are located in Appendix A.

Aortic valve

Mitral valve

Pulmonic valve

Tricuspid valve

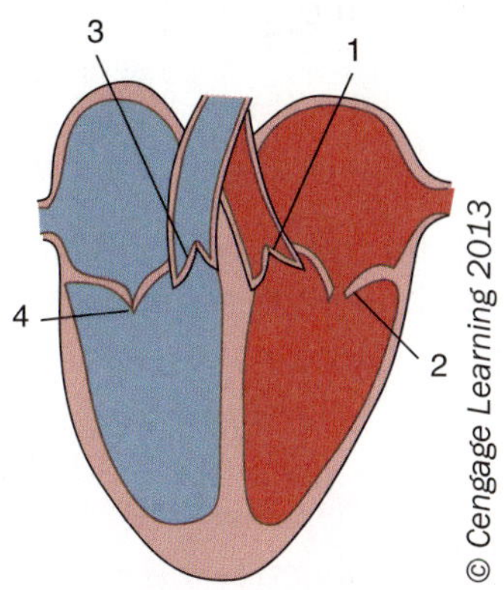

Figure 7-1

Check Your Clinical Knowledge

Circle one of the selections provided in parentheses to complete the following sentences. Answers are located in Appendix A.

1. The patient's blood pressure is 150/85. The number 85 is referred to as the ___________ pressure. (diastolic, systolic)
2. A(n) _______________ is a blood clot that forms in the vessel and *does not* move to another area of the body. (embolus, thrombus)

3. As a result of a stroke, the patient has difficulty swallowing and is ordered therapy for treatment of ________________. (dysphagia, dysphasia)
4. The documentation in the health records indicates that the patient has a rapid heart rate, which supports the diagnosis of ____________________. (brachycardia, tachycardia)
5. The surgeon documented that the _______________ artery in the neck was occluded and caused the stroke. (carotid, coronary)

Coding

Assign ICD-10-CM codes to the following. Answers to exercises 1–10 are located in Appendix A, and the remaining answers are only provided to educators through the instructor online companion.

1. Acute, diastolic congestive heart failure ______________
2. Rheumatic aortic valve stenosis ______________
3. Pulmonary embolism with acute cor pulmonale ______________
4. Acute posterolateral-transmural myocardial infarction (ST elevation [STEMI]) ______________
5. Hypertensive heart disease with chronic (systolic and diastolic) heart failure ______________
6. Cerebrovascular accident due to thrombosis of left vertebral artery ______________
7. Premature ventricular contractions ______________
8. Cerebrovascular infarction due to embolism of right middle cerebral artery ______________
9. Left bundle branch block ______________
10. Patient treated in the outpatient clinic for dysphagia (pharyngeal phase) as a residual from a previous intracerebral hemorrhage ______________
11. Chronic aortic regurgitation ______________
12. Patent ductus arteriosus ______________
13. Mitral valve prolapse syndrome ______________
14. Hypertensive heart disease with chronic stage 5 kidney disease ______________
15. Atrial paroxysmal tachycardia ______________
16. Residual hemiplegia, left nondominant side (patient suffered cerebral infarction several months earlier) ______________

17. 3 weeks after sustaining an STEMI of the inferior wall, the patient is seen in the physician's office for a follow-up appointment ______________

18. Patient currently treated as an inpatient for acute cerebrovascular infarction (thrombosis of left cerebellar artery) with resulting hemiplegia on the right dominant side ______________

19. Acute bacterial (*Staphylococcus aureus*) endocarditis ______________

20. Arteriosclerotic heart disease (ASHD) with angina; no history of bypass surgery ______________

21. Healed MI ______________

22. Silent myocardial ischemia ______________

23. Chronic cor pulmonale ______________

24. Giant cell myocarditis ______________

25. Sinoatrial block ______________

CHAPTER

8 Diseases of the Respiratory System

The respiratory system contains many combination codes because related conditions overlap in the disease process. The following are some of the unique characteristics of coding in this chapter.

Example 1

Disease	With Chronic Bronchitis	Without Chronic Bronchitis
Emphysema	J44.- Other chronic obstructive pulmonary disease	J43.- Emphysema

Example 2

Disease	With Chronic Obstructive Pulmonary Disease	Without Chronic Obstructive Pulmonary Disease
Asthma	J44.- Other chronic obstructive pulmonary disease **Coders are instructed to also code the type of asthma (J45.-) if applicable*	J45.- Asthma

Check Your Knowledge of Anatomy

Label Figure 8-1 correctly by using the following terms. Answers are located in Appendix A.

Bronchus	Nasal cavity
Pharynx	Mouth
Larynx	Right lung
Alveoli	Bronchiole
Trachea	

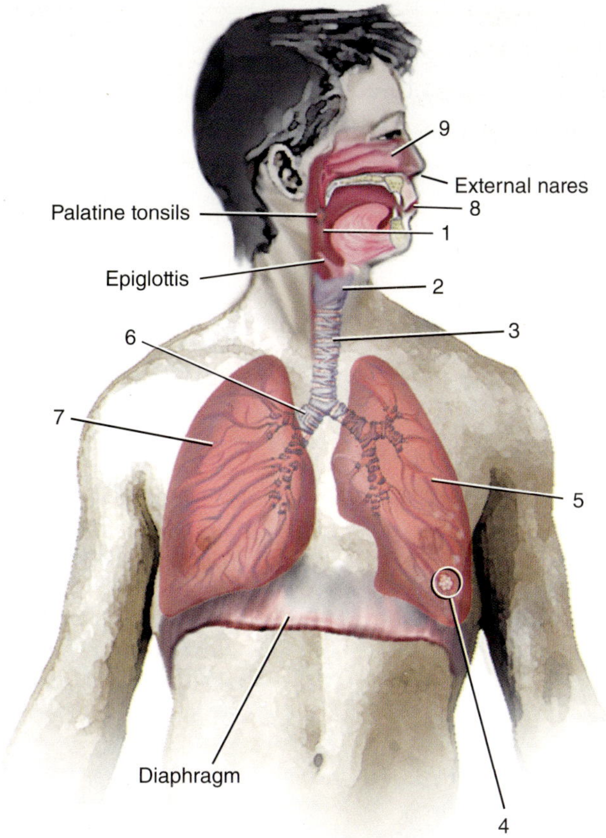

Figure 8-1

Check Your Clinical Knowledge

Circle one of the selections provided in parentheses to complete the following sentences. Answers are located in Appendix A.

1. The patient has a piece of candy stuck in his throat that is causing irritation. The physician documents examination of the _________________. (pharynx, larynx)
2. The physician documents that the patient has a buildup of fluid in the air sacs of the lungs. This documentation supports the diagnosis of _______________. (pneumothorax, pulmonary edema)
3. The physician documents that the patient has wheezing, shortness of breath, and chest tightness. It was noted that the family recently adopted a cat. The documentation supports the diagnosis of ________________. (asthma, bronchitis)
4. The physician notes that there is swelling and mucus buildup in the smallest air passages in the lungs, or the ________________. (bronchioles, pleura)
5. The physician documents that the patient has a bacterial pneumonia. The laboratory test revealed ________________ as the organism. (histoplasmosis, *Pseudomonas*)

Coding

Assign ICD-10-CM codes to the following. Answers to exercises 1–10 are located in Appendix A, and the remaining answers are only provided to educators through the instructor online companion.

1. Hypertrophic adenoids and tonsils ______________
2. Chronic pulmonary edema ______________
3. Obstructive rhinitis ______________
4. Chronic obstructive pulmonary disease (COPD) with acute bronchitis ______________
5. Bilateral, complete cleft palate with cleft lip ______________
6. Maxillary nasal polyp ______________
7. Severe, persistent asthma with acute exacerbation ______________
8. Bronchopneumonia due to *staphylococci* ______________
9. Acute pharyngitis due to influenza ______________
10. A 6-year-old child is seen for acute respiratory distress syndrome ______________
11. Asthmatic bronchitis ______________
12. Patient presents with cough, fever, and a stuffy nose. Diagnosis: Influenza due to novel influenza A virus ______________
13. Acute laryngitis ______________
14. Chronic obstructive asthma with acute exacerbation ______________
15. Acute bronchitis with bronchiectasis ______________
16. COPD with chronic bronchitis and pulmonary emphysema ______________
17. Acute bronchiolitis with bronchospasm ______________
18. Acute and chronic respiratory failure ______________
19. The surgeon documents that the patient is experiencing acute pulmonary insufficiency immediately following a partial lobectomy ______________
20. Patient seen in the emergency department for a piece of chicken bone lodged in pharynx that is causing discomfort and scraping ______________

21. Chronic tonsillitis and adenoiditis ______________

22. Bilateral paralysis of glottis ______________

23. Edema of pharynx ______________

24. Coalworker's lung disease ______________

25. Pulmonary alveolar proteinosis ______________

CHAPTER

9 Diseases of the Digestive System

As with other chapters within ICD-10-CM, the chapter for the digestive system also contains many combination codes. Many coding assignments depend on documentation to identify whether bleeding, perforation, gangrene, or another condition complicated the diagnosis. Note the following examples that depict the detailed diagnostic information within the code selections:

Code Category	**With** presence of complication(s)	**Without** presence of complication(s)
K57 Diverticular disease of intestine	K57.01 Diverticulitis of small intestine *with* perforation and abscess with bleeding	K57.12 Diverticulitis of small intestine *without* perforation or abscess without bleeding
K51.5 Left-sided colitis	K51.511 Left-sided colitis *with* rectal bleeding K51.512 Left-sided colitis *with* intestinal obstruction	K51.50 Left-sided colitis *without* complications
K43 Ventral hernia	K43.11 Incisional hernia *with* gangrene K43.19 Other ventral hernia, *with* gangrene	K43.91 Incisional hernia, *without* obstruction or gangrene

Check Your Knowledge of Anatomy

Label Figure 9-1 correctly by using the following terms. Answers are located in Appendix A.

Esophagus	Ascending colon
Duodenum	Oral cavity
Appendix	Ileum
Pharynx	Anus
Rectum	Sigmoid colon
Jejunum	Descending colon

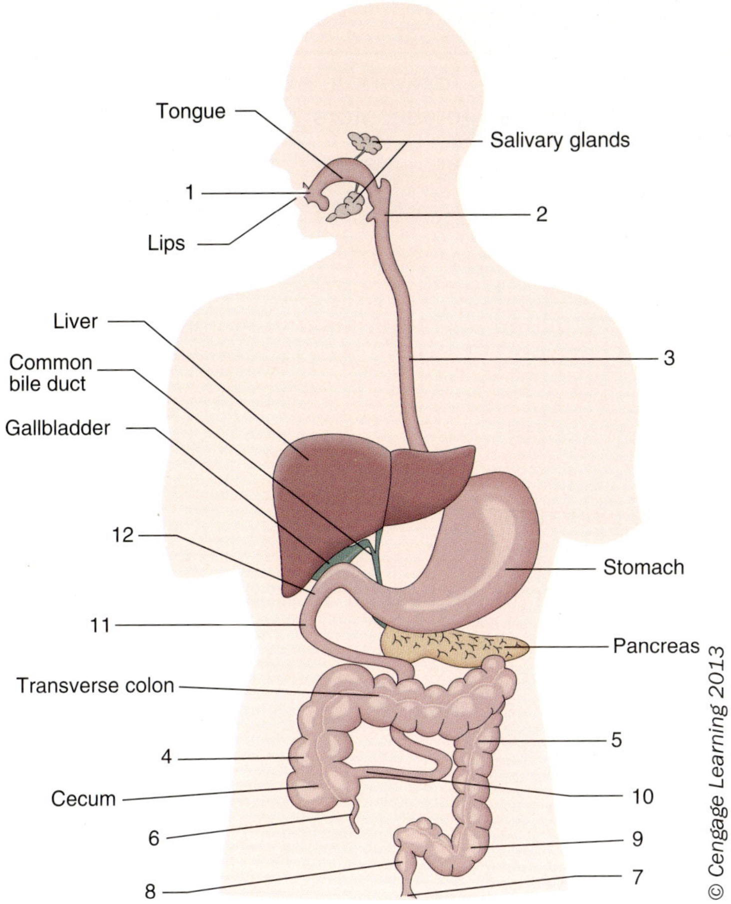

Figure 9-1

Check Your Clinical Knowledge

Circle one of the selections provided in parentheses to complete the following sentences. Answers are located in Appendix A.

1. The surgeon noted that stones were located in the bile duct and documented the diagnosis of __________. (cholelithiasis, choledocholithiasis)

2. The operative report explained that an excessive amount of fluid was located in the peritoneal cavity. This statement was consistent with the postoperative diagnosis of __________. (ascites, varices)

3. The pathology report revealed that the gallbladder was inflamed, which supported the postoperative diagnosis of __________. (cholecystitis, cholangitis).

4. The physical examination revealed a protrusion of the intestine through a weakening of the abdominal wall near the groin. This finding supports the diagnosis of a __________hernia. (hiatal, femoral)

5. The operative report revealed a stricture in the small intestine, supporting documentation of a narrowing of the __________. (rectum, ileum)

Coding

Assign ICD-10-CM codes to the following. Answers to exercises 1–10 are located in Appendix A, and the remaining answers are only provided to educators through the instructor online companion.

1. Recurrent distal esophageal stricture ______________
2. Chronic hepatic failure ______________
3. Gastrointestinal bleeding due to angiodysplasia of stomach and duodenum ______________
4. Alcoholic hepatitis with ascites ______________
5. Perforated acute duodenal ulcer ______________
6. Preoperative diagnosis: Polyp of the colon. Pathology report states adenocarcinoma of the ascending colon ______________
7. Diverticulosis of ileum with hemorrhaging ______________
8. External hemorrhoids ______________
9. Acute gastritis with hemorrhaging ______________
10. Ulcerated esophageal varices ______________
11. Choledocholithiasis with acute cholecystitis ______________
12. Paraesophageal hernia ______________
13. Acute appendicitis with subsequent rupture and widespread peritonitis ______________
14. Chronic peptic ulcer with both hemorrhage and perforation ______________
15. Diverticulitis of duodenum ______________
16. Acute gingivitis ______________
17. Gastroesophageal reflux disease (GERD) ______________
18. Irritable bowel syndrome with frequent bouts of diarrhea ______________
19. Left-strangulated femoral hernia causing obstruction ______________
20. Crohn's disease of ileum with abscess ______________

21. Sciatic hernia _______________

22. Ulcerative proctitis with fistula _______________

23. Left-sided colitis _______________

24. Acute intestinal infarction _______________

25. Paralysis of bowel _______________

CHAPTER

10 Diseases of the Skin and Subcutaneous Tissue

This chapter of ICD-10-CM contains codes that report various diseases of the skin and subcutaneous tissue with great specificity at the fourth and fifth character levels. Instructional notations are used to instruct the coder to:

- Code first any associated condition
- Code first underlying disease
- Use additional code to identify organism
- Code first (T36-T65) to identify drug or substance

Check Your Knowledge of Anatomy

Label Figure 10-1 correctly by using the following terms. Answers are located in Appendix A.

Arrector pili muscle
Dermis
Epidermis
Hair follicle
Hair shaft
Papilla of hair
Sebaceous (oil) gland
Sweat gland
Sweat pore
Subcutaneous fatty tissue

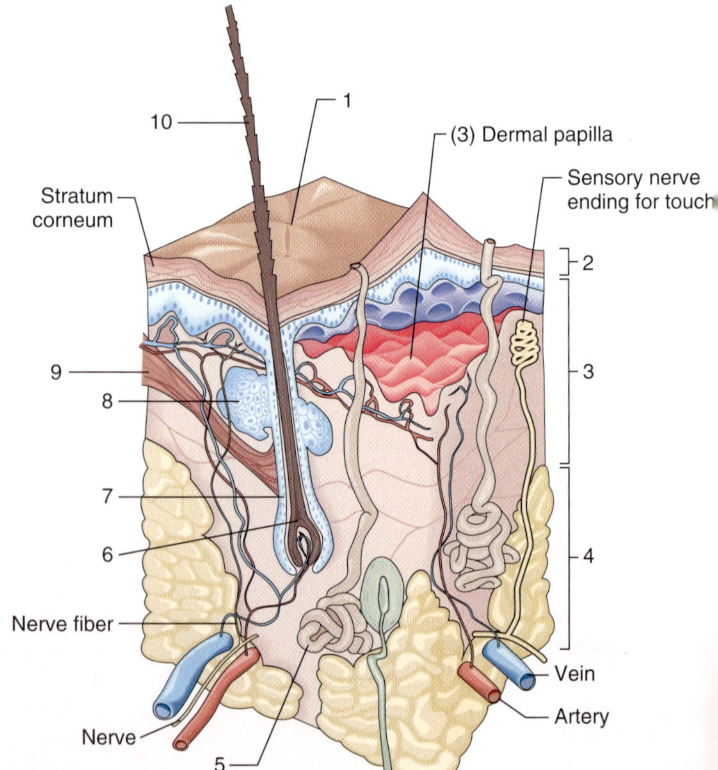

Figure 10-1

Check Your Clinical Knowledge

Circle one of the selections provided in parentheses to complete the following sentences. Answers are located in Appendix A.

1. __________ is an extremely contagious skin disease that most commonly affects the face and hands and is caused by *Streptococcus* and staphylococcal bacteria. (Plantar warts, Impetigo)
2. __________, a noncontagious chronic skin disease, is characterized by a rapid replacement of epidermal cells that appears as red raised lesions with silvery colored scales. (Psoriasis, Candidiasis)
3. Skin redness, also known as __________, is a common sign that occurs for many conditions of the integumentary system. (hematoma, erythema)
4. Erosion of the skin or mucous membrane that results in tissue loss due to prolonged pressure on the affected area is known as a pressure ulcer or a __________ ulcer. (decubitus, papule)
5. A boil, also known as a __________, is a small abscess that occurs in the tissues of the skin generally around a hair follicle. (furuncle, carbuncle)

Coding

Assign ICD-10-CM codes to the following. Answers to exercises 1–10 are located in Appendix A, and the remaining answers are only provided to educators through the instructor online companion.

1. Acute lymphadenitis of axilla ______________
2. Circumscribed neurodermatitis ______________
3. Yellow nail syndrome ______________
4. Urticaria due to cold ______________
5. Acute lymphangitis of left arm ______________
6. Dry skin dermatitis ______________
7. Pressure sore of elbow, stage I ______________
8. Pilonidal cyst with abscess ______________
9. Allergic dermatitis due to contact with chromium, initial visit ______________
10. Androgenic alopecia ______________
11. Postprocedural hematoma of skin following a dermatologic procedure ______________
12. Acne necrotica miliaris ______________

13. Chronic infantile eczema ____________

14. Infectious eczematoid dermatitis ____________

15. Psoriatic arthritis mutilans ____________

16. Sixth visit to treat chronic radiodermatitis due to exposure to laser radiation ____________

17. Dermatosis papulosa nigra ____________

18. Stage IV pressure ulcer of tailbone area with gangrene ____________

19. Third-degree sunburn ____________

20. Primary focal hyperhidrosis on palms of hands ____________

21. Impetigo neonatorum ____________

22. Recurrent periodic urticaria ____________

23. Nail dystrophy ____________

24. Psoriasis, arthropathic ____________

25. Retiformis parapsoriasis ____________

Diseases of the Musculoskeletal System and Connective Tissue

CHAPTER 11

Laterality and anatomical specificity are used for many of the codes that report diseases of the musculoskeletal system and connective tissue. Seventh-character extensions are used to provide additional information. Instructional notations are used to alert coders to add additional codes and the notations of "Code first..." denote code sequencing.

Check Your Knowledge of Anatomy and Disorders

Label the figures correctly by using the following terms. Answers are located in Appendix A.

A. Terms for Figures 11-1, 11-2, and 11-3

Kyphosis

Lordosis

Scoliosis

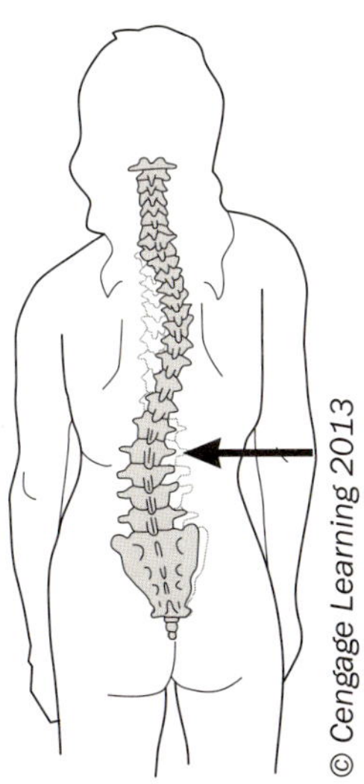

Figure 11-1

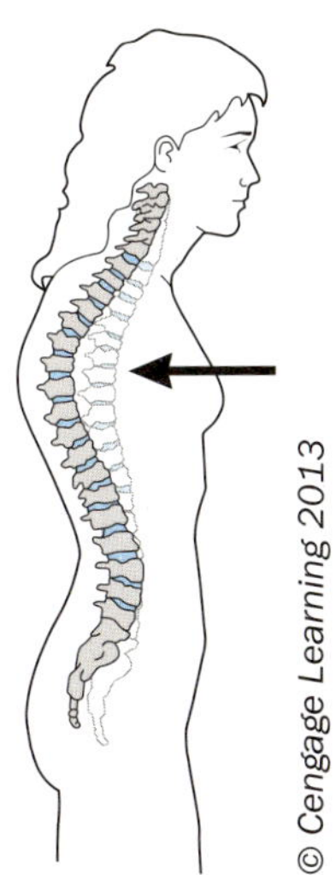

Figure 11-2

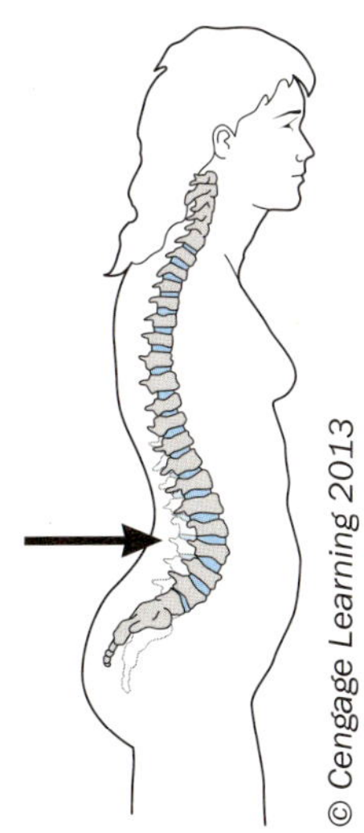

Figure 11-3

B. Terms for Figure 11-4

Cervical vertebrae

Coccyx

Intervertebral disc

Lumbar vertebrae

Sacrum

Thoracic (dorsal) vertebrae

Vertebral body

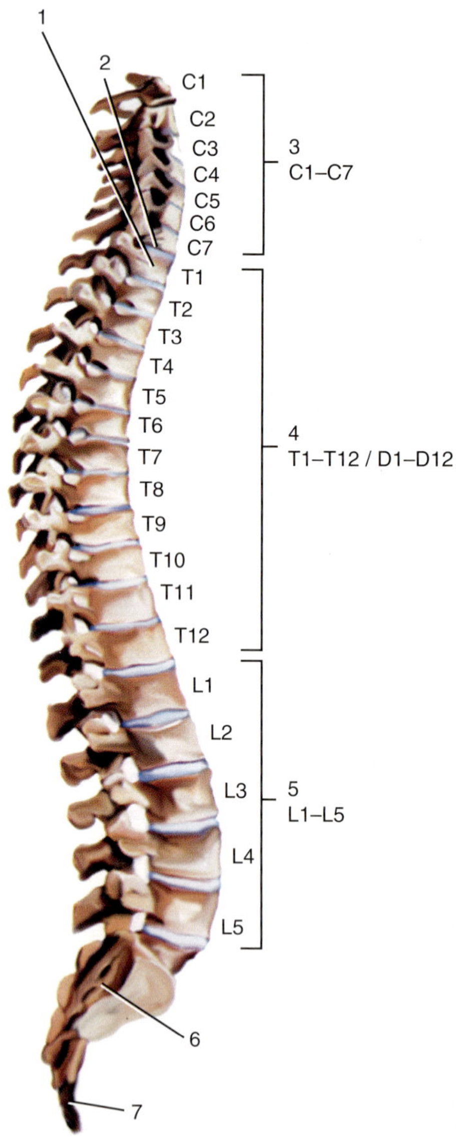

Figure 11-4

Check Your Clinical Knowledge

Circle one of the selections provided in parentheses to complete the following sentences. Answers are located in Appendix A.

1. ____________________ is a metabolic disease that causes the bone to have a Swiss cheese–like appearance that leads to bone mass loss. (Arthritis, Osteoporosis)
2. The term "bunion" is commonly used for ________________, a deformity that affects the metatarsophalangeal joint of the big toe. (hallux valgus, rheumatoid arthritis)
3. The physician documents the following: "In the patient's right hand there is fusion and total loss of joint function." This would suggest that the patient has _________ of the hand. (ankylosis, bursitis)
4. ______________ is caused by a deficiency of vitamin D and results in the softening of the bones. (Osteomalacia, Osteomyeltis)
5. A(n) _______________ is used to evaluate muscle disorders by inserting a small needle into the muscle tissue and recording the electrical activity. (dual-energy X-ray absorptiometry scan, electromyography)

Coding

Assign ICD-10-CM codes to the following. Answers to exercises 1–10 are located in Appendix A, and the remaining answers are only provided to educators through the instructor online companion.

1. Juvenile osteochondrosis of pelvis _______________
2. Rheumatoid vasculitis with rheumatoid arthritis of left shoulder _______________
3. Rheumatoid bursitis of the right foot and ankle _______________
4. Acute gout flare _______________
5. Left foot, acquired hallux rigidus _______________
6. Acquired clubfoot of right foot _______________
7. Recurrent subluxation of patella, left knee _______________
8. Loose body in third left toe joint _______________
9. Myositis ossificans progressiva, left upper arm _______________
10. Right hip abscess of bursa caused by *Staphylococcus aureus* _______________
11. Calve's disease of lumbosacral region _______________
12. Acute hematogenous osteomyelitis, left humerus _______________

13. Osteitis deformans of left fingers ______________

14. Osteolysis of right tibia ______________

15. Hypertrophy of left ulna ______________

16. Adult osteochondrosis of right knee ______________

17. Acquired hallux varus of left foot ______________

18. Wrist drop of right hand ______________

19. Acquired bow leg of left side ______________

20. Chondromalacia of right patella ______________

21. Idiopathic gout, right hand ______________

22. Effusion of left hip ______________

23. Stiffness of right ankle ______________

24. Instability of left elbow ______________

25. Right shoulder osteitis condensans ______________

Diseases of the Genitourinary System

CHAPTER 12

Diseases of both the male and female genitourinary systems are classified to ICD-10-CM Chapter 14. Instructional notations appear throughout the chapter to direct the coder to "use additional codes," to "code first," or to "code also associated underlying conditions." Many of the codes are expanded at the fourth and fifth character levels to include specific codes for acute, chronic, or unspecified states of a disease. Codes for diseases that impact the breast include fifth characters to indicate laterality.

Check Your Knowledge of Anatomy and Disorders

Label the figures correctly by using the following terms. Answers are located in Appendix A.

A. Terms for Figure 12-1

Adrenal suprarenal

Left kidney

Left renal artery

Prostate gland

Renal cortex

Renal medulla

Right kidney

Right and left ureters

Ureteral orifices

Urethra

Urethral meatus

Urinary bladder

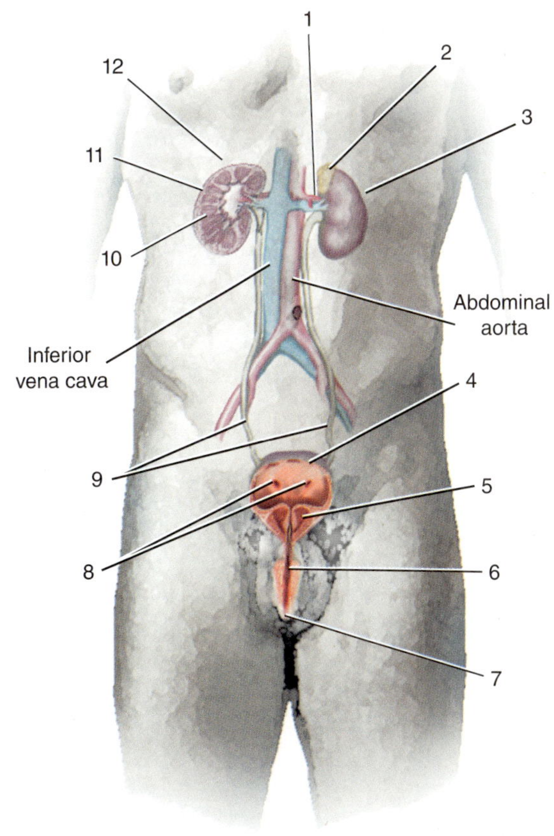

Figure 12-1

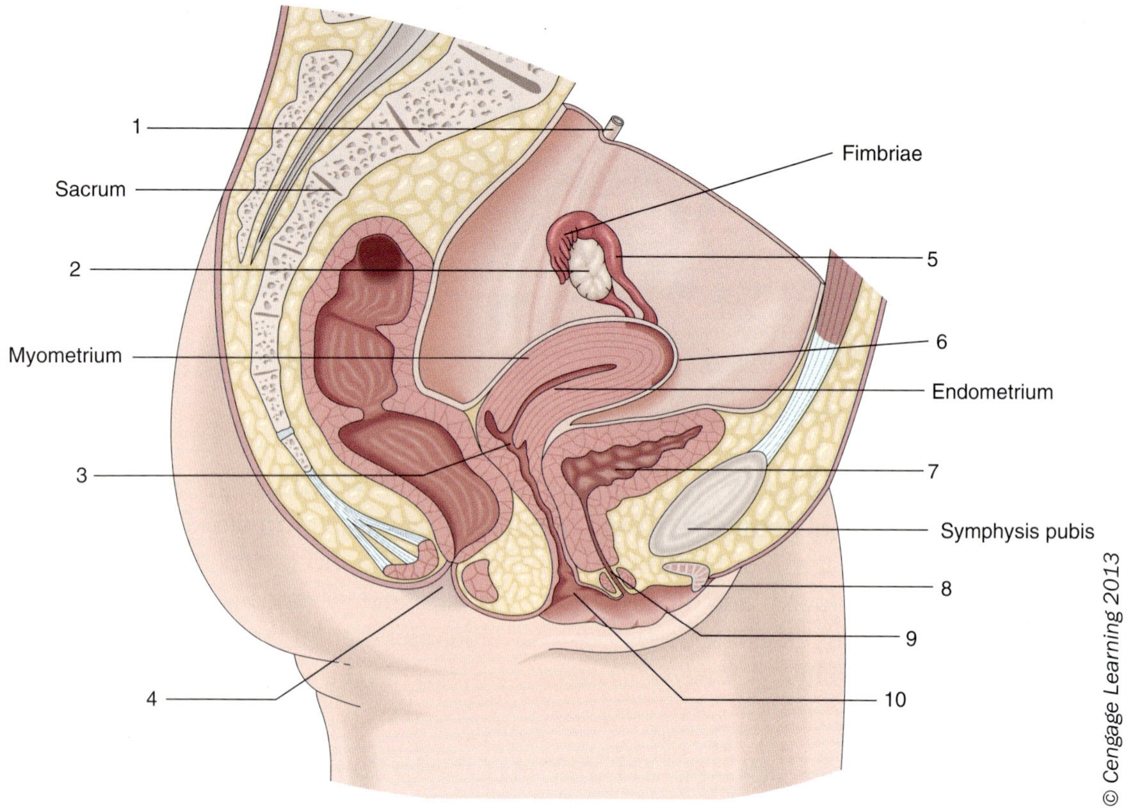

Figure 12-2

B. Terms for Figure 12-2

Anus	Ovary
Body of uterus	Ureter
Cervix of uterus	Urethra
Clitoris	Urinary bladder
Fallopian tube	Vagina

Check Your Clinical Knowledge

Circle one of the selections provided in parentheses to complete the following sentences. Answers are located in Appendix A.

1. An inflammation of the fallopian tube is known as ____________. (oophoritis, salpingitis)
2. Patients with end-stage renal disease require ______________. (dialysis, insulin)
3. A test used to determine the levels of urea nitrogen or waste products in the blood is a ___________ test. (BUN, urine C&S)
4. __________, an inherited disease, causes enlargement of both kidneys due to the formation of multiple grape-like cysts. (Polycystic disease, Renal failure)
5. __________ incontinence occurs when a person is unable to hold urine when he or she coughs, sneezes, or laughs. (Overflow, Stress)

Coding

Assign ICD-10-CM codes to the following. Answers to exercises 1–10 are located in Appendix A, and the remaining answers are only provided to educators through the instructor online companion.

1. Calculus in urethra ______________
2. Urinary tract obstruction ______________
3. Prostatitis ______________
4. Irregular periods ______________
5. Paravaginal cystocele ______________
6. Segmental fat necrosis of breast ______________
7. Benign cyst of prepuce ______________
8. Acquired bladder-neck stenosis ______________
9. Destrusor muscle hyperactivity ______________
10. Acute nephritis ______________
11. Interstitial nephritis ______________
12. Bilateral small kidney ______________
13. Acute salpingitis and oophoritis ______________
14. Bilateral vesicoureteral-reflux with reflux nephropathy with hydroureter ______________

15. Stage III chronic kidney disease ________________

16. Renal tubular acidosis ________________

17. Trigonitis with hematuria ________________

18. Chronic interstitial cystitis with hematuria ________________

19. Single spermatocele of epididymis ________________

20. Mammary duct ectasia of left breast ________________

21. Right breast fibroadenosis ________________

22. Breast atrophy ________________

23. Chronic salpingitis ________________

24. Bartholin's gland abscess ________________

25. Intestinal endometriosis ________________

CHAPTER

Pregnancy, Childbirth, and the Puerperium

13

Chapter 15 of ICD-10-CM classifies conditions occurring during pregnancy, childbirth, and the puerperium as well as encounters for the supervision of high-risk pregnancies. Codes from this chapter of ICD-10-CM are used only for coding of the records of mothers. Seventh characters are used for some codes to identify multiple gestations. The trimester in which the condition occurs is identified for some codes.

A code from category Z37, Outcome of Delivery, should be included on every maternal record when a delivery has occurred. These codes are not to be used on subsequent records or on the newborn record.

Check Your ICD-10-CM Knowledge

Circle one of the selections provided in parentheses to complete the following sentences. Answers are located in Appendix A.

1. ICD-10-CM defines the ________ trimester from 14 weeks 0 days to less than 28 weeks 0 days. (second, third)
2. A seventh character of 0 for code O33.5xx0 denotes __________. (single gestation, fetus 1)
3. Obstetric ________ is reported with code O71.7. (hematoma of vulva, damage to coccyx)
4. _______ is classified to code O00.1. (Rupture of fallopian tube due to pregnancy, Mural pregnancy)
5. A young primigravida, as defined by ICD-10-CM, is a woman who is less than ______ years old at expected date of delivery. (16, 18)

Check Your Clinical Knowledge

Circle one of the selections provided in parentheses to complete the following sentences. Answers are located in Appendix A.

1. The most common location of an ectopic pregnancy is the _______. (fallopian tubes, cervix)
2. Excessive vomiting during pregnancy is known as ____________. (hyperemesis gravidarum, miscarriage)
3. _________ is the abnormal positioning of the placenta in the lower uterus. (Abruptio placentae, Placenta previa)

4. The letters in HELLP syndrome refer to __________, elevated liver function, and low platelet level. (hypertension, hemolysis)
5. Pre-eclampsia is a serious condition of pregnancy characterized by hypertension, ________, and proteinuria. (coma, edema)

Coding

Assign ICD-10-CM codes to the following. Answers to exercises 1–10 are located in Appendix A, and the remaining answers are only provided to educators through the instructor online companion. For this exercise, assign an Outcome of Delivery code when prompted.

1. Missed abortion at 17 weeks' gestation with retention of dead fetus ______________
2. 24-week OB visit for 14-year-old primigravida patient ______________
3. Tubal abortion ______________
4. Eclampsia during 29th week of pregnancy ______________
5. Antepartum hemorrhage with coagulation defect at 30 weeks' gestation ______________
6. Diabetes mellitus arising during pregnancy controlled by diet ______________
7. Premature separation of placenta with afibrinogememia, at 31 weeks' gestation ______________
8. *Streptococcus* group A infection of bladder following delivery ______________
9. Cracked nipple due to breast-feeding ______________
10. Cesarean delivery of 7-pound 11-ounce baby girl *(assign an Outcome of Delivery code)* ______________
11. 30-week gestational patient with pre-existing hypertension complicating the pregnancy ______________
12. Triplet pregnancy at 35 weeks' gestation with transverse presentation of fetus three ______________
13. Annular detachment of the cervix complicating delivery ______________
14. Delayed delivery after artificial rupture of membranes ______________
15. Obstetric hematoma of vagina complicating delivery ______________
16. Rupture of uterus before onset of labor at 16-week gestation ______________

17. Placenta percreta, 18 weeks ______________

18. Braxton Hicks contractions ______________

19. UTI following induced termination of pregnancy ______________

20. Obstetric fat embolism, 35 weeks ______________

21. Primary agalactica ______________

22. Puerperal thyroiditis ______________

23. Gonorrhea complicating pregnancy at 12 weeks ______________

24. Anemia complicating pregnancy at 19 weeks ______________

25. Physical abuse complicating pregnancy at 8 weeks ______________

CHAPTER

14 Certain Conditions Originating in the Perinatal Period and Congenital Malformations, Deformations, and Chromosomal Abnormalities

Conditions originating in the fetal or perinatal period (before birth through the first 28 days after birth) are classified to Chapter 16 of ICD-10-CM. These codes are used on the records of the newborns. Chapter 17 of ICD-10-CM classifies congenital malformations, deformations, and chromosomal abnormalities. Codes from this chapter are not for use on maternal or fetal records.

Check Your Knowledge of Conditions

From the conditions listed below, place a check mark in front of the diagnostic statement if it reflects congenital malformations, deformations, or chromosomal abnormalities. Answers are located in Appendix A.

_____ **1.** Pentalogy of Fallot

_____ **2.** Respiratory distress syndrome

_____ **3.** Sepsis of newborn due to *E. coli*

_____ **4.** Cleft palate with bilateral cleft lip

_____ **5.** Neonatal cerebral ischemia

_____ **6.** Transposition of colon

_____ **7.** Complex syndactyly of fingers with synostosis

_____ **8.** Traumatic glaucoma of newborn

_____ **9.** Neonatal melena

_____ **10.** Van der Woude's syndrome

Check Your Clinical Knowledge

Circle one of the selections provided in parentheses to complete the following sentences. Answers are located in Appendix A.

1. ___________ is a congenital disorder in which the posterior portion of the vertebrae of the bony spinal column fails to close over the spinal cord. (Cerebral palsy, Spina bifida)

2. ___________ is a combination of four defects of the heart. (Tetralogy of Fallot, Hemophilia)

3. ____________ typically impacts the sigmoid colon and is due to an absence of nerves therefore causing a lack of peristalsis. (Hypospadias, Hirschsprung's disease)

4. Congenital varicella is a congenital _________ disease. (bacterial, viral)

5. __________ occurs early in gestation and is a severe form of neural tube deficit with the failure of the cephalic aspect of the neural tube to close. (Anencephaly, Talipes equinovarus)

Coding

Assign ICD-10-CM codes to the following. Answers to exercises 1–10 are located in Appendix A, and the remaining answers are only provided to educators through the instructor online companion.

1. Lumbar spina bifida with hydrocephalus ______________
2. Rupture of the liver due to birth injury ______________
3. Newborn impacted by in utero exposure to tobacco smoke ______________
4. Newborn type II, respiratory distress syndrome ______________
5. Cephalhematoma due to birth injury ______________
6. Congenital funnel chest ______________
7. Birth weight of newborn, 525 grams ______________
8. Acidosis of newborn ______________
9. Transient neonatal diabetes mellitus ______________
10. Neonatal rectal hemorrhage ______________
11. Congenital accessory eye muscle ______________
12. Congenital pneumonia due to *Staphylococcus* ______________
13. Ostium primum atrial septal defect, type I ______________
14. Hypospadias with intersex state ______________
15. Translocation, trisomy 18 ______________
16. Megalocornea with glaucoma ______________

17. Congenital stenosis of larynx __________

18. Newborn affected by prolapsed cord __________

19. Mild HIE __________

20. Sodium balance disturbance of newborn __________

21. Meconium ileus __________

22. Neonatal peritonitis __________

23. Neonate potassium balance disturbance __________

24. Esophageal reflux of neonate __________

25. Noninfective mastitis of newborn __________

Symptoms, Signs, and Abnormal Clinical and Laboratory Findings, Not Elsewhere Classified

CHAPTER 15

Chapter 18 of ICD-10-CM is used to report the following:

- Cases for which no specific diagnosis can be made even after all the facts bearing on the case have been investigated
- Signs or symptoms existing at the time of initial encounter that proved to be transient and whose causes could not be determined
- Provisional diagnosis in a patient who failed to return for further investigation or care
- Cases referred elsewhere for investigation or treatment before the diagnosis has been made
- Cases in which a more precise diagnosis was not available for any other reason
- Certain symptoms, for which supplementary information is provided, that represent important problems in medical care in their own right

Check Your Knowledge

For the symptoms and signs listed below state the main body system (e.g., digestive system) that would be associated with the condition. Answers are located in Appendix A.

1. Precordial friction ____________________
2. Nocturia ____________________
3. Pruritus ____________________
4. Dyspnea ____________________
5. Dysphagia ____________________

Check Your Clinical Knowledge

Match the abnormal finding with the disease that the finding could indicate. Answers are located in Appendix A.

_____ **1.** elevated PSA — **A.** seizure activity

_____ **2.** abnormal EKG — **B.** visual impairment

_____ **3.** abnormal EEG — **C.** prostate cancer

_____ **4.** abnormal ERG	**D.** diabetes mellitus
_____ **5.** elevated fasting glucose	**E.** myocardial infarction

Coding

Assign ICD-10-CM codes to the following. Answers to exercises 1–10 are located in Appendix A, and the remaining answers are only provided to educators through the instructor online companion.

1. Elevated CRP _____________

2. Fluid retention _____________

3. Painful urination _____________

4. Spastic gait _____________

5. Abnormal bowel sounds _____________

6. Abnormal level of cocaine in the blood _____________

7. Abnormal liver function study _____________

8. Elevated levels of steroids in urine _____________

9. Decreased sexual desire _____________

10. Patient is a 10-day-old infant with excessive crying _____________

11. Night sweats _____________

12. Postprocedural fever _____________

13. Weak urinary stream _____________

14. Elevated glucose tolerance _____________

15. Idiopathic vasovagal attack _____________

16. Senile debility _____________

17. Painful respiration _____________

18. Inability to swallow _____________

19. Abnormal result of Mantoux test ________________

20. Excessive thirst ________________

21. Abnormal weight loss ________________

22. Elevated erythrocyte sedimentation rate ________________

23. Increased fasting glucose ________________

24. Recurrent convulsions ________________

25. Postimmunization fever ________________

CHAPTER

16 Injuries, Poisoning, and Certain Other Consequences of External Causes

Chapter 19 of ICD-10-CM is used to report injuries, poisonings, and certain other consequences of external causes. For most of the codes found in this chapter, ICD-10-CM seventh characters are used. The final character typically identifies an initial encounter, subsequent encounter, or sequelae. Prior to code selection, coders need to review not only medical documentation but also any reports of X-rays and imaging to support more specificity in the coding assignment.

Check Your Knowledge of Anatomy

Label Figure 16-1 correctly by using the following terms. Answers are located in Appendix A.

Carpals
Clavicle
Femur
Fibula
Humerus
Ilium
Ischium
Mandible
Maxilla
Metacarpals
Metatarsals
Patella
Phalanges of foot
Phalanges of hand
Pubis
Radius
Ribs
Skull
Sternum
Tarsals
Tibia
Ulna
Vertebral column

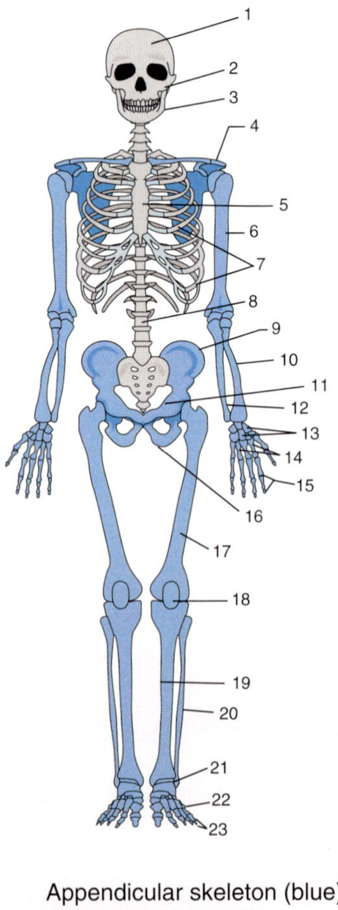

Appendicular skeleton (blue)
Axial skeleton (grey)

Figure 16-1

Coding

Assign ICD-10-CM codes to the following. Answers to exercises 1–10 are located in Appendix A, and the remaining answers are only provided to educators through the instructor online companion. For each exercise, assume an initial encounter unless it is otherwise noted in the diagnostic statement.

1. Complete traumatic amputation of left ear ____________
2. Subsequent encounter for puncture wound of the scalp ____________
3. Right eye, penetrating wound of orbit ____________
4. Posterior displaced Type II dens fracture, subsequent encounter with routine healing ____________
5. Contusion of left front wall of thorax ____________
6. Rejection of bone marrow transplant ____________
7. Sexual abuse of child ____________
8. Local infection due to port-a-cath ____________
9. Open transverse fracture of the shaft of the right femur, displaced ____________
10. Sprain in left hip iliofemoral ligament, third follow-up visit ____________
11. Crushing injury of right thigh ____________
12. Laceration of right knee with foreign body ____________
13. Sprain of lateral collateral ligament of left knee ____________
14. Displaced bile duct prosthesis ____________
15. Necrosis of amputated stump of left arm ____________
16. Shock from electric current ____________
17. Dislocation of right clavicle ____________
18. Open wound of right ankle, subsequent encounter ____________
19. Traumatic partial amputation between hip and knee on right side of body ____________
20. Poisoning by ampicillin, accidental ____________

21. Dislocation of mandible ______________

22. Patient seen in ER for abrasion of throat ______________

23. Subsequent visit for concussion of thoracic spinal cord ______________

24. Blister on left shoulder ______________

25. Splinter in left knee ______________

CHAPTER

17

External Causes of Morbidity

Chapter 20 of ICD-10-CM is used to report environmental events and circumstances that are the cause of injury and other adverse effects. These codes are to be used as secondary codes to describe the circumstance that was the external cause of morbidity. The following table provides an overview of the types of codes that appear in this chapter. Note that codes with four or five characters that require a seventh-character extension will be completed with the use of "x" placeholders.

Codes	Description (assume all encounters are the initial encounter)
V02.01xA	Pedestrian on roller-skates injured in collision with two- or three-wheeled motor vehicle in nontraffic accident
W21.01xA	Struck by football
W93.01xA	Contact with dry ice
X98.2xxA	Assault by hot fluids

Check Your Knowledge

Refer to the beginning of the Tabular section of Chapter 20 and reference the definitions of transport vehicles. For each statement below, complete the missing term that relates to definitions for transport accidents. For example, special construction vehicles include bulldozers, diggers, earth levelers, dump trucks, backhoes, front-end loaders, pavers, and mechanical shovels. Answers are located in Appendix A.

1. A hot-air balloon is a type of ________ device.
2. A bus is a motor vehicle designed to carry more than ________ passengers.
3. A ___________ accident is any vehicle accident that occurs entirely in any place other than a public highway.
4. A motor-driven tricycle or a motorized rickshaw is considered a ___________ motor vehicle.
5. A person changing a tire that is involved in an accident is considered a ___________.

Coding

Assign ICD-10-CM V00-Y99 codes for the following statements. Do not assign the code for the injury. This exercise is to practice the selection of External Causes of Morbidity codes from Chapter 20 of ICD-10-CM. Assign Place of Occurrence (Y92) and Activity codes (Y93) when prompted in the exercise. For assignment of seventh-character extension, assume initial encounter unless otherwise stated. Answers to exercises 1–10 are located in Appendix A, and the remaining answers are only provided to educators through the instructor online companion.

1. Tripping over carpet at patient's single family home in bedroom while rough housing *[in addition to an External Cause code, assign a code for both the Place of Occurrence (Y92-) and Activity (Y93-)]* ____________
2. Bitten by horse ____________
3. Fall into hole ____________
4. Gored by goat ____________
5. Hypodermic needle stick ____________
6. Subsequent encounter due to helicopter crash causing injury to occupant ____________
7. Tree accidentally falling on person ____________
8. Injury from walking into lamppost, subsequent encounter ____________
9. Struck by softball ____________
10. Evaluation of injury to foot by being skated over by sharp skate blades ____________
11. Suicide attempt by hanging ____________
12. Injuries from an assault caused by being pushed in front of a train ____________
13. Injury by cigar burn ____________
14. Cut from broken glass ____________
15. Driver of car injured as a result of a collision with a van on downtown street ____________
16. Skin damage due to exposure to sunlight, subsequent visit ____________
17. Skin damage caused by tanning bed ____________
18. Suicide attempt by cutting right leg with knife ____________
19. Accidental suffocation in burning building ____________
20. Accidental drowning in swimming pool at the neighborhood community pool *[in addition to an External Cause code, assign a code for both the Place of Occurrence (Y92-) and Activity (Y93-)]* ____________

21. Fall out of bed _______________

22. Seven-year-old jumped into water and sustained multiple injuries _______________

23. Injury from nail gun _______________

24. Stepped on by elephant _______________

25. Gunshot wound _______________

CHAPTER

18 Factors Influencing Health Status and Contact with Health Services

The reasons for encounters are reported in ICD-10-CM with the use of Z codes that are found in Chapter 21 of ICD-10-CM. These codes are reported to indicate that a person may or may not be sick but encounter health care services for a specific purpose, or to indicate a circumstance or problem that influences the person's health status but is not in itself a current illness or injury. Instructional notations are present throughout the chapter that instruct coders to "Use additional codes" or "Code first."

Check Your Knowledge

For each statement state whether the statement is true (T) or false (F). Answers are located in Appendix A.

_____ **1.** Category codes from Z37, Outcome of Delivery, would be reported on the newborn's record.

_____ **2.** Codes from Chapter 21 of ICD-10-CM can be reported only as secondary codes.

_____ **3.** When a patient has an encounter for a medical examination and an abnormal finding is documented, the coder should report a code for the medical examination and the finding.

_____ **4.** Separate code categories exist for encounters for medical observations and encounters for screenings.

_____ **5.** Only one code is reported from Chapter 21 of ICD-10-CM when a child is seen for a routine childhood examination and immunization.

Coding

Assign ICD-10-CM Z codes for the cases. Answers to exercises 1–10 are located in Appendix A, and the remaining answers are only provided to educators through the instructor online companion.

1. Carrier of typhoid _____________

2. Type AB, Rh-negative blood _____________

3. Patient seen in the office for a sports physical _____________

4. Screening for HPV _____________

5. Occupational exposure to dust __________

6. Problems related to child living in a group home __________

7. Lack of adequate sleep __________

8. Underachievement in school __________

9. History of estrogen therapy __________

10. Encounter for checking of IUD __________

11. Patient admitted for cosmetic procedure __________

12. History of malignant neoplasm of the rectum __________

13. Counseling for sexual education __________

14. Family history of leukemia __________

15. Patient had a vasectomy 3 years earlier __________

16. Patient has a partial artificial right arm (status) __________

17. Patient seen in the physician's office for removal of postsurgical abdominal drain __________

18. Adjustment of infusion pump __________

19. Whole blood donor __________

20. Adjustment of cerebral ventricular shunt __________

21. Adult health checkup, no findings __________

22. Hearing examination following failed hearing screening __________

23. Paternity testing __________

24. Observation for alleged adult rape, ruled out __________

25. Carrier of hepatitis B surface antigen [HbsAg] __________

CHAPTER

19 Transition from ICD-9-CM to ICD-10-CM

Transitioning from ICD-9-CM to ICD-10-CM will have a great impact on the health care industry. To facilitate the transition, the National Centers for Health Statistics has developed Diagnosis Code Set General Equivalence Mappings (GEM) to be used as a translational tool. The GEM presents the information in an easy-to-use table format that maps ICD-9-CM codes to ICD-10-CM codes. It should be noted that there is not always a one-to-one mapping of codes. Coders cannot use the GEM in place of the ICD-10-CM code book. The GEM files can be found on the NCHS website at http://www.cdc.gov/nchs/icd/icd10cm.htm#10update. The files contain the codes without the code titles and were designed to be used by the health care industry for the creation of mapping applications.

Coding

For each statement below, assign the correct ICD-9-CM and ICD-10-CM codes. Answers to exercises 1–10 are located in Appendix A, and the remaining answers are only provided to educators through the instructor online companion.

1. Open wound of the nose, initial visit
ICD-9-CM: ______________________
ICD-10-CM: ______________________

2. Congenital salivary fistula
ICD-9-CM: ______________________
ICD-10-CM: ______________________

3. Acute tonsillitis
ICD-9-CM: ______________________
ICD-10-CM: ______________________

4. Collapsed lung
ICD-9-CM: ______________________
ICD-10-CM: ______________________

5. Lung mass
ICD-9-CM: ______________________
ICD-10-CM: ______________________

6. Bronchial stenosis
ICD-9-CM: ____________________
ICD-10-CM: ____________________

7. Chronic hepatitis C
ICD-9-CM: ____________________
ICD-10-CM: ____________________

8. Alcohol withdrawal
ICD-9-CM: ____________________
ICD-10-CM: ____________________

9. Panic disorder
ICD-9-CM: ____________________
ICD-10-CM: ____________________

10. Obsessive-compulsive disorder
ICD-9-CM: ____________________
ICD-10-CM: ____________________

11. Portal hypertension
ICD-9-CM: ____________________
ICD-10-CM: ____________________

12. Herniated cervical disc, mid-cervical region
ICD-9-CM: ____________________
ICD-10-CM: ____________________

13. Initial visit for closed rib fracture on right side
ICD-9-CM: ____________________
ICD-10-CM: ____________________

14. Ulcerative colitis
ICD-9-CM: ____________________
ICD-10-CM: ____________________

15. Rheumatoid arthritis
ICD-9-CM: ____________________
ICD-10-CM: ____________________

16. Second visit for fatigue fracture of right fibula with routine healing
ICD-9-CM: ____________________
ICD-10-CM: ____________________

17. Infarction of spleen
ICD-9-CM: ____________________
ICD-10-CM: ____________________

18. Obstruction of gallbladder
ICD-9-CM: ____________________
ICD-10-CM: ____________________

19. Congenital polycystic kidney
ICD-9-CM: ____________________
ICD-10-CM: ____________________

20. Calculus of kidney
ICD-9-CM: ______________________
ICD-10-CM: ______________________

21. Prostatic hemorrhage
ICD-9-CM: ______________________
ICD-10-CM: ______________________

22. Endometriosis of uterus
ICD-9-CM: ______________________
ICD-10-CM: ______________________

23. Uterine cyst
ICD-9-CM: ______________________
ICD-10-CM: ______________________

24. Endometriosis of ovary
ICD-9-CM: ______________________
ICD-10-CM: ______________________

25. Restricting type of anorexia nervosa
ICD-9-CM: ______________________
ICD-10-CM: ______________________

26. Hyperemesis gravidarium, at week 19
ICD-9-CM: ______________________
ICD-10-CM: ______________________

27. Delivery of single child complicated by prolapse of cord
ICD-9-CM: ______________________
ICD-10-CM: ______________________

28. Supervision of normal first pregnancy at 6 weeks
ICD-9-CM: ______________________
ICD-10-CM: ______________________

29. Aortic value stenosis
ICD-9-CM: ______________________
ICD-10-CM: ______________________

30. Second visit for whiplash injury
ICD-9-CM: ______________________
ICD-10-CM: ______________________

31. Initial visit for traumatic pneumothorax
ICD-9-CM: ______________________
ICD-10-CM: ______________________

32. Encounter of palliative care
ICD-9-CM: ______________________
ICD-10-CM: ______________________

33. Encounter for hearing examination following failed hearing screening
ICD-9-CM: ______________________
ICD-10-CM: ______________________

34. Preoperative cardiovascular examination
ICD-9-CM: ____________________
ICD-10-CM: ____________________

35. Threatened premature labor at 30 weeks, not delivered
ICD-9-CM: ____________________
ICD-10-CM: ____________________

36. Cellulitis of finger
ICD-9-CM: ____________________
ICD-10-CM: ____________________

37. Seborrheic dermatitis
ICD-9-CM: ____________________
ICD-10-CM: ____________________

38. Cervical spondylosis with myelopathy
ICD-9-CM: ____________________
ICD-10-CM: ____________________

39. Cervical postlaminectomy syndrome
ICD-9-CM: ____________________
ICD-10-CM: ____________________

40. Rotator cuff syndrome of right shoulder
ICD-9-CM: ____________________
ICD-10-CM: ____________________

41. Postlaminectomy kyphosis
ICD-9-CM: ____________________
ICD-10-CM: ____________________

42. Spina bifida with hydrocephalus
ICD-9-CM: ____________________
ICD-10-CM: ____________________

43. Newborn affected by knot in cord
ICD-9-CM: ____________________
ICD-10-CM: ____________________

44. Chronic respiratory distress occurring in the perinatal period
ICD-9-CM: ____________________
ICD-10-CM: ____________________

45. Hemolytic disease of newborn
ICD-9-CM: ____________________
ICD-10-CM: ____________________

46. Neonatal dehydration
ICD-9-CM: ____________________
ICD-10-CM: ____________________

47. Anemia of prematurity
ICD-9-CM: ____________________
ICD-10-CM: ____________________

48. Enlargement of lymph nodes
ICD-9-CM: ______________________
ICD-10-CM: ______________________

49. Sequelae of complete lesion L4 of lumbar spinal cord
ICD-9-CM: ______________________
ICD-10-CM: ______________________

50. Late effect of physeal fracture or upper end of right femur
ICD-9-CM: ______________________
ICD-10-CM: ______________________

Coding with ICD-10-PCS

CHAPTER 20

ICD-10-PCS is unique in its format and organization. The system was developed to replace Volume III (procedure codes) in ICD-9-CM. ICD-10-PCS codes were designed to identify hospital inpatient procedures; however, providers may elect to use the codes for other data collection purposes. The Centers for Medicare & Medicaid Services (CMS) requires ICD-10-PCS codes only for inpatient services. The classification system includes seven characters, each character representing an aspect of the procedure. For example, the first character represents the section, which may indicate Medical/Surgical, Obstetrics, or Mental Health.

The workbook exercises are designed in a step-by-step approach for building a code by focusing on the selection of individual characters that comprise the entire code. The last exercise will allow practice for assigning the entire ICD-10-PCS code. The following is a snapshot of an ICD-10-PCS code, illustrating the building blocks for the seven characters.

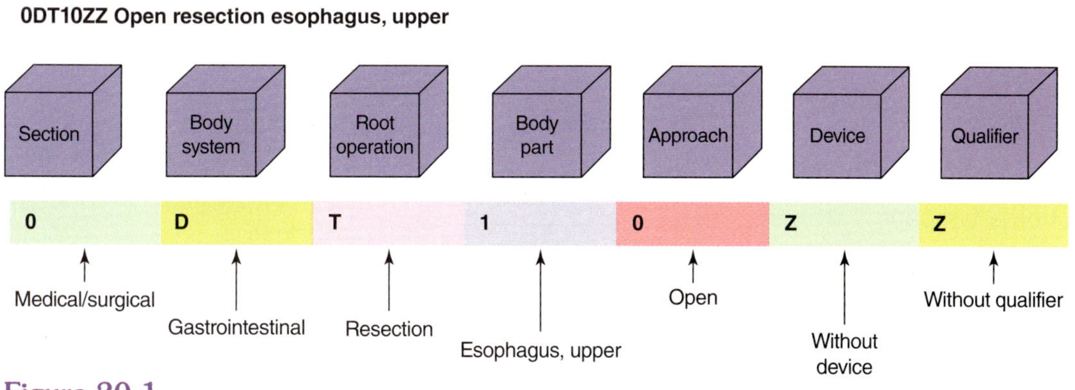

Figure 20-1

United States Department of Health and Human Services (2012): Illustration derived from https://www.cms.gov/ICD10/Downloads/pcs_final_report2012.pdf

Alphabetic Index

ICD-10-PCS (referred to as PCS) provides an Alphabetic Index to guide coders to the appropriate section of the code book Tables. In addition, the Index provides classification reference for body parts and devices. The Index is a tool but coders must rely on their knowledge of format and organization and master the definitions of Root Operations. The Alphabetic Index may provide the entire seven-digit character for the complete code or a portion of the code to reference in the Tables. Coders must always check the PCS tables for the final decision. A review of the Alphabetic Index will reveal that the organization is based on Root Operations (e.g., Excision, Resection) as well as instructional notes.

Examples of Instructional Notes:

Prodisc-C *use* Synthetic Substitute

Medial popliteal nerve *use* Nerve, Tibial

Graft

see Replacement

see Supplement

(This entry asks the coder to review the documentation to determine if the graft was used as a Replacement or Supplement. These Root Operations will be discussed in a later exercise.)

The instructional notes support consistent application of definitions and help to support the integrity of the classification system.

Alphabetic Index Exercise

Search the Alphabetic Index for the following procedures, body parts, or devices. Document the instructional note. Answers to exercises 1–5 are located in Appendix A, and the remaining answers are only provided to educators through the instructor online companion.

1. Incision, abscess ____________________
2. PTCA ____________________
3. Lumpectomy ____________________
4. Hepatogastric ligament ____________________
5. Chorda tympani ____________________
6. Clipping, aneurysm ____________________
7. Quadrate lobe ____________________
8. Posterior scrotal nerve ____________________
9. Colonic Z-Stent ____________________
10. Radial collateral ligament ____________________

Reading the ICD-10-PCS Tables

The Alphabetic Index is designed to lead the coder to the PCS Table to make the final coding selection. The following case study will help to explain the workflow for selecting the correct PCS code based on definitions and use of both the Alphabetic Index and PCS Table.

Case Study: The surgeon documents that a percutaneous needle drainage was performed to remove excessive fluid from the right pleural cavity. As a first step, search the Alphabetic Index for *Drainage, Pleural Cavity, Right* which provides the first four characters of the code (0W99). Reference PCS Table (Figure 20-2) to see that the decision making begins with the Approach column. The definitions for the Root Operations, Approaches, Devices, and Qualifiers will be the focus of future workbook ıctivities, but this lesson will serve as an overview. The documentation that the procedure was ɔerformed with a needle indicates a percutaneous approach; therefore, the fifth character will be 3-Percutaneous. Next, review the coding selections for the last two columns: Device and Qualifier. Note that the exact same body parts and approaches are repeated in different rows.

Official ICD-10-PCS Coding Guidelines (see Appendix E) **A9** states that within a PCS table, valid codes nclude all combinations of choices in characters 4 through 7 contained in the same row of the table.

In other words, coders should not choose characters from different rows of the PCS Table. The ormat of the rows guides the coder to make appropriate choices. In this case, the choices are guiding the coding selection based on if the drainage procedure was performed for diagnostic or herapeutic reasons. The surgeon inserted the tube for continuous drainage, for excessive fluid; herefore, this indicates it was performed for therapeutic purposes and the Device would be 0. Note that the last column for Qualifier does not provide an option for "X" (Diagnostic). It would be a contradiction if the character 0 (Drainage Device) would be selected with a Qualifier of "X"—for diagnostic. The diagnostic procedure would require a sample of fluid for laboratory analysis and his was not the intent of this procedure.

The correct coding assignment for this case study would come from the top row of the table:)W9930Z

Section 0 Medical and surgical *Body system* W Anatomical regions, general *Operation* 9 Drainage: Taking or letting out fluids and/or gases from a body part			
Body part	*Approach*	*Device*	*Qualifier*
0 Head **1** Cranical cavity **2** Face **3** Oral cavity and throat **4** Upper jaw **5** Lower jaw **6** Neck **8** Chest wall **9** Pleural cavity, right **B** Pleural cavity, left **C** Mediastinum **D** Pericardial cavity **F** Abdominal wall **G** Peritoneal cavity **H** Retroperitoneum **J** Pelvic cavity **K** Upper back **L** Lower back **M** Perineum, male **N** Perineum, female	**0** Open **3** Percutaneous **4** Percutaneous endoscopic	**0** Drainage device	**Z** No qualifier

Figure 20-2

United States Department of Health & Human Services. (2011). Retrieved from http://www.cms.gov/ICD10/Downloads/pcs_whats_new_2011.pdf

⊃CS Table Exercise

Refer to Figure 20-3 to answer the following questions. Assign PCS codes using the table. All ınswers are located in Appendix A.

1. The surgeon performed a craniotomy to insert a neurostimulator generator within the skull bone of the patient ________________

2. Insertion of percutaneous growth stimulator ________________

Section	0	Medical and surgical		
Body system	N	Head and facial bones		
Operation	H	Insertion: Putting in a nonbiological appliance that monitors, assists, performs, or prevents a physiological function but does not physically take the place of a body part		

Body part	*Approach*	*Device*	*Qualifier*
0 Skull	**0** Open	**4** Internal fixation device **5** External fixation device **M** Bone growth stimulator **N** Neurostimulator generator	**Z** No qualifier
0 Skull	**3** Percutaneous **4** Percutaneous endoscopic	**4** Internal fixation device **5** External fixation device **M** Bone growth stimulator	**Z** No qualifier

Figure 20-3

United States Department of Health & Human Services. (2011). Retrieved from http://www.cms.gov/ICD10/Downloads/pcs_whats_new_2011.pdf

Character 1: Section

For inpatient surgical procedures, the majority of the codes will be selected from the Medical and Surgical section that begins with the numeric character 0. The Medical and Surgical Related Sections begins with the Obstetrics section (1) and continues with a variety of sections, including Measurement and Monitoring (4), Imaging (B), and Mental Health (H).

The following list displays all of the sections in ICD-10-PCS. This exercise will explore the organization of this first character for coding.

Sections

0- Medical and Surgical
1- Obstetrics
2- Placement
3- Administration
4- Measurement and Monitoring
5- Extracorporeal Assistance and Performance
6- Extracorporeal Therapies
7- Osteopathic
8- Other Procedures
9- Chiropractic
B- Imaging
C- Nuclear Medicine
D- Radiation Oncology
F- Physical Rehabilitation and Diagnostic Audiology
G- Mental Health
H- Substance Abuse Treatment

Section Exercise

Using the reference above and on the previous page, write the character that represents the section in ICD-10-PCS on the line that is provided. Answers to exercises 1–5 are located in Appendix A, and the remaining answers are only provided to educators through the instructor online companion.

1. _____ Hypothermia treatment (whole body)

2. _____ Open reduction and internal fixation of fractured femur

3. _____ Nasal packing

4. _____ Narcosynthesis
5. _____ Spiritual group counseling for treatment of cocaine abuse
6. _____ Beam radiation of the pancreas
7. _____ CT scan of the cervical spine (low osmolar)
8. _____ Blood transfusion–red blood cells (infused via central artery)
9. _____ Hysteroscopy
10. _____ Monitoring of urinary flow

Character 2: Body System

Character 2 in ICD-10-PCS is reserved for "Body System." The following is a subset for body systems in the Medical and Surgical section.

Body Systems

5- Upper Veins
6- Lower Veins
7- Lymphatic and Hemic Systems
8- Eye
9- Ear, Nose, Sinus
C- Mouth and Throat
D- Gastrointestinal System
F- Hepatobiliary System and Pancreas
J- Subcutaneous Tissue and Fascia
P- Upper Bones
Q- Lower Bones
W-Anatomical Regions

Body System Exercise

The second character in ICD-10-PCS represents the body systems, which also includes anatomical regions. Using the subset listed in the preceding box, write the correct character that classifies the body system for the following procedures on the line that is provided. Use the Alphabetic Index as your guide for this exercise. Answers to exercises 1–5 are located in Appendix A, and the remaining answers are only provided to educators through the instructor online companion.

Example: Mediastinoscopy (Alphabetic Index provides the second character "W" which represents Anatomical Regions.)

1. _____ Right hemicolectomy
2. _____ Scapulectomy
3. _____ Dilation of left lacrimal duct
4. _____ Percutaneous mechanical thrombectomy—femoral vein
5. _____ Laparoscopic cholecystectomy
6. _____ Insertion of peritoneal dialysis catheter
7. _____ Esophagoscopy for removal of foreign body
8. _____ Total sinus ethmoidectomy
9. _____ Splenectomy
10. _____ Insertion of pacemaker generator in subcutaneous tissue of chest wall

Character 3: Root Operation

The Root Operation represents the third character position in the ICD-10-PCS code. Identification of the Root Operation is a key decision-making component for the code selection. Coders must determine the intent of the procedure for an accurate assignment. Appendix C includes a list of Root Operations and definitions, explanations, and examples to guide coder decisions. There are a total of 31 Root Operations that are divided into 9 general categories. The following outline displays the nine categories and their corresponding Root Operations:

1. Take Out Some or All of a Body Part
   - *Excision, Resection, Extraction, Destruction, Detachment*
2. Put In/Put Back or Move Some or All of a Body Part
   - *Transplantation, Reattachment, Reposition, Transfer*
3. Take Out or Eliminate Solid Matter, Fluids, or Gases from a Body Part
   - *Drainage, Extirpation, Fragmentation*
4. Involve Only Examination of Body Parts and Regions
   - *Inspection, Map*
5. Alter the Diameter/Route of a Tubular Body Part
   - *Bypass, Dilation, Occlusion, Restriction*
6. Always Involve a Device
   - *Insertion, Replacement, Supplement, Removal, Change, Revision*
7. Involve Cutting or Separation Only
   - *Division, Release*
8. Define Other Repairs
   - *Control, Repair*
9. Define Objectives
   - *Alteration, Creation, Fusion*

In the decision-making process, first consider the nine categories instead of the entire suite of 31 Root Operations. For example, if the main intent of the procedure is to insert a feeding tube, the choices of Root Operations would fall under category 6: Always Involve a Device. The following decision tree (Figure 20-4) exhibits the process for distinguishing between the three Root Operations that are in the category for procedures that Take Out or Eliminate Solid Matter, Fluids, or Gases from a Body Part: Drainage, Extirpation, and Fragmentation.

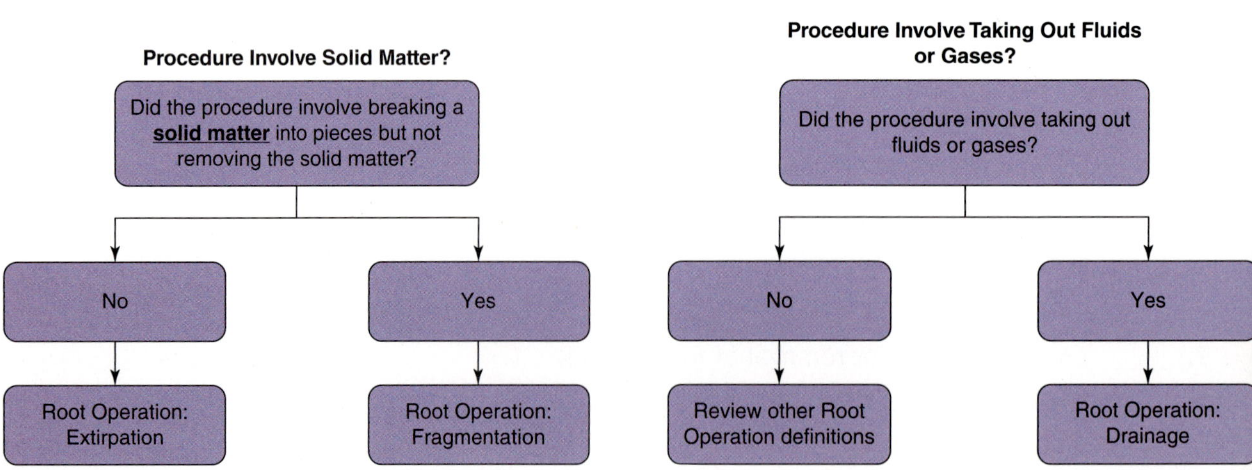

Figure 20-4

Root Operation Exercise 1

For this exercise, distinguish between the three Root Operations from the category That Take Out or Eliminate Solid Matter, Fluids or Gases from a Body Part. Use Appendix C to compare the definitions for Drainage, Extirpation, and Fragmentation. In addition, refer to the decision trees in Figure 20-4. All of the answers are located in Appendix A.

1. Lithotripsy for calculus of the right ureter __________
2. Esophagoscopy for removal of a chicken bone from the throat __________
3. Thoracentesis for drainage of fluid from pleural cavity __________
4. ESWL for kidney stone __________
5. Thrombectomy __________

Excision vs. Resection

For this second exercise on Root Operations, the focus will be on distinguishing between the two of the five Root Operations from the category That Take Out Some or All of a Body Part: Excision and Resection. Use Appendix C to compare the definitions between Excision and Resection. Excision is defined as cutting out or off, without replacement, a *portion* of a body part. An example would be removing a colon polyp. Resection is cutting out or off, without replacement, *all* of a body part. Although this appears to be straightforward, this process is more difficult because coders must reference the Alphabetic Index and/or PCS Tables for final determination.

Note the following guideline (referenced in Appendix E):

Guideline B3.8 Excision vs. Resection

PCS contains specific body parts for anatomical subdivisions of a body part, such as lobes of the lungs or liver and regions of the intestine. Resection of the specific body part is coded whenever all of the body part is cut out or off, rather than coding Excision of a less specific body part.

The following decision process will help to differentiate between Excision and Resection. Note that the step includes referring to the Alphabetic Index to determine if there is a selection for Resection of a body part.

Did the surgeon cut out or off, without replacement, a portion of a body part?

Although this is the definition for Excision, the next step is to analyze if that portion of a body part can be "resected" in PCS. As mentioned in Guideline B3.8, subdivisions of body parts may be resected. During early training, coders will not be familiar with the classification of excision vs. resection; therefore, it is necessary to review the Alphabetic Index for guidance. For example, if the surgeon states that the right upper lobe of the lung was removed, the coder must check in the Alphabetic Index to determine if there is a unique body part entry for resection of the right upper lobe in the Index. Note the following Alphabetic Index entry:

Resection
  Lung
    Upper Lobe
      Right 0BTC

Because PCS provides an entry for coding resection of this portion of the lung, Resection is the correct Root Operation.

Example:

The procedure the surgeon performed was "removal of the antrum of the stomach." Note that in the Alphabetic Index, there is no entry under Resection of the antrum of the stomach; therefore, the correct Root Operation is Excision. The surgeon removed a subdivision of a body part (stomach), *but* this subdivision is not classified as such under Resection in the Alphabetic Index. In addition, the PCS Table would not provide a selection under Resection. Refer to the following Alphabetic entry for the first four characters of the code:

Excision
    Stomach 0DB6

Root Operation Exercise 2

Refer to the Alphabetic Index to determine if the following procedures are classified as Excision or Resection. Write the correct partial characters (three or four characters) and indicate if it was found under the Root Operation *Excision* or *Resection*. Answers to exercises 1–3 are located in Appendix A, and the remaining answers are only provided to educators through the instructor online companion.

1. Cholecystectomy *(surgeon removed the entire gallbadder)* __________
2. The surgeon removed the lingula of the bronchus __________
3. The surgeon removed the tail of the pancreas __________
4. The surgeon removed the left lobe of the liver __________
5. Bilateral total orchiectomy __________
6. The surgeon removed the lower esophagus __________
7. The surgeon removed the distal section of the jejunum __________

Root Operation Exercise 3

Reference Appendix C to assign Root Operations for the following procedures. Only assign Root Operations; do not attempt to assign codes at this point. Answers to exercises 1–5 are located in Appendix A, and the remaining answers are only provided to educators through the instructor online companion.

1. Adjustment of displaced pacemaker lead __________
2. Corneal transplant __________
3. ERCP with balloon dilation of common bile duct __________
4. Closed reduction of distal radical fracture __________
5. Fetal spinal tap, open __________
6. Laparoscopic vaginal hysterectomy __________
7. Lumpectomy, left breast __________
8. Diagnostic colonoscopy __________
9. Placement of central venous catheter __________

10. Liposuction of thighs (cosmetic) ________________

11. Postpartum bilateral tubal ligation ________________

12. Removal of a leiomyosarcoma of the stomach ________________

13. Extracorporeal shock wave lithotripsy of ureter ________________

14. Laparoscopy with lysis of adhesions ________________

15. Percutaneous endoscopic gastrostomy (PEG) tube change ________________

16. Diagnostic left thoracentesis ________________

17. Laparoscopic inguinal herniorrhaphy ________________

18. Right groin sentinel lymph node biopsy ________________

19. Lateral interbody fusion at L3-4 and L4-5 ________________

20. Removal of retained intrauterine contraceptive device ________________

Character 4: Body Part

The fourth character in ICD-10-PCS identifies the specific body part for the procedure. There are two main resources for guidance with selecting the correct body part:

1. Reference the Alphabetic Index under the name of body part for classification.
2. Reference the PCS Table for final coding decision.

The next two exercises will focus on the use of these two resources.

Body Part Exercise 1

For the Body Part Exercise 1, refer to the Alphabetic Index for the appropriate body part classification. Write the body part reference term. Follow the Root Operation to the correct table and document the first several characters of the PCS Code.

For example: The surgeon documents that he performed a division of the left hamate bone. Searching under the Root Operation-Division, note that there is no entry for hamate bone. Reference the term Hamate bone in the Alphabetic Index and note that it states to classify to Carpal, left. Next, in the Alphabetic Index, reference Division, Carpal, Left for the first four characters: 0P8N.

All of the answers are located in Appendix A.

1. _______ Transfer of the left extensor hallucis brevis muscle
2. _______ Excision of medial plantar nerve
3. _______ Repair of the right circumflex iliac artery

Body Part Exercise 2

For the Body Part Exercise 2, refer to the following excerpt from the ICD-10-PCS Table for the Root Operation *Excision* in the body system *Gastrointestinal* (Figure 20-5). For visualization of the anatomic body parts, refer to Appendix B of this workbook. Rely on your knowledge of anatomy to assist with this exercise. Write the character for the body part (e.g., character 5 for Esophagus) on the line that is provided. All of the answers are located in Appendix A.

1. _____ The surgeon excised a polyp from the first portion of the small intestine.
2. _____ A biopsy was performed from the region of the stomach where it connects to the small intestine.
3. _____ The surgeon excised a lesion located on the sphincter muscle that connects the small intestine to the large intestine.

Section	**0**	Medical and surgical	
Body system	**D**	Gastrointestinal system	
Operation	**B**	Excision: Cutting out or off, without replacement, a portion of a body part	
Body part	*Approach*	*Device*	*Qualifier*
1 Esophagus, upper **2** Esophagus, middle **3** Esophagus, lower **4** Esophagogastrlc junction **5** Esophagus **6** Stomach, pylorus **7** Small intestine **8** Duodenum **A** Jejunum **B** Ileum **C** Ileocecal valve **E** Large intestine **F** Large intestine, right	**0** Open **3** Percutaneous **4** Percutaneous endoscopic **7** Via Natural or artificial opening **8** Via Natural or artificial opening endoscopic	**Z** No device	**X** Diagnostic **Z** No qualifier

Figure 20-5

United States Department of Health and Human Services. (2012). Retrieved from http://www.cms.gov/ICD10

Character 5: Approach

The Approach character identifies the surgical technique used to reach the procedure site. This information will come from the documentation in the Operative Report. CMS provides definitions for the approaches (as well as other unique characters) on their website. The following table identifies the most common approaches with definitions for the medical/surgical cases.

Approach	**Definition**
External	Procedures performed directly on the skin or mucous membrane and procedures performed indirectly by the application of external force through the skin or mucous membrane.
Open	Cutting through the skin or mucous membrane and any other body layers necessary to expose the site of the procedure.
Percutaneous	Entry, by puncture or minor incision, of instrumentation through the skin or mucous membrane and any other body layers necessary to reach the site of the procedure.
Percutaneous endoscopic	Entry, by puncture or minor incision, of instrumentation through the skin or mucous membrane and any other body layers necessary to reach and *visualize* the site of the procedure.
Via natural or artificial opening	Entry of instrumentation through a natural or artificial external opening to reach the site of the procedure.
Via natural or artificial opening endoscopic	Entry of instrumentation through a natural or artificial external opening to reach and *visualize* the site of the procedure.
Via natural or artificial opening with percutaneous endoscopic assistance	Entry of instrumentation through a natural or artificial external opening and entry, by puncture or minor incision, of instrumentation through the skin or mucous membrane and any other body layers necessary to aid in the performance of the procedure.

Approach Exercise 1

View the following surgical illustrations (Figures 20-6 through 20-10) and match the visual with the definitions of approaches listed in the previous table. All of the answers are located in Appendix A.

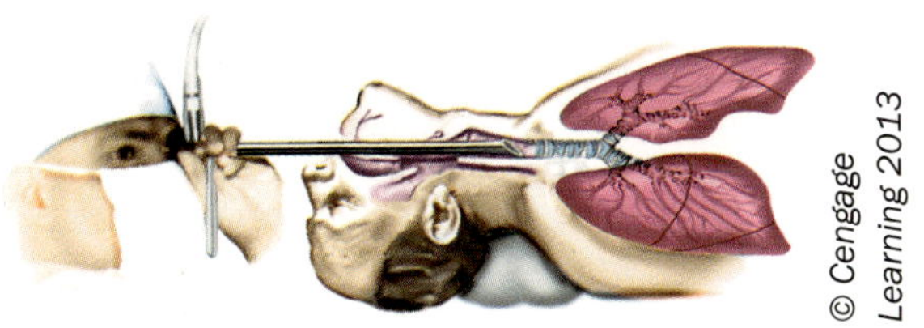

1.

Figure 20-6 Rigid bronchoscopy

____

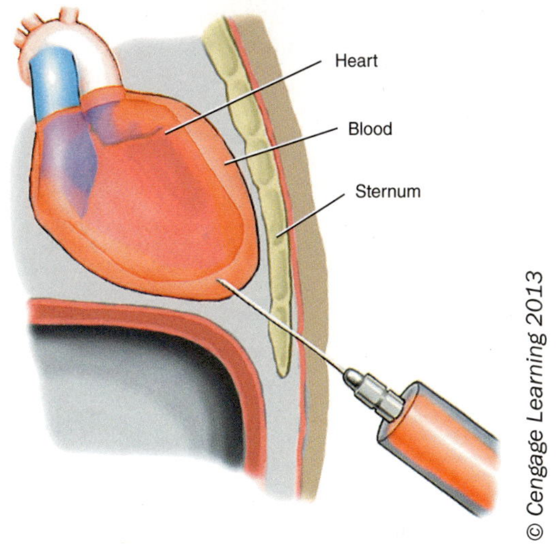

2.

Figure 20-7 Cardiac tamponade: pericardial aspiration with needle and syringe

____

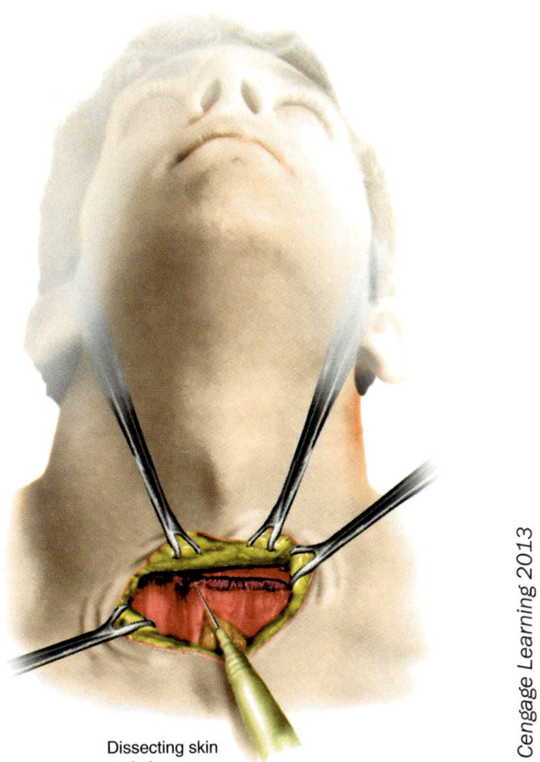

3.

Figure 20-8 Thyroidectomy: Insicion

____

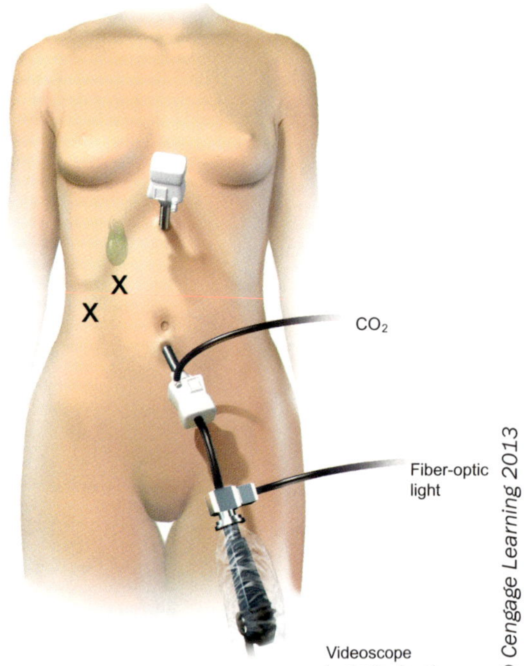

4.

Figure 20-9 Camera and additional trocars are placed

____

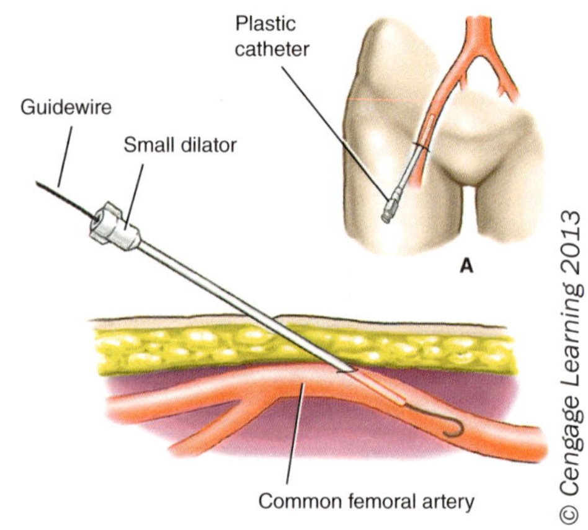

5.

Figure 20-10 Intra-aortic balloon pump insert (A) Needle cannula assembly is inserted into fe artery, (B) small dilator is threaded over guidew

____

Approach Exercise 2

Apply the definitions from the previous table to the following procedures. Identify if the procedure is percutaneous, percutaneous endoscopic, via natural or artificial opening, via natural or artificial opening endoscopic, or via natural or artificial opening with percutaneous endoscopic assistance. Answers to exercises 1–5 are located in Appendix A, and the remaining answers are only provided to educators through the instructor online companion.

1. Esophagogastroduodenoscopy (EGD) ______________
2. Open reduction of distal tibia fracture ______________
3. Sterile dressing applied to the wound of the shoulder ______________
4. Thyroidectomy ______________
5. Colonoscopy ______________
6. Laparoscopic appendectomy ______________
7. Digital rectal examination ______________
8. Total abdominal hysterectomy ______________
9. Endotracheal intubation ______________
10. Percutaneous bone marrow biopsy ______________

Approach Exercise 3

This exercise includes excerpts from Operative Reports that describe the approach. Review the documentation and refer to the definitions to classify the approach. If you are unfamiliar with the procedure, perform a web search that further describes the technique. Write the name of the approach next to the excerpt. Answers to exercises 1–3 are located in Appendix A, and the remaining answers are only provided to educators through the instructor online companion.

1. Description of procedure: The patient was brought emergently to the cardiac catheterization lab. Sedation was given with a total of 250 mcg of fentanyl and 5 mg of versed. Local anesthesia was given in the right groin with 1% lidocaine. The right common femoral artery was accessed using the modified Seldinger technique, and a 6-French sheath was placed.

   ____

2. The patient had general anesthesia and positioned supine; the right knee was prepped and draped in the routine fashion. The knee was elevated and tourniquet inflated to 300 mmHg. A midline incision was opened over the patella and sharp dissection carried down to the extensor mechanism.

   ____

3. The patient was taken to the operating room and was induced with general endotracheal anesthesia. The abdomen was prepped and draped in sterile fashion. An umbilical incision was made and a Veress needle was introduced and abdomen was insufflated to 3 liters. A 10 mm supraumbilical trocar was introduced with a Visiport. Under direct visualization, two right lateral and one left-sided trocar were introduced.

   ____

4. The colonoscope was inserted via the anus and advanced under direct vision until the cecum was reached.

   ____

5. After careful consideration of the area, appropriate needle placement was found and marked. The area was then sterilely prepped and draped in the usual fashion with chlorhexidine swab. The area was then anesthetized with 10cc of 1% lidocaine. A #11 blade was used to make a small skin nick, through which an 8-French, 18-gauge needle/catheter system was advanced under direct guidance into the fluid collection system.

   ____

6. The patient was prepped and draped in sterile fashion and 20 mL of 0.25% Marcaine with epinephrine was used to inject the skin. A 10-blade scalpel was used to skin incision and the prior craniotomy flap was reflected anteriorly and held in place with fishhooks over a Ray-Tec sponge. The temporalis muscle was also reflected anteriorly so that the perimeter of the craniotomy flap could be identified.

   ____

7. After this patient was prepped and draped, I began by placing a 21-French rigid cystoscope with a 12 degree lens into the urethra and bladder.

   ____

Character 6: Device

The sixth character appears only in sections that are applicable; otherwise, the default of Z (no device) is assigned. Definitions are provided by CMS and classification guidance is provided from the Alphabetic Index. Only devices that remain at the conclusion of the procedure are coded. Exploration of PCS tables will reveal consistent terminology (classification) such as intraluminal, extraluminal, and internal fixation.

Device Exercise 1

To maintain consistency in the classification system, the Alphabetic Index provides numerous references for common surgical devices. Refer to the Alphabetic Index to determine the classification for the following devices. Answers to exercises 1–4 are located in Appendix A, and the remaining answers are only provided to educators through the instructor online companion.

Example:

CONSERVE® PLUS Total Resurfacing Hip System use Resurfacing Device in Lower Joints

1. Formula™ Balloon-Expandable Renal Stent System __________
2. Ex-PRESS™ mini glaucoma shunt __________
3. Impella® (2.5) (5.0) (LD) cardiac assist device __________
4. Nitinol framed polymer mesh __________
5. Cobalt/chromium head and socket __________
6. Bard® Dulex™ mesh __________
7. Paclitaxel-eluting peripheral stent __________
8. InterStim® Therapy lead __________

Device Exercise 2

Refer to the following excerpt from a table in ICD-10-PCS (Figure 20-11) and identify the device (tissue substitutes) described in the following procedures. Research any unfamiliar terms using the web. All of the answers are located in Appendix A.

Device
7 Autologous tissue substitute **8** Zooplastic tissue **J** Synthetic substitute **K** Nonautologous tissue substitute

United States Department of Health and Human Services. (2012). Retrieved from http://www.cms.gov/ICD10

Figure 20-11

1. Repair of bladder with tissue that was created from the patient's own bladder tissue

____

2. A laboratory-produced skin tissue was used on the burn victim

____

3. Mitral valve replacement with porcine tissue

____

Character 7: Qualifier

The last character in ICD-10-PCS is called a qualifier. The qualifiers provide additional information and are used only in certain sections; the default is Z for "no qualifier." In a previous exercise, the Qualifier "X" was used to identify a Diagnostic procedure. For the following exercise, refer to the ICD-10-PCS Table excerpt for hip joint replacement (Figure 20-12).

9 Hip joint, right **B** Hip joint, left	**0** Open	**1** Synthetic substitute, metal **2** Synthetic substitute, metal on polyethylene **3** Synthetic substitute, ceramic **4** Synthetic substitute, ceramic on polyethylene **J** Synthetic substitute	**9** Cemented **A** Uncemented **Z** No qualifier

Figure 20-12

United States Department of Health and Human Services. (2012). Retrieved from http://www.cms.gov/ICD10

Qualifier Case Study

This case is a Replacement of the left hip joint. Refer to the Root Operation Replacement and search for Joint, Hip, Left. The Alphabetic Index provides the first four characters (0SRB). It is an open procedure; therefore, decisions need to be made only for the Device and Qualifier. From the following documentation, complete the codes with choosing the correct Device and Qualifier. Answer is located in Appendix A.

OPERATIVE NOTE

PREOPERATIVE DIAGNOSIS: Left severe hip arthritis.

POSTOPERATIVE DIAGNOSIS: Left severe hip arthritis.

PROCEDURE: Press-fit total hip arthroplasty.

Femoral head and neck were removed and sent to pathology for review. The ball and socket of the hip joint were replaced with titanium prosthesis and polyethylene surface. What is the appropriate code for this case?

____

Building an ICD-10-PCS Code

Assign ICD-10-PCS codes to the following procedures. Answers to exercises 1–5 are located in Appendix A, and the remaining answers are only provided to educators through the instructor online companion.

1. Bilateral liposuction of upper arms (elective procedure) ______________
2. Laparoscopic-assisted total vaginal hysterectomy (LAVH) ____________
3. Advancement flap skin graft covering left forearm __________________
4. Open reduction with internal fixation, displaced left lateral ankle fracture ________________
5. ERCP with balloon dilation of common bile duct ______________
6. Needle biopsy of liver, right lobe ______________
7. Debridement-excision of right hip pressure ulcer down to and including the subcutaneous layer and fascia ______________
8. Colonoscopy with removal of polyp using hot biopsy forceps in ascending colon. The surgeon explained that the polyp looked suspicious and was awaiting pathological analysis. _____________
9. Complete thyroidectomy ______________
10. Repair of left thumb, flexor pollicis longus tendon ______________

Coding Operative Reports

Assign ICD-10-PCS codes to the procedures documented in the following Operative Reports. Answers to exercises 1–5 are located in Appendix A, and the remaining answers are only provided to educators through the instructor online companion.

OPERATIVE REPORT 1

PREOPERATIVE DIAGNOSIS: Abnormal right mammogram.

POSTOPERATIVE DIAGNOSIS: Abnormal right mammogram.

PROCEDURE PERFORMED: Right breast lumpectomy.

ESTIMATED BLOOD LOSS: Minimal.

INDICATIONS FOR PROCEDURE: The patient had an area of abnormal thickening noted on a mammogram, just lateral to the nipple–areolar complex.

DESCRIPTION OF THE PROCEDURE: The patient was taken to the operating room and placed in the supine position. After general endotracheal anesthesia was administered, the patient was prepped and draped in the usual sterile manner.

The patient had a right lateral circumareolar incision made. A generous lumpectomy was performed around this area. There were no dominant masses. The specimen was removed and sent to pathology. The biopsy cavity was inspected, and hemostasis was achieved. The dermal tissue was reapproximated with 3-0 Polysorb in an interrupted fashion. The skin was closed with a 4-0 Caprosyn in a running subcuticular fashion. The wound was infiltrated with 0.5% Marcaine and 1% lidocaine. The patient had Steri-Strips and a sterile dressing applied.

The patient was awakened from anesthesia, having suffered no apparent intraoperative complications.

ICD-10-PCS Code(s): ______________________________

OPERATIVE REPORT 2

PREOPERATIVE DIAGNOSIS: Unstable left distal radial metaphyseal fracture.

POSTOPERATIVE DIAGNOSIS: Unstable left distal radial metaphyseal fracture.

PROCEDURE PERFORMED: Open reduction and internal fixation of left distal radius.

ANESTHESIA: General.

PROCEDURE IN DETAIL: After obtaining informed consent, the patient was brought to the operating room whereupon the smooth induction of general anesthesia was performed. The patient was positioned in a supine fashion on the operating room table and all bony prominences were well padded. The left upper extremity was placed on a radiolucent arm board. A tourniquet was placed in the left upper extremity and the left upper extremity was prepped and draped in a standard sterile fashion from the distal arm to the fingertips. After exsanguination of the left upper extremity with an Ace wrap, the tourniquet was inflated to 200 mmHg.

A 6-cm incision was made over the volar aspect of the wrist just radial to the flexor carpi radialis (FCR) tendon, which was palpable. The skin was dissected sharply and the subcutaneous tissue was dissected bluntly down to the level of the antebrachial fascia. This was incised sharply in line with the incision under direct visualization. The FCR tendon and median nerve were retracted in an ulnar direction. The radial artery and attendant leash of veins were retracted in a radial direction. In this manner the pronator quadratus was identified. It was released from its radial insertion to expose the volar aspect of the distal radius. The distal radial transverse metaphyseal fracture was thus visualized. This fracture was mobilized with a Freer and reduction was checked with intraoperative fluoroscopy in the AP and lateral views. After mobilization of this callus, a three-hole Synthes-locked distal radial plate was selected and contoured to fit the volar aspect of the distal radius. Holding the plate slightly off the radial shaft, three locking screws were placed through the plate and into the distal fragment just below the subchondral bone. Once these screws were in place, the plate was brought down onto the radial shaft, thus achieving the reduction. The plate was held in position with 3.5-mm fully threaded standard cortical screws. Reduction was checked on AP and lateral views and found to be anatomic.

The wound was then copiously irrigated with normal saline and closed. The skin was then closed using interrupted 4-0 nylon suture in a horizontal mattress fashion. A sterile dressing and a well-padded, well-molded sugar-tong splint were placed.

The patient was awoken from anesthesia and taken to the recovery room in stable condition.

ICD-10-PCS Code(s): ____

OPERATIVE REPORT 3

PROCEDURE PERFORMED: Esophagogastroduodenoscopy with cautery.

INDICATIONS: Gastrointestinal (GI) bleed and angiodysplasia of the stomach.

PREOPERATIVE DIAGNOSES: GI bleed and angiodysplasia of the stomach.

POSTOPERATIVE DIAGNOSES: GI bleed and angiodysplasia of the stomach.

INSTRUMENT AND MEDICATIONS: The Olympus video system was used. The patient was given a total of 2 mg of IV Versed and 25 mcg of IV fentanyl. Throat was sprayed and epinephrine as well as bipolar cautery was used.

DESCRIPTION OF THE PROCEDURE: The scope was passed through the hypopharynx with ease. The esophagus, stomach, and duodenum to the second portion were all well evaluated, including retroflexion of the GE junction from below. The findings were within normal limits in the duodenum and the esophagus, but in the stomach I could see two spots of angiodysplasia. This is shown in photograph 2. I injected this with approximately 1.5 mL of 1:10,000 epinephrine. It blanched rather nicely. I then used the Gold probe and on a setting of 16 watts using 2-second pulses. I was able to fulgurate this. The patient tolerated the procedure well.

ICD-10-PCS Code(s): ____

OPERATIVE REPORT 4

PREOPERATIVE DIAGNOSIS: Screening for colon cancer.

POSTOPERATIVE DIAGNOSIS: Normal colon to the level of the cecum.

PROCEDURE: Colonoscopy.

ANESTHESIA: Titrated increments of fentanyl and Versed.

COMPLICATIONS: None.

DESCRIPTION OF PROCEDURE: The patient was brought to the endoscopy suite where he was confirmed to be in stable condition. His history and physical examinations were essentially unchanged from the time of dictation. His questions were again addressed prior to initiation of the procedure. With confirming of hemodynamic stability, the patient was given titrated increments of fentanyl and Versed to achieve IV sedation.

The colonoscope was introduced and I was able to navigate through to the level of the cecum, with clear visualization of the ileocecal valve. The scope was then very carefully brought back for careful inspection and readvancement of the scope to ensure good visualization. With careful inspection and withdrawal time of approximately 10 minutes, the scope was then retroflexed and then withdrawn.

Overall, the patient tolerated the procedure well and he is stable to recovery.

FINDINGS: Normal colon to the level of the cecum.

ICD-10-PCS Code(s): ______________________________

OPERATIVE REPORT 5

PREOPERATIVE DIAGNOSIS: Right nasal foreign body.

POSTOPERATIVE DIAGNOSIS: Right nasal foreign body.

DESCRIPTION OF THE PROCEDURE: This patient was placed in the supine position under satisfactory general anesthesia by mask. His nose was examined and a small cotton foreign body was removed from the anterior aspect of the nose. This seemed to be the entire content of the foreign body and his nose was examined and no further foreign body was noted. He was then awakened and taken to recovery in satisfactory condition.

ICD-10-PCS Code(s): ______________________________

OPERATIVE REPORT 6

PROCEDURE: Thoracentesis.

INDICATION: Large fluid collection on the left side.

CONSENT: Informed consent was obtained from the patient. The risks, benefits, and alternatives to the procedure were explained, and the patient agreed to proceed with thoracentesis.

DESCRIPTION OF THE PROCEDURE: The left posterior lower thorax was cleansed with iodine. Using standard sterile technique, the fluid was identified with a fine needle in a place of dullness. Subsequently, the skin was incised with a scalpel for about 2 mm. Catheter was inserted over the needle in the pleural space without difficulty. Opaque greenish-colored fluid was collected in suction bottles; 1.9 liters of fluid was removed, and at the end of the procedure, intermittent drainage occurred, and eventually the drainage stopped, at which time the procedure was terminated. The patient had some cough while the fluid was being removed. Overall, he tolerated the procedure very well, and there were no complications.

ICD-10-PCS Code(s): ______________________________

OPERATIVE REPORT 7

DIAGNOSIS: Pneumonia with severe hypoxemia.

PROCEDURE: Endotracheal intubation.

Patient was sedated with Versed 3 mg, Fentanyl 25 mcg, and Etomidate 10 mg. Patient was intubated with 8.0 ETT using the Glidescope with direct visualization of vocal cords. Patient tolerated the procedure well without complications.

ICD-10-PCS Code(s): ______________________________

OPERATIVE REPORT 8

PREOPERATIVE DIAGNOSIS: Incisional hernia.

POSTOPERATIVE DIAGNOSIS: Incisional hernia.

PROCEDURE: Laparoscopic incisional herniorrhaphy with mesh.

INDICATIONS: The patient is a 70-year-old gentleman who has previously undergone a vertical-banded gastroplasty and this was converted to a Roux-en-Y gastric bypass. He has had a single midline incision and now has developed a painful mass in his epigastrium. Clinical evaluation and CT scanning has confirmed the diagnosis of a symptomatic incisional hernia and he will now undergo repair.

FINDINGS: Incisional hernia, not incarcerated.

PROCEDURE IN DETAIL: The patient was brought to the operating room and placed supine on the operating table. General endotracheal anesthesia was induced and his abdomen was prepped and draped sterilely. Then 0.25% Marcaine was infiltrated into his surgical sites for postoperative analgesia.

A small nick was made in the left upper quadrant. A Veress needle was inserted into the abdomen through this nick. After confirming intraabdominal position of the needle, pneumoperitoneum to 15 mm Hg was generated. A 5-mm port was placed in the left side of the abdomen using an Optiview technique. Under direct vision, a second right-sided port and a left-sided port were placed. Utilizing these three 5-mm ports, adhesions to the anterior abdominal wall were taken down with combination of sharp dissection and electrocautery. This exposed a Swiss cheese–type hernia defect in the upper portion of his abdomen. All fat and these hernia defects were reduced. Adhesions were taken down up underneath the diaphragm to allow for placement of the mesh into this position. Once this was completed, an 8 inch × 10 inch piece of Physiomesh was brought to the operating field. A suture was placed in the superior and inferior aspects of the mesh. The superior suture was placed approximately 1 inch from the mesh edge to allow it to be placed in the subxiphoid position and have the mesh flip up underneath the diaphragm to be tacked under the diaphragm. The mesh was then inserted into the abdomen and unfolded. The epigastric suture was brought through counter incisions on the anterior abdominal wall. The intraabdominal pressure was then turned down to 8. The mesh was then stretched inferiorly and a mark was made on the anterior abdominal wall inferiorly where all defects would be covered and the mesh would be tensioned appropriately. A counter incision was made in this location and the preplaced 0 PDS suture was brought through the anterior abdominal wall. These two sutures were held on tension. With the intraabdominal pressure still at 8, two rows of tacks were placed circumferentially through the anterior abdominal wall. To facilitate this, two further 5-mm ports were needed to be placed in the lateral aspects of the abdomen. Once the tacking of the mesh was completed, two more transfascial sutures were placed in the lateral aspects of the mesh. This was done by passing a 0 PDS suture transfascially lateral to the mesh through one of the 5-mm port site incisions. The endo close was then passed through the mesh and the suture grasped and brought back out through the anterior abdominal wall. This was done on both the right and left sides of the abdomen. With the four transfascial sutures now in place, the mesh was inspected and found to be appropriately positioned. All of these sutures were tied. The ports were removed and the pneumoperitoneum released. To facilitate placement of the mesh, one of the 5-mm ports was changed out for an 11-mm port and this port site fascial defect was encircled with an 0 Vicryl suture to occlude its fascial defect. The pneumoperitoneum was released by removing the remainder of the ports. The skin incisions were closed with 4-0 Monocryl subcuticular suture and Steri-Strips. The patient tolerated the procedure well, there were no complications, and estimated blood loss was minimal. He was taken to recovery in satisfactory condition.

ICD-10-PCS Code(s): ______________________________

OPERATIVE REPORT 9

PREOPERATIVE DIAGNOSIS: Right nasal foreign body.

POSTOPERATIVE DIAGNOSIS: Right nasal foreign body.

DESCRIPTION OF PROCEDURE: This patient was placed in the supine position under satisfactory general anesthesia by mask. His nose was examined and a small cotton foreign body was removed from the anterior aspect of the nose. This seemed to be the entire content of the foreign body and his nose was examined and no further foreign body was noted. He was then awakened and taken to recovery in satisfactory condition.

ICD-10-PCS Code(s): ________________________________

OPERATIVE REPORT 10

PREOPERATIVE DIAGNOSIS: Retained hardware right tibia with hardware bursitis.

POSTOPERATIVE DIAGNOSIS: Retained hardware right tibia with hardware bursitis.

PROCEDURE: Right tibia hardware removal.

INDICATIONS: This 60-year-old lady underwent intramedullary nailing of her right tibia about a year ago. The patient has since then healed her tibia fracture and had had symptoms reminiscent of hardware bursitis. She is agreeable to the decision to remove the hardware.

PROCEDURE: Under general anesthesia and tourniquet control, the right leg was prepped and draped using normal sterile technique. Prior to surgery the patient's previous incisions were marked for reference. The three short incisions were utilized to remove the transfixing screws. All three screws were easily removed without difficulty. The wounds were irrigated and closed with staples. Next, the patient's longitudinal incision over the medial patellar tendon area was utilized to approach the proximal end of the tibial rod. Soft tissue was cleaned out of the proximal rod and the end cap was easily removed. Once the end cap was removed, the inserter/extractor attachment was inserted into the proximal end of the rod and using a slap hammer the rod was gently removed. The knee wound was irrigated and closed with absorbable sutures repairing the medial retinaculum to the patellar tendon followed by absorbable sutures on the subcutaneous tissues and staples on the skin. A light dressing was applied, one at the knee and the other at the ankle. Tourniquet time was 40 minutes. Blood loss was minimal. There were no complications.

ICD-10-PCS Code(s): ________________________________

CHAPTER

21

Application of Coding Guidelines

This section is designed to test your knowledge of the ICD-10-CM Official Guidelines for Coding Reporting developed by the Centers for Medicare & Medicaid Services and the National Center for Health Statistics. Answers to exercises 1–10 are located in Appendix A, and the remaining answers are only provided to educators through the instructor online companion.

Instructions: For each question select the appropriate answer.

1. The 32-year-old patient is at a dinner party, drinking wine with her dinner. At 6 PM she takes prescribed Allegra and then experiences severe dizziness and nausea. She is taken to the emergency department to be seen because the symptoms are so severe. After examination the provider concludes that the dizziness and nausea were caused by the combination of the Allegra and wine. This would be reported as a(n):
   - a. poisoning.
   - b. overdose.
   - c. abuse of drugs.
   - d. adverse effect.

2. Tachycardia after taking a correct dosage of prescribed Lortab would be reported as a(n):
   - a. poisoning.
   - b. adverse reaction to a drug.
   - c. abuse of drugs.
   - d. underdosing.

3. A patient is undergoing hemodialysis for end-stage renal disease in the outpatient department of an acute care hospital. The patient develops what is believed to be severe heartburn, but is sent to observation for several hours, at which time the patient is admitted to inpatient care for further workup. At the time of admission to observation, the admitting physician feels that the patient has unstable angina. The consulting cardiologist diagnoses the patient's problem as a myocardial infarction. What is the principal diagnosis for the acute hospital stay?
   - a. Complications of hemodialysis
   - b. Myocardial infarction
   - c. Unstable angina
   - d. Renal disease

4. A patient is admitted for treatment of cough, fever, and congestion. The physician makes the diagnosis of pneumonia. The coder would:
   - a. assign codes for cough, fever, congestion, and pneumonia.
   - b. assign codes for congestion and pneumonia.
   - c. query the physician for the causal relationship between symptoms and pneumonia.
   - d. assign code only for pneumonia.

5. A female patient has just undergone a hysterectomy. Documentation indicates that she lost 800 mL of blood during surgery. Her hemoglobin and hematocrit are monitored following surgery. Subsequently she is given a blood transfusion. The physician documents anemia as a secondary diagnosis. The coder would:
   a. query the physician to clarify the type of anemia as acute blood loss.
   b. assign a code for unspecified anemia.
   c. assign a code for acute blood loss anemia.
   d. assign a code for low hemoglobin and hematocrit.

6. The 34-year-old patient is admitted for a compound fracture of the left tibia. He also has an abrasion and several superficial lacerations in the same area. The coder should:
   a. query the physician to determine if the abrasions and lacerations should be coded.
   b. code the fracture of the tibia only.
   c. code the fracture of the tibia and code the abrasion if the abrasion is treated.
   d. code the fracture, abrasion, and lacerations.

7. Which of the following is *not* considered a poisoning?
   a. Overdose of Oxycontin intentionally taken to commit suicide.
   b. Error made in the administration of the prescribed drug gabapentin by a nurse.
   c. Allergic reaction to Rozerem that was correctly prescribed and properly administered.
   d. Error made in a drug prescription by a physician for Zocar.

8. According to the Official Coding Guidelines, which of the following statements is true in relation to the assignment of code O80?
   a. Code O80 can be assigned with any other codes from Chapter 15 of ICD-10-CM.
   b. Code O80 is always assigned as the principal diagnosis.
   c. When the outcome of delivery is liveborn, twins code O80 can be assigned.
   d. Code O80 can be assigned if the patient had an unresolved antepartum complication at the time of delivery.

9. A fracture of the radius without any further clarification is coded as:
   a. closed and displaced.
   b. closed and nondisplaced.
   c. open and displaced.
   d. open and nondisplaced.

10. An HIV-infected asymptomatic patient is admitted to the hospital as an inpatient with acute appendicitis. A laparoscopic appendectomy is performed. What is the appropriate principal diagnoses code for this case?
    a. AIDS
    b. Acute appendicitis
    c. Admission for surgical procedure
    d. Any of the above

11. When a symptom is followed by a contrasting or comparative diagnoses, which of the following is correct when selecting a principal Diagnosis?
    a. The contrasting diagnoses are listed first.
    b. The comparative diagnoses are listed first.
    c. The symptom code is sequenced first.
    d. Any of the above can occur.

12. A patient is admitted with fever, abdominal pain, and an elevated WBC. Acute appendicitis is confirmed. What diagnoses should be reported for this case?
    a. Fever and abdominal pain
    b. Only acute appendicitis
    c. Fever, abdominal pain, and elevated WBC
    d. Acute appendicitis is reported as the principal and fever, abdominal pain, and elevated WBC are reported as secondary diagnoses

13. The following appeared in the documentation for an outpatient visit: Patient's blood pressure is 140/98 mm Hg. The patient has experienced vomiting for three days. The patient was treated for gastritis and the blood pressure will be monitored on the next visit. Which of the following would be correct?
    a. Assign a code for gastritis and hypertension.
    b. Assign a code for gastritis.
    c. Assign a code for gastritis and for high or elevated blood pressure without a firm diagnosis of hypertension.
    d. Assign a code for gastritis, vomiting, and hypertension.

14. The patient has a third-degree burn of the forearm and a second-degree burn on the leg. What is the correct coding action?
    a. Code both burns and sequence the burn of the forearm first.
    b. Code only the burn of the forearm.
    c. Query the physician.
    d. Code both and sequence the leg first.

15. The 28-year-old female was seen in the outpatient department with chronic abdominal pain for the last 7 days. After the examination the physician records: rule out ovarian cyst. What should be coded as the patient's diagnosis?
    a. Observation and evaluation without need for further medical care
    b. Diagnosis of unknown etiology
    c. Ovarian cyst
    d. Abdominal pain

16. When the phrase "code first underlying disease" appears in the ICD-10-CM code book, the coder should:
    a. code the underlying disease only when selecting codes in the inpatient setting.
    b. view this as mandatory depending on the chapter of ICD-10-CM in which the phrase appears.
    c. view this as a mandatory instruction.
    d. treat the phrase as a suggestion only.

17. Given the diagnosis "carcinoma of brain and lymph nodes, metastatic from lungs," what is the primary cancer site(s)?
    a. Lungs
    b. Lymph nodes
    c. Lungs and lymph nodes
    d. Brain

18. The 54-year-old female was admitted to the ambulatory care unit for a planned cholecystectomy for cholelithiasis. Shortly before surgery, she developed tachycardia and the surgery was cancelled. After a workup for the tachycardia, she was discharged. The first-listed diagnosis would be a code for:
    a. an encounter for cholecystectomy.
    b. tachycardia.
    c. observation status.
    d. cholelithiasis.

19. The 28-year-old female has had abdominal pain for several weeks and has been spitting up blood for 5 days. She was admitted and the following procedures were completed: abdominal X-ray, CT of abdomen with contrast, and esophagogastroduodenscopy (EGD) with biopsy. The diagnostic testing confirmed gastritis. Which is the principal diagnosis and procedure for this admission?
    a. Abdominal pain, abdominal X-ray
    b. Gastritis, CT of abdomen with contrast
    c. Abdominal pain, EGD with biopsy
    d. Gastritis, EGD with biopsy

20. The patient was in a house fire and sustained first-, second-, and third-degree burns on his left arm. He was admitted as an inpatient. This case should be coded by selecting a code for:
    a. the third-degree burn only.
    b. the second-degree burn only.
    c. the first- and second-degree burns.
    d. each degree of burn separately.

21. An 86-year-old man was admitted for a repair of a hiatal hernia. The hernia was repaired and on the second day of admission the patient fell and fractured his mandible. He also experienced chest pain and dizziness. A cardiac catheterization and percutaneous transluminal coronary angioplasty (PTCA) was completed to rule out cardiac findings. The principal diagnosis is:
    a. chest pain.
    b. dizziness.
    c. hiatal hernia.
    d. fractured mandible.

22. Which of the following is coded as an adverse effect in ICD-10-CM?
    a. Mental retardation due to cranial abscess
    b. Rejection of transplanted lung
    c. Nonfunctioning cardiac pacemaker
    d. Conjunctivitis due to allergic reaction after administration of eye drops

23. A 29-year-old female patient was admitted in active labor. She delivered her fifth child and following the delivery a sterilization procedure was performed for contraceptive reasons. The code for sterilization, Z30.2, would be:
    a. not assigned because it is the same admission as the delivery.
    b. not assigned because it was performed for contraceptive reasons.
    c. assigned as a secondary diagnosis.
    d. assigned as a principal diagnosis.

24. Which of the following is ***false*** in regards to chronic kidney disease?
    a. Mild chronic kidney disease is reported with code N18.3.
    b. ICD-10-CM classifies chronic kidney disease based on severity.
    c. If both a stage of chronic kidney disease and end-stage renal disease is documented, assign code N18.6 only.
    d. Patients who have undergone kidney transplant may still have some form of CKD; therefore, assign the appropriate N18 code for the patient's stage of CKD and code Z94.0, kidney transplant status.

25. When a patient is admitted for management of dehydration due to a malignancy and only the dehydration is being treated, the coder should:
    a. list the code for the malignancy only.
    b. list the code for dehydration only.
    c. list the code for the malignancy first and then the code for the dehydration.
    d. list the code for the dehydration first followed by the code for the malignancy.

CHAPTER 22

Coding Case Studies

This section of the workbook will allow you to put it all together by selecting codes and following the ICD-10-CM Official Guidelines for Coding and Reporting. Read each case study and for each case select the correct ICD-10-CM and/or ICD-10-PCS codes(s) based on correct coding principles and sequence codes according to the Official Guidelines for Coding and Reporting. Answers to exercises 1–10 are located in Appendix A, and the remaining answers are only provided to educators through the instructor online companion.

1. A 35-year-old female patient was admitted due to heavy uterine bleeding and generalized abdominal pain. A diagnostic hysteroscopy with D&C was completed, which showed bright red blood in the vagina. The discharge diagnosis was uterine cyst and acute blood loss anemia. Select the appropriate codes for this admission.

ICD-10-CM code(s): ______________________

ICD-10-PCS codes(s): ______________________

2. The patient is 6 weeks post mastectomy for carcinoma of the right breast and is now admitted for chemotherapy. She has no other medical conditions.

ICD-10-CM code(s): ______________________

3. The following appeared in the documentation for an outpatient visit:

Patient's blood pressure is 140/98 mm Hg. There is no documentation of a previous elevated BP. Cardiac: No findings.

Lungs: No rales, within normal limits.

Gastrointestinal System: The patient has experienced vomiting for 3 days.

Assessment: Acute gastritis, elevated BP

Plan: E prescription sent to pharmacy.

ICD-10-CM code(s): ______________________

4. The patient presented for a laparoscopic cholecystectomy due to gallstones. The laparoscopic procedure was started but was converted to an open procedure. Discharge summary was documented:

Diagnosis: Gallstones

Procedure: Cholecystectomy

ICD-10-CM code(s): ______________________

ICD-10-PCS code(s): ______________________

5. This 35-year-old female patient was seen in Dr. Jones' office with a chief complaint of chronic abdominal pain for the last 5 days. After the examination the physician records rule out ovarian cyst and order an ultrasound to be completed at the hospital.

ICD-10-CM code(s): ______________________

6. The patient is admitted to an acute care hospital with alcohol withdrawal and is suffering with delirium. The patient has been previously diagnosed with chronic alcoholism. She is being treated for the withdrawal and delirium.

   ICD-10-CM code(s): ______________________

7. A 55-year-old male was admitted and described as having prolonged and intractable wheezing; airway obstruction that was not relieved by bronchodilators, and lab values showed decreased respiratory function. The discharge summary recorded a final diagnosis of asthma with chronic obstructive pulmonary disease with an acute exacerbation.

   ICD-10-CM code(s): ______________________

8. The patient was undergoing hemodialysis for end-stage renal disease in the outpatient department of an acute care hospital. After the treatment she complained of severe heartburn and was sent to observation for several hours, at which time the patient is admitted to inpatient care for further workup. The cardiologist diagnoses the patient's problem as unstable angina. The code for the principal diagnosis for the inpatient admission should be:

   ICD-10-CM code(s): ______________________

9. The patient is admitted with a comminuted displaced fracture of the shaft of the left tibia with multiple abrasions in the same area on his leg. An open reduction of a fracture of the left tibia was performed.

   ICD-10-CM code(s): ______________________

   ICD-10-PCS code(s): ______________________

10. A woman, who is a known alcoholic, gave birth via a vaginal delivery to a 5-pound, 3-ounce female infant. The infant was born in the hospital and was diagnosed with fetal alcohol syndrome and remained in the hospital for 3 weeks. At the time of discharge for the infant the codes to report should be:

    ICD-10-CM code(s): ______________________

11. A 60-year-old patient was admitted with a diagnosis of hyperthyroidism due to ectopic thyroid tissue with thyroid storm. During this admission the patient had an open complete thyroidectomy.

    ICD-10-CM code(s): ______________________

    ICD-10-PCS code(s): ______________________

12. An 81-year-old patient is admitted with fever, cough, and shortness of breath. Because of previous concerns a bronchoscopy of the right lung was completed and confirmed pneumonia. Lab testing additionally confirmed a streptococcal, group B, infection. The discharge summary recorded: group B streptococcal pneumonia.

    ICD-10-CM code(s): ______________________

    ICD-10-PCS code(s): ______________________

13. A 23-year-old female patient presented to the office with painful urination. A urine test showed a UTI due to *E. coli.*

    ICD-10-CM code(s): ______________________

14. A 2-year-old child presents to the office today. His mother states that she feels that he has placed an object in his ear. Both ears were examined and there appears to be a foreign object in his right ear. Because of his age he was referred to ENT for further exam and treatment.

    ICD-10-CM code(s): ______________________

15. The patient had a 4-day hospital stay and the discharge diagnoses recorded as:

    Principal dx: ASHD, native artery with unstable angina

    Secondary dx: type 1 diabetic with diabetic nephropathy

    ICD-10-CM code(s): ______________________

16. The patient presents today with red eyes for the last 2 to 3 days. The patient states that his eyes are becoming more and more irritated. After examination the patient was found to have a chalazion of the right upper eyelid and an infected meibomian gland of the left lower eyelid. Prescriptions were written.

    ICD-10-CM code(s): ___________________________

17. A 17-year-old male presents to the emergency department. He was at a party drinking alcohol and accidently overdosed on speed and vodka tonics. His blood tests showed an alcohol level of 50 mg/100 mi. He was stabilized and referred to the Addiction Unit for evaluation.

    ICD-10-CM code(s): ___________________________

18. An 89-year-old patient has resided at Sunny Valley Skilled Nursing Facility for 8 months. The facility physician examined her at the request of the nursing staff. Examination of the skin reveals that there is a chronic ulceration of the skin of the left heel and mid foot. There is no breakdown into the fatty layer, muscle, or bone. This will be monitored by the staff.

    ICD-10-CM code(s): ___________________________

19. The patient was seen today in the office for primary hypertension. Her medications were reviewed and scripts were written. Impacting her status, it should be noted that she has a history of tobacco dependence.

    ICD-10-CM code(s): ___________________________

20. The 25-year-old patient took Percodan as prescribed and now presents to the office due to extreme nausea. It is determined that he is having an adverse effect of Percodan.

    ICD-10-CM code(s): ___________________________

21. The patient is seen in the physician's office for a follow-up after suffering an anterolateral myocardial infarction 4 weeks ago. The patient is also evaluated for Type 1 diabetes mellitus with associated polyneuropathy.

    ICD-10-CM code(s): ___________________________

22. The 45-year-old male was seen in the ambulatory surgery center for tubular adenoma of the rectum. The surgeon performs a colonoscopy and excision of the adenoma.

    ICD-10-CM code(s): ___________________________

    ICD-10-PCS code(s): ___________________________

23. The 54-year-old female is admitted with carcinoma of the lower-outer quadrant of the left breast. The surgeon performs a radical mastectomy.

    ICD-10-CM code(s): ___________________________

    ICD-10-PCS code(s): ___________________________

24. A 62-year-old male was seen in the emergency department for chest pain. He has been previously diagnosed with atherosclerotic heart disease and has a history of hypertension that is treated with medication. No history of surgical procedures. ED physician documents the following diagnosis:

    ASHD with unstable angina

    Hypertension

    ICD-10-CM code(s): ___________________________

25. The 19-year-old patient was seen in the physician's office for nausea and upset stomach as a result of taking too much Robitussin (dextromethorphan) for a cough.

    ICD-10-CM code(s): ___________________________

CHAPTER

23 Decision-Based Coding

This chapter will focus on the skill of decision-based coding. The case study exercises have been assigned ICD-10-CM diagnosis and ICD-10-PCS procedure codes. The decision-based coding process requires the coding professional to defend the code selection based on integrated knowledge and the supportive documentation that tells the patient's clinical story. This task is a change to the traditional coding workflow process of producing a code. This change requires analysi of coded data to *support* or *not support* the selected code assignment. These skills can be applied to the auditing function as well as in the role of clinical code editor in the world of computer-assiste coding (CAC).

Computer-Assisted Coding (CAC)

For many years, software vendors have developed technological solutions to assist with coding. In addition to encoders, editing tools, and searchable database of resources, the next generation of technological tools is being introduced to the industry: CAC. CAC software involves a complicated logic technological process that relies on systems such as national language processing or structured text input.

With CAC, coders will be asked to *accept or not accept* the computer-generated codes based on analysis of the patient's clinical story documented in the health record and application of all the knowledge and skill required of clinical coders. Coding professionals need to base their decisions o a combined knowledge of disease processes, coding principles, and clinical concepts. The clinical editor role must recognize inconsistencies and inappropriate application of coding guidelines.

Case Study Exercises

The intent of this exercise is to apply all of the knowledge and skills to support or reject the codes that have been assigned. Many facilities plan to use ICD-10-PCS for data collection for outpatient surgery cases. For that reason, the case studies were selected from both the inpatient and outpatient settings.

Read the following case studies to assimilate the patient's clinical picture. Reference the listed ICD-10-CM and ICD-10-PCS codes and compare this assignment to the documentation. Validate the coding selection and in the "Rationale" section of the table, document what key points drove your decision. If the code is incorrect, assign the correct code and note the difference.

Answers to case studies 1–5 are located in Appendix A, and the remaining answers are only provide to educators through the instruction online companion.

Case Study 1

OPERATIVE REPORT

PREOPERATIVE DIAGNOSIS: Left hip mass.

POSTOPERATIVE DIAGNOSIS: Hemangioma, left hip.

OPERATIVE PROCEDURE: Excision of mass from hip.

ANESTHESIA: General endotracheal anesthesia.

INDICATIONS: This 1-year-old child presents with a mass on her left hip area, which is soft, moveable, and in the subcutaneous tissue.

DESCRIPTION OF PROCEDURE: Under satisfactory general anesthesia, the patient was placed in the supine position. The abdomen and left hip were prepped with Betadine gel and draped in a routine fashion. Marcaine was injected over the mass just below her birthmark and the previously marked incision. The incision was made with a scalpel and dissection carried through the superficial fascia with the cautery. The underlying 0.6-cm mass was then slowly dissected free from the surrounding subcutaneous fibrofatty tissue. It had several small vessels feeding it, which were cauterized. There were several lobules of small tufts of vascular tissue, suggesting a hemangioma. They tended to insinuate in fingers in the subcutaneous tissue in various directions. These were all gently dissected free superiorly toward the iliac crest and inferiorly, medially, and laterally. The supplying vessels were doubly clamped, divided, and ligated with 3-0 Vicryl suture. A No. 10 Blake drain was placed into the cavity after assuring hemostasis and irrigating it with saline. It was brought out through a separate skin incision and secured to the skin with 4-0 nylon. Specimen was sent to pathology for confirmed diagnosis.

The subcutaneous tissue was reapproximated with an interrupted 5-0 undyed Vicryl suture and the skin was closed with Steri-Strips. Sterile dressings were placed on the wounds and the patient, having tolerated the procedure well, was returned to the recovery room in satisfactory condition with vital signs stable.

Coding Assignment	Rationale
ICD-10-CM Code(s): D18.01 Hemangioma of skin and subcutaneous tissue	
ICD-10-PCS Code(s): 0JBL0ZZ	

Case Study 2

OPERATIVE REPORT

PREOPERATIVE DIAGNOSIS: Biliary colic

POSTOPERATIVE DIAGNOSIS: Biliary colic

PROCEDURE PERFORMED: Laparoscopic cholecystectomy

FINDINGS: The patient had normal anatomy. The cystic duct was small; therefore, a cholangiogram catheter could not be introduced into the duct.

DESCRIPTION OF THE PROCEDURE: The patient was taken to the operating room and placed in the supine position. The patient was prepped and draped in the usual sterile manner. Endotracheal anesthesia was administered.

An infraumbilical incision was made and the abdomen was entered using the open Hasson technique. The abdomen was insufflated with CO_2 without difficulty. The laparoscope was inserted and no injuries were identified. An 11-mm VersaStep trocar was placed in the mid-epigastric region and two 5-mm trocars were placed in the right lateral abdomen. These were all placed under direct visualization of the laparoscope. The cystic duct was bluntly dissected out. A clip was placed proximally on the gallbladder and a ductotomy was performed. The patient had a very small cystic duct. This would not allow introduction of the cholangiocatheter. The cystic duct was then doubly clipped and transected. The cystic artery was doubly clipped and transected. The gallbladder was then removed from the liver bed using the Hook laser cautery. There was no spillage of stones or bile. The gallbladder was placed in an Endobag and removed through the infraumbilical port site. The liver bed was inspected and hemostasis was achieved. The trocars were removed under visualization of the laparoscope. The infraumbilical fascia was approximated with 0 Vicryl in an interrupted fashion. The skin was closed with 4-0 Caprosyn in a running subcuticular fashion. The wounds were infiltrated with 0.5% Marcaine with epinephrine. The patient had Steri-Strips and a sterile dressing was applied.

The patient was taken to recovery with no apparent intraoperative complications.

Coding Assignment	Rationale
ICD-10-CM Code(s): K80.50 Calculus of bile duct without cholangitis or cholecystitis without obstruction	
ICD-10-PCS Code(s): 0FT44ZZ	

Case Study 3

OPERATIVE REPORT

PREOPERATIVE DIAGNOSIS: Retained hardware right tibia

POSTOPERATIVE DIAGNOSIS: Retained hardware right tibia

PROCEDURE: Hardware removal right tibia

INDICATIONS: This 16-year-old male previously underwent an intramedullary nailing of his right tibial shaft fracture. His tibia has healed and he now is seeking removal of the hardware.

DESCRIPTION OF PROCEDURE: Under general anesthesia and tourniquet control, the patient's right leg was prepped and draped using normal sterile technique. The previous incisions were used to approach the proximal and distal screw holes. The proximal screw was approached first. Next, the distal screw was approached and it was easily identifiable and it was removed without difficulty. Dissection proximally was tedious, and the proximal screw was not readily apparent. Image intensification was used to approach the proximal screw. The lateral portion of the proximal screw was palpated percutaneously and the end was identified. This was used as a marker. A single drill hole was made in the tibia and the screw head was identified slightly anterior to the drill hole itself. The vast majority of the screw head was overgrown with bone. The overgrown bone was removed without difficulty. The screw was backed out. Next, image intensifier was used to approach the proximal end of the rod. The proximal end was identified, and bone was cleared away from the proximal end of the rod. This bone also invaded the screw cap. The bone was removed from the screw cap, and the screw cap was removed. In order to place the inserter/extractor bolt, the proximal rod had to be drilled to remove bone from the center portion of the rod. Once the bone was drilled, the inserter extractor screw was tightened. The tuning fork hammer was used to remove the rod. This was done once the rod had broken free from the bone nearby. All hardware was removed to be sterilized and given to the patient. The wounds were copiously irrigated and closed with absorbable sutures on the subcutaneous tissues, and the skin was closed with staples. Marcaine was instilled and a light dressing was placed at the knee and ankle.

TOURNIQUET TIME: 85 minutes.

BLOOD LOSS: Minimal.

COMPLICATIONS: None.

PLAN: The patient was given a prescription for 30 Vicodin for postoperative pain control. He will return to see me in the office in a week for dressing removal and a week later for removal of all staples. Next week we can remove some of the staples. We should also get an X-ray of his right tibia, two views, at that time.

Coding Assignment	Rationale
ICD-10-CM Code(s): S82.201A Unspecified fracture of shaft of right tibia	
ICD-10-PCS Code(s): 0QPGX4Z	

Case Study 4

OUTPATIENT SURGERY CENTER

PROCEDURE PERFORMED: Esophagogastroduodenoscopy (EGD) with biopsy

INSTRUMENT USED: Olympus GAF-160 upper video endoscope

MEDICATIONS ADMINISTERED: Fentanyl 150 mcg intravenously, Versed 3 mg intravenously, and Hurricaine spray topically.

INDICATION: Dysphagia

HISTORY: Patient has had a history of difficulty when swallowing. Conservation treatment has failed, and diagnostic/surgical intervention was recommended.

DESCRIPTION OF PROCEDURE: The patient was brought to the outpatient operative suite and placed in left lateral decubitus position. His throat was anesthetized with Hurricaine spray. Conscious sedation was induced and maintained with the intravenous medications listed earlier.

The endoscope was passed by direct vision into the oropharynx and upper esophagus and then advanced carefully and without difficulty under direct vision to a depth of the proximal small bowel. Retroflexion of the scope was performed in the stomach, with a clear view of the fundus and cardia obtained.

FINDINGS: The esophagus showed some irregularity to the Z line. It was difficult to tell exactly where the esophagus ended and the stomach began. A biopsy was taken from the distal esophagus to rule out Barrett's esophagus. There were no ulcerations or erosions. There were no strictures or rings. The scope passed easily into the gastric remnant. No lesions were seen within the gastric remnant. The first portion of the small bowel was then explored for several centimeters and no lesions were seen. He tolerated the procedure well and without apparent immediate complication.

IMPRESSION: Dysphagia.

Long-standing gastroesophageal reflux disease (GERD), rule out Barrett's esophagus.

RECOMMENDATION: We will await the patient's biopsy results regarding Barrett's esophagus.

Coding Assignment	Rationale
ICD-10-CM Code(s): R13.10 Dysphagia, unspecified K21.9 Gastro-esophageal reflux disease without esophagitis K22.70 Barrett's esophagus without dysplasia	
ICD-10-PCS Code(s): 0DB38ZZ	

Case Study 5

OUTPATIENT SURGERY DEPARTMENT

PROGRESS NOTE: Patient has cardiac arrhythmia. The patient's loop recorder currently is at end-of-life. The patient comes now for removal of the cardiac event recorder device.

OPERATIVE NOTE: The patient has no known allergies. She received 1 g of Ancef intravenously periprocedurally. The left periclavicular area, the location of the device, was prepped and draped in the usual fashion. Using local anesthetic was administered lidocaine without epinephrine. The wound was opened and sutures, that were holding the device, were removed. The device was removed and the wound was cleaned with Betadine swabs. Subsequently, saline was used to remove the Betadine. Hemostasis was achieved without needing cautery. The wound was closed in two layers. The first layer was 3-0 interrupted Vicryl. The second layer was 4-0 interrupted Vicryl subcuticular. The patient tolerated the procedure well. There was no immediate complication.

Coding Assignment	Rationale
ICD-10-CM Code(s): Z45.09 Encounter for adjustment and management of other cardiac device I49.9 Cardiac arrhythmia, unspecified	
ICD-10-PCS Code(s): 0WP80YZ	

Case Study 6

OUTPATIENT SURGERY DEPARTMENT

PREOPERATIVE PROGRESS NOTE: This 35-year-old patient, Gravida 5, Para 4, AB 0, desires sterilization. The consequences and risks have been explained to the patient.

OPERATIVE REPORT

PREOPERATIVE DIAGNOSIS: Desires permanent sterilization

POSTOPERATIVE DIAGNOSIS: Desires permanent sterilization

OPERATION PERFORMED: Laparoscopic bilateral tubal sterilization using bipolar cautery

ANESTHESIA: General

FINDINGS: The uterus, ovaries, and fallopian tubes were normal in size and appearance.

PROCEDURE: In the operating room general anesthesia was administered and the patient was positioned into low lithotomy with feet apart in Allen stirrups. She was sterilely prepped and draped for laparoscopy. Foley catheter was placed. The HUMI catheter was inserted into the uterus. A small vertical subumbilical incision was made with the scalpel in the abdomen and centered in an open laparoscopy fashion. A 10-mm Hasson trocar was inserted bluntly through the subumbilical incision in the usual fashion and secured with 0 Polysorb suture previously placed in the fascia on either side of the trocar. The abdomen was insufflated with CO_2 gas to a pressure of 15 PSI. Pelvis was examined. A small suprapubic incision was made with a scalpel and the 5-mm trocar was inserted under direct visualization. Starting on the left side, 3 to 4 cm of fallopian tube was cauterized with bipolar cautery until disconnected. This was done on the right side in the same fashion. Hemostasis was excellent. Then all instrumentation was removed from the abdominal wall, and the gas was expelled from the abdominal cavity. The fascia below the subumbilical incision was approximated with uninterrupted 0 Polysorb figure-of-eight suture. The subumbilical skin incision was closed with 3-0 Polysorb running subcuticular suture. The lower abdominal incision was approximated with Steri-Strips and benzoin on the skin. Both skin incisions were infiltrated with 0.5% Marcaine with epinephrine 1:2,000 and dressings were applied. She was cleaned and undraped. She was awakened from anesthesia. Patient was transferred to a gurney and taken to recovery in satisfactory condition.

ESTIMATED BLOOD LOSS: Minimal.

SPECIMENS: Cauterized segments of right and left fallopian tubes.

DRAINS AND PACKS: Foley catheter was removed in the operating room just prior to leaving for PACU.

NEEDLE AND SPONGE COUNT: Reported as correct.

PROGNOSIS: Immediate and remote are both good.

COMPLICATIONS: None.

Coding Assignment	Rationale
ICD-10-CM Code(s): Z30.2 Encounter for sterilization	
ICD-10-PCS Code(s): 0UB74ZZ	

Case Study 7

OPERATIVE REPORT

PREOPERATIVE DIAGNOSIS: Comminuted right closed mid shaft clavicle fracture

POSTOPERATIVE DIAGNOSIS: Comminuted right closed mid shaft clavicle fracture

PROCEDURE: Open reduction internal fixation right clavicle

ANESTHESIA: General.

DESCRIPTION OF PROCEDURE: After providing informed consent, Levi was brought to the operating room whereupon smooth induction of general anesthesia was performed, the patient was positioned in a beach chair position on the operating room table, and all bony prominences were well padded. A bump was placed under the proximal thoracic spine to allow the scapula and shoulder to retract on the right. The right upper extremity was prepped and draped in the standard sterile fashion from the neck to the midline of the chest to the fingertips. An alcohol pre-prep was used. The clavicle fracture was readily palpable about the mid shaft. A longitudinal incision overlying the subcutaneous border of the clavicle centered on the deformity was made and length was approximately 10 cm. The skin and subcutaneous tissue were carefully dissected sharply down to the level of the periosteum overlying the clavicle. Hemostasis was carefully obtained using Bovie cautery. The clavicle fracture was dissected free of early soft callus in a subperiosteal fashion superiorly and anteriorly. The medial and lateral fragments were identified. The central comminution was noted to be severe with at least three fragments making up the central area in addition to the larger medial and lateral fragments. The fracture margins were carefully cleaned using suction, a small rongeur, and a small curet. Following this, a careful anatomic reduction was obtained manually and held using multiple bony reduction clamps. Care was taken throughout the operation to protect the subclavian vessels about the inferior surface of the clavicle.

Once the provisional reduction had been achieved and was maintained with bone clamps, two interfragmentary lag screws from the Acumed precontoured clavicle plate set (titanium) were used to hold the provisional reduction and this was successful. An eight-hold right-sided precontoured clavicle titanium plate was then removed from the set and placed over the fracture. The right-sided plate was the least bend was found to fit well. However, it fit better in a reverse position with the intended medial end facing laterally. This was because the fracture encompassed more of the more lateral bend of the clavicle as opposed to the medial bend. The plate required some contouring medially and this was done with plate benders. The plate was then solidly fixed to the bone in a noncompression fashion using 3.5-mm fully threaded cortical titanium screws from the set. All eight holes were filled. Three lateral screws and two medial screws were fully in the lateral and medial fragments respectively. The three central screws were attached to portions of the lateral and medial fragments as well as the intervening comminution. Screw length was checked by direct palpations and intraoperatively using a flat plate X-ray. The reduction of the fracture and position of the hardware was confirmed and the wound was copiously irrigated with normal saline. It was then closed in layers using 0 Vicryl suture in a simple interrupted fashion for the deep fascia. The subcutaneous tissue was closed using interrupted 3-0 Monocryl suture in a simple buried fashion. A subcuticular 4-0 Prolene suture was then used to close skin. Steri-Strips and a sterile compressive dressing were applied and the patient was placed in a right upper extremity sling. He was awakened from anesthesia and taken to the recovery room in stable condition. Estimated blood loss was 250 mL. There were no intraoperative complications. Postoperatively he will be strictly non–weight bearing on the right upper extremity with use of a sling. He will have PO pain medicine for pain control. If he requires admission for pain control, I expect this to be less than 24 hours.

Coding Assignment	Rationale
ICD-10-CM Code(s): S42.021A Displaced fracture of shaft of right clavicle	
ICD-10-PCS Code(s): 0PSB34Z	

Case Study 8

OPERATIVE REPORT

PREOPERATIVE DIAGNOSIS: Left breast lump, large 2+ cm.

POSTOPERATIVE DIAGNOSIS: Left breast lump, large 2+ cm.

PROCEDURE PERFORMED: Left breast lumpectomy through a circumareolar incision.

ANESTHESIA: General.

COMPLICATIONS: None.

DESCRIPTION OF PROCEDURE: The patient was placed in the supine position, and the breast was prepped and draped. A marking pen was used to mark the line of incision, which was from about 12 o'clock to the 3 o clock position in the circumareolar area. The incision was made, the skin was raised with skin hooks, and using sharp and blunt dissection I was able to dissect all the way to the palpable lump. A lumpectomy was performed, removing the lump in toto, not cutting into the lesion at all. Hemostasis was then achieved by electrocautery. The wound was then closed with 3-0 Vicryl suture and subcuticular 4-0 Monocryl suture and Steri-Strips. There were no problems or complications. The patient left the OR in good condition.

Coding Assignment	Rationale
ICD-10-CM Code(s) N63 Lump in breast	
ICD-10-PCS Code(s): 0HBU0ZX	

Case Study 9

OPERATIVE REPORT

PREOPERATIVE DIAGNOSIS: Primary osteoarthritis of the right knee.

POSTOPERATIVE DIAGNOSIS: Primary osteoarthritis of the right knee.

PROCEDURE: Right posterior stabilized total knee arthroplasty.

ANESTHESIA: General plus right femoral block.

IMPLANTS: DePuy Sigma System size 4 right posterior stabilized femoral component, size 3 modular tibial tray with 8 mm non-crosslinked polyethylene spacer, and 35 mm × 8.5 mm thick patella. Antibiotic cement was used.

PROCEDURE IN DETAIL: The patient was brought to the OR and positioned in supine fashion with all bony prominences well padded. A bump was placed under the right hip, and a tourniquet was placed on the right proximal thigh. A gram of Kefzol was given intravenously. The right lower extremity was prepped and draped in standard sterile fashion for arthroplasty including an alcohol pre-prep.

After exsanguination of the extremity with an Ace wrap, the tourniquet was inflated to 300 mmHg. An approximately 6-inch longitudinal incision was made about the anterior aspect of the knee centered on the inferior pole of the patella. The skin and subcutaneous tissue were dissected sharply down to the level of the fascia, and a medial parapatellar incision was made in the fascia with the medial most split proximally. The patella was everted, and the knee was flexed. Care was taken to protect the patellar tendon insertion. The osteophytes about the femoral notch were removed, and a partial resection of the posterior patellar fat pad was carried out. No significant medial release was carried out because of the valgus deformity of the knee. The femoral canal was entered with a drill, and the sword with distal femoral cutting guide was attached set for a resection of 10 mm at 6 degrees of valgus. The lateral femoral condyle was noted to be eroded distally and posteriorly. However, a 10-mm cut was sufficient for the distal cut.

Using anterior-referenced system, the femur was sized to a size 4. Rotation was set at 3 degrees external rotation. This was checked using the epicondylar axis. The four-in-one cutting guide was then applied, and the distal femoral anterior and posterior cuts as well as chamfer cuts were completed. This went well. Care was taken to protect the collateral ligaments during these cuts. The femoral notch was then completed using the notch-cutting guide supplied with the system. Once this was done, attention was turned to the tibia. Using an external referenced guide, a tibial cut was made with a zero degree posterior slope with 2 mm off the low (lateral) side. This resection resulted in a similar amount of resection medially and laterally. The tibia was exposed using a Homan placed posteriorly and laterally. The osteophytes were removed laterally and posteriorly.

At this point the osteophytes about the posterior femoral condyles were removed using a curved osteotome under direct visualization. Care was taken to protect the posterior structures. The tibia was then sized to a size 3. A thin cut was then made for the modular tibial tray system. An 8-mm posterior stabilized trial spacer, size 3 tibial tray, and size 4 femur were then applied. The knee was taken through a range of motion, and there was a tightness noted laterally. The lateral collateral ligament was recessed slightly off the lateral femoral condyle. Following this, stability was symmetric medially and laterally. The patella was then prepared. The osteophytes were removed with a rongeur, and the thickness was measured to be 25 mm. An 8.5-mm resection was made down to 16.5 mm, and a 16.5 × 35 mm patellar trial was applied after the cut was completed. Stability of this component was then trialed, and it was found to be excellent.

The trial components were removed, and the knee was copiously irrigated with normal saline. The final components were then cemented in place in the sizes mentioned earlier. Order of cement was patella, tibia, femur. The tibial tray was placed and the knee brought out into full extension to compress the tibial and femoral components. Again, antibiotic gentamicin-containing cement was used. The wound was then cleared of excess cement and bony debris and irrigated one final time. It was then closed in layers over a ConstaVac drain. Number 1 Vicryl was used for the extensor fascia and Scarpa fascia in a simple interrupted fashion, 3_0 Monocryl was used for the subcutaneous tissue in a simple buried fashion, and staples were placed at the level of the skin.

A sterile dressing was placed. The ConstaVac drain extension and reservoir were attached and activated, and a compressive wrap was placed from the toes to the thigh. The tourniquet was released for a total tourniquet time of 112 minutes. EBL was minimal. There were no intraoperative complications. Postoperatively the patient was taken to the recovery room in stable condition. She will begin CPM today. She will begin weightbearing as tolerated with physical therapy on postoperative day 1. ConstaVac, Foley, PCA, and antibiotics will be used for 24 to 48 hours. DVT prophylaxis will be with Coumadin and foot pumps.

Coding Assignment	Rationale
ICD-10-CM Code(s) M17.11 Osteoarthritis of knee	
ICD-10-PCS Code(s): 0SRC0JA	

Case Study 10

DIAGNOSIS: Deep Vein Thrombosis-legs

PROCEDURE: Inferior vena cava filter placement

DESCRIPTION OF THE PROCEDURE: The patient was taken to the cath lab, placed in supine position, and prepped and draped in a routine manner. Right femoral vein access was obtained guided by the venacavagram. The filter was then advanced under fluoroscopic guidance and deployed at the L1-L2 interspace. It appeared to be fully expanded and stable in position. The introducer sheath was withdrawn. A single 4-0 Vicryl suture was placed in the groin skin. Pressure was applied to the right groin access site for 5 minutes. At this point, the wound appeared to be hemostatic. Dressings were applied. The patient was then returned to the ward appearing to have tolerated the procedure well.

Coding Assignment	Rationale
ICD-10-CM Code(s) I80.209 Thrombosis	
ICD-10-PCS Code(s): 06H00DZ	

Appendix A: Answer Key

Answers for Chapter 1: Infectious and Parasitic Diseases

Check Your Knowledge of Infectious Diseases

Column A	Column B
1. __B__ bacterial organism	**A.** histoplasmosis
2. __D__ viral infection	**B.** *staphylococcus*
3. __A__ fungal infection	**C.** malaria
4. __C__ protozoal disease	**D.** herpes zoster

Check Your Clinical Knowledge

1. **Pneumococcal pneumonia** is the most common infectious disease complication of both measles and influenza. *Clostridium difficile* (called *C. diff*) is a bacterial infection that causes diarrhea. *C. diff* is not related to measles or influenza.
2. **Lyme disease** is the most frequently transmitted tick-borne disease. Chagas disease is caused by a parasite that is common in South and Central America.
3. The **Epstein-Barr virus** causes infectious mononucleosis. Human papillomavirus (HPV) is the most common sexually transmitted infection.
4. ***Staphylococcus aureus*** is the most common pathogen for pneumonia. *Escherichia coli* (bacteria) can cause diarrhea and often is associated with urinary tract infections. Although it can be associated with pneumonia, it is not the most common pathogen.
5. **Karposi sarcoma** is most commonly associated with AIDS. The sarcoma is an opportunistic infection, meaning that it takes advantage of debilitated patients. Merkel cell carcinoma is primarily a skin cancer and not commonly associated with AIDS.

Coding

1. Western equine encephalitis

   A83.1 Western equine encephalitis

   Index: Encephalitis, Western equine
2. Cytomegaloviral mononucleosis

   B27.10 Cytomegaloviral mononucleosis without complications

   Index: Mononucleosis, infection, cytomegaloviral
3. Chickenpox

   B01.9 Varicella without complication

   Index: Chickenpox, *see Varicella*
4. Meningitis due to Lyme disease

   A69.21 Meningitis due to Lyme disease

   Index: Meningitis, in (due to) Lyme disease
5. Gonococcal conjunctivitis of the left eye

   A54.31 Gonococcal conjunctivitis

   Index: Conjunctivitis, in (due to) gonococci
6. Acute viral hepatitis C

   B17.10 Acute hepatitis C without hepatic coma

   Index: Hepatitis, viral, acute (this entry leads to unspecified code). Coders may review series of codes in this section to locate more specified code.

   Index: Hepatitis, C (viral), acute leads to B17.10

7. Shingles of the eyelids

   B02.39 Other herpes zoster eye disease

   Index: Shingles—*see Herpes, zoster*

   Herpes, zoster, eye (lid)

8. Toxic shock syndrome (*staphylococcus* identified as organism)

   A48.3 Toxic shock syndrome

   B95.8 Unspecified *staphylococcus* as the cause of disease classified elsewhere

   Index: Syndrome, toxic shock

   See note that states "use additional code to identify organism (B95, B96).

9. Severe gastroenteritis due to *Salmonella* food poisoning

   A02.0 Salmonella enteritis

   Index: Poisoning, food, due to *salmonella* with gastroenteritis

10. Vulvovaginitis due to chlamydial infection

    A56.02 Chlamydial vulvovaginitis

    Index: Chlamydia, vulvovaginitis

Answers for Chapter 2: Neoplasms

Check Your Knowledge of Neoplasms

__B__ **1.** Adenoma of prostate

__M__ **2.** Infiltrating duct carcinoma of the breast

__B__ **3.** Osteofibroma of the femur (refers coder to bone)

__U__ **4.** Endometrioid adenoma (pathology report states borderline malignancy)

__M__ **5.** Hepatic mesenchymal sarcoma (refers coder to connective tissue)

Check Your Clinical Knowledge

1. The pathology report states that the patient has carcinoma in situ of the cervix. This morphology indicates that the cancer cells have **not invaded the surrounding tissues.**
2. **Melanoma** is most often identified as skin cancer.
3. A uterine leiomyoma is commonly known as a **fibroid.**
4. Condylomas are commonly known as **genital warts**.
5. An adenomatous polyp in the colon would be identified as a **benign** tumor.

Coding

1. Myxofibrosarcoma of the neck

   C49.0 Malignant neoplasm of connective and soft tissue of head, face, and neck

   Index: Myxofibrosarcoma—*see Neoplasm, connective tissue, malignant*

2. Female patient was diagnosed with carcinoma of the lower-inner quadrant of the right breast

   C50.311 Malignant neoplasm of lower-inner quadrant of right female breast

   Index: *see also Neoplasm by site, malignant*

   Neoplasm Table: primary site listed as C50.31- (must refer to Tabular List for sixth character, which identifies the laterality [right breast])

3. Malignant melanoma of the skin of the cheek

   C43.39 Malignant melanoma of other parts of the face

   Index: Melanoma, skin, cheek

4. Carcinoma of the upper lobe of the right lung with metastasis to the bone (spinal column)

   C34.11 Malignant neoplasm of upper lobe, right bronchus or lung

   C79.51 Secondary malignant neoplasm of bone

   Index: *see also Neoplasm by site, malignant*

   Code for lung from malignant primary column in Neoplasm table. Code for bone from malignant secondary column.

5. Adenocarcinoma of the prostate

   C61 Malignant neoplasm of prostate

   Index: Adenocarcinoma—*see also Neoplasm, malignant*

   Refer to Neoplasm table for site from Malignant Primary column.

6. Osteofibroma of the right femur

   D16.21 Benign neoplasm of long bones of right lower limb

   Index: Osteofibroma—*see Neoplasm bone, benign*

7. Condyloma acuminatum of the penis

   A63.0 Anogenital (venereal) warts

   Index: Condyloma, acuminatum

   Note that this code is located in the Infectious and Parasitic Diseases chapter.

8. Diffuse lymphoblastic lymphoma (of lymph nodes of left axilla and arm)

   C83.54 Lymphoblastic (diffuse) lymphoma, lymph nodes of axilla and upper limb

   Index: Lymphoblastic—*see condition*

   Lymphoma, lymphoblastic C83.5-

9. Mixed glioma of the right optic nerve

   C72.31 Malignant neoplasm of right optic nerve

   Index: Glioma, mixed, specific site—*see Neoplasm, malignant*

   Neoplasm table: Nerve, optic (from Malignant primary column) C72.3-

10. Malignant melanoma of forehead

    C43.39 Malignant melanoma, other parts of the face

    Index: Melanoma, skin, forehead

Answers for Chapter 3: Diseases of the Blood and Blood-Forming Organs

Check Your Clinical Knowledge

Clinical Description	Diagnosis
1. __C__ 34-year-old man experiences excessive bleeding after surgery, reports that he bruised easily.	A. sickle cell disease
2. __A__ 5-year-old African American child reports abdominal pain and trouble breathing. Clinician notes delayed growth.	B. vitamin B deficiency
3. __B__ 22-year-old woman, who is a vegetarian, reports chronic fatigue, generalized aching, and insomnia.	C. von Willebrand disease
4. __E__ 5-year-old child is pale, tired, and irritable. Recently treated for digestive disorder. Reddish tint to urine.	D. Christmas disease (hemophilia B)
5. __D__ Child experiences excessive bleeding following circumcision Lab results reveal hereditary clotting disorder.	E. hemolytic uremic syndrome

Coding

1. Posttraumatic cyst of the spleen

   D73.4 Cyst of spleen

   Index: Cyst, spleen NEC D73.4

2. Christmas disease (hemophilia B)

   D67 Hereditary factor IX deficiency

   Index: Christmas disease

3. Normocytic chronic blood loss anemia

   D50.0 Iron deficiency anemia secondary to blood loss (chronic)

   Index: Anemia, normocytic, due to blood loss (chronic)

4. Vitamin B12 deficiency anemia—vegan anemia

   D51.3 Other dietary vitamin B12 deficiency anemia

   Index: Anemia, vegan

5. Coagulation disorder, factor X

   D68.2 Hereditary deficiency of other clotting factors

   Index: Disorder, coagulation—*see also Defect, coagulation*

   Defect, coagulation—*see also Deficiency, factor*

   Deficiency, factor, X

Answers for Chapter 4: Endocrine, Nutritional, and Metabolic Diseases

Check Your Clinical Knowledge: Case Studies

Case Study # 1

This profile would best support which of the following diagnoses?

a. Type 1 diabetes mellitus

b. **Type 2 diabetes mellitus**

c. Graves disease

d. Hypothyroidism

Case Study # 2

This profile would best support which of the following diagnoses?

a. Type 1 diabetes mellitus

b. Type 2 diabetes mellitus

c. **Graves disease**

d. Hypothyroidism

Case Study # 3

This profile would best support which of the following diagnoses?

a. **Type 1 diabetes mellitus**

b. Type 2 diabetes mellitus

c. Graves disease

d. Hypothyroidism

Case Study # 4

This type of skin ulcer would be classified as:

a. Decubitus

b. Pressure ulcer

c. **Nonpressure ulcer**

Coding

1. Graves disease

   E05.00 Thyrotoxicosis, with diffuse goiter, without thyrotoxic crisis or storm

   Index: Graves—*see Hyperthyroidism, with goiter*

2. Hyperkalemia

   E87.5 Hyperkalemia

   Index: Hyperkalemia

3. Vitamin B12 deficiency

   E53.8 Deficiency of other specified B group vitamins

   Index: Deficiency, vitamin B12

4. Diabetic cataract, Type 1 diabetic patient

   E10.36 Type 1 diabetes mellitus with diabetic cataract

   Index: diabetes, Type 1, with cataract

5. Type 1 diabetes with diabetic chronic skin ulcer of the left heel and midfoot *(breakdown of skin only)*

   E10.622 Type 1 diabetes mellitus with other skin ulcer *(see note that states to use additional code to identify the site of the ulcer [L code section])*

   L97.421 Nonpressure chronic ulcer of left heel and midfoot limited to breakdown of skin *(see note under L97 that instructs the coder to code first any associated underlying condition)*

   Index: diabetes, Type 1, with skin ulcer

   Ulcer, heel (see lower limb), heel, left, with skin breakdown only

Answers for Chapter 5: Mental, Behavioral and Neurodevelopmental Disorders

Check Your Clinical Knowledge

Clinical Description	Diagnosis
1. __D__ inattentive, impulsive, and hyperactive	**A.** panic disorder
2. __C__ loss of interest, no pleasure in life	**B.** schizophrenia

3. __A__ episodes of palpitations, diaphoresis, fear of losing control

4. __E__ flashbacks, nightmares, intrusive memories

5. __B__ delusional, hallucinations, disorganized thinking

C. depression

D. attention-deficit disorder

E. posttraumatic stress syndrome

Coding

1. Anorexia nervosa—patient alternates between binge eating and purging

   F50.02 Anorexia nervosa, binge eating/pursing type

   Index: Anorexia, binge eating, with purging

2. Posttraumatic stress disorder, acute

   F43.11 Posttraumatic stress disorder, acute

   Index: Disorder, posttraumatic stress

3. Complete auditory hallucinations

   R44.0 Auditory hallucinations

   Index: hallucinations, auditory

   Note: This condition is classified in the chapter on Symptoms, Signs, and Abnormal Clinical and Laboratory Findings.

4. Bipolar disorder (current episode of depression), mild

   F31.31 Bipolar disorder, current episode depressed, mild

   Index: Disorder, biopolar, current episode, depressed without psychotic features, mild

5. Schizotypal personality disorder

   F21 Schizotypal disorder

   Index: Disorder, personality, schizotypal

Answers for Chapter 6: Diseases of Nervous System (Eyes and Ears)

Check Your Clinical Knowledge

1. The physician documents that the patient's middle ear infection was producing pus. Producing pus would be classified as **purulent.**
2. The elderly patient's eyelids were drooping and causing problems with vision. The physician scheduled the patient for surgery with the diagnosis of **dermatochalasis.**
3. The physician noted that the patient's **intractable** pain was severe, constant, and not curable.
4. The documentation states that the patient's eye (iris and ciliary body) is swollen and inflamed. The physician concludes with the diagnosis of **iridocyclitis.**
5. The pathology report describes the **pterygium** as a noncancerous growth of the conjunctiva.

Coding

1. Left ulnar nerve entrapment at the elbow

   G56.22 Lesion of ulnar nerve, left side

   Index: Entrapment, nerve—*see Neuropathy entrapment*

   Index: Neuropathy, entrapment, ulnar nerve G56.2-

2. Left tympanic membrane perforation

   H72.92 Unspecified perforation of tympanic membrane, left ear

   Index: Perforation, tympanic H72.9-

3. Intracranial meningioma

   D32.0 Benign neoplasm of cerebral meninges

   Index: Meningioma—*see Neoplasm, meninges, benign*

4. Retinal detachment, left eye

H33.22 Serous retinal detachment, left eye

Index: Detachment, retina H33.2-

5. Carpal tunnel compression, left, severe

G56.02 Carpal tunnel syndrome, left side

Index: Compression, nerve, median (in carpal tunnel)—*see Syndrome, carpal tunnel*

Index: Syndrome, carpal tunnel G56.0-

Note: On this case, knowledge of anatomy is important. Reference a website for clarification of the disease process associated with carpal tunnel syndrome.

6. Patient seen in emergency department as a result of an injury at work. Diagnosis: Foreign body of left eye—sliver of metal located in cornea

T15.02XA Foreign body, in cornea, left eye (seventh character for "initial encounter")

Index: Foreign body, cornea T15.0 or reference Foreign body, eye cornea—*see Foreign body cornea T15.0-*

Note: This is not in the Eye chapter but classified in the Injury category.

7. Dermatochalasis of bilateral upper eyelids

H02.834 Dermatochalasis of left upper eyelid

H02.831 Dermatochalasis of right upper eyelid

Index: Dermatochalasis, left and right, upper

8. Acute otitis media, left, producing pus

H66.002 Acute suppurative otitis media without spontaneous rupture of ear drum, left ear

Index: Otitis, media, acute, purulent—*see Otitis, media, suppurative, acute. Note that* purulent *means "pus producing."*

9. Classic migraine, intractable with aura

G43.119 Migraine with aura, intractable, without status migrainosus

Index: Migraine, with aura, intractable, without status migrainosus

10. Spastic hemiplegia of right (dominant) side

G81.11 Spastic hemiplegia affecting right dominant side

Index: Hemiplegia, spastic G81.1-

Note under G81 specifies that this category is only used when there is not further specificity. If the hemiplegia follows a stroke, coders are referred to the I69 code section.

Answers for Chapter 7: Diseases of the Circulatory System

Check Your Knowledge of Anatomy

Refer to Figure A-1

1. Aortic valve
2. Mitral valve
3. Pulmonic valve
4. Tricuspid valve

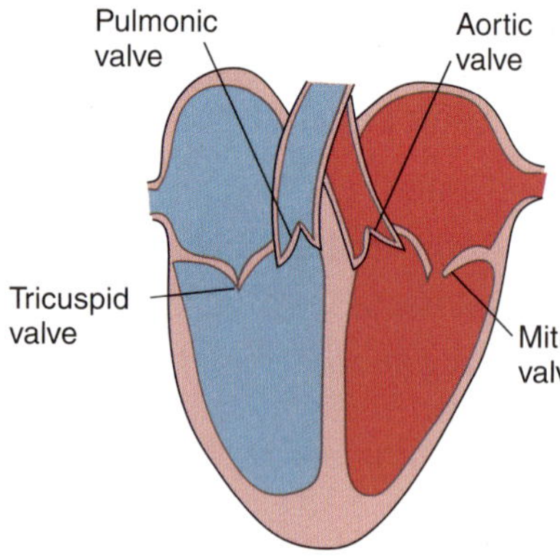

Figure A-1

Check Your Clinical Knowledge

1. The patient's blood pressure is 150/85. The number 85 is referred to as the **diastolic** pressure.
2. A(n) **thrombus** is a blood clot that forms in the vessel and *does not* move to another area of the body.
3. As a result of a stroke, the patient has difficulty swallowing and is ordered therapy for the treatment of **dysphagia.**
4. The documentation in the health records indicates that the patient has

a rapid heart rate, which supports the diagnosis of **tachycardia.**

5. The surgeon documented that the **carotid** artery in the neck was occluded and caused the stroke.

Coding

1. Acute, diastolic congestive heart failure

   I50.31 Acute diastolic (congestive) heart failure

   Index: Failure, heart, diastolic, acute

2. Rheumatic aortic valve stenosis

   I06.0 Rheumatic aortic stenosis

   Index: Stenosis, aortic, rheumatic

3. Pulmonary embolism with acute cor pulmonale

   I26.09 Other pulmonary embolism with acute cor pulmonale

   Index: Embolism, pulmonary, with acute cor poulmonale

4. Acute posterolateral-transmural myocardial infarction (ST elevation)

   I21.29 ST Elevation myocardial infarction (STEMI) involving other sites

   Index: Infarction, myocardial, ST elevation, posterior

5. Hypertensive heart disease with chronic (systolic and diastolic) heart failure

   I11.0 Hypertensive heart disease with heart failure

   I50.42 Chronic combined systolic (congestive) and diastolic (congestive) heart failure

   Index: Disease, heart, hypertensive—*see Hypertension, heart*

   Index: Hypertensive, heart with heart failure

   See note under code I11.0 to use additional code to identify type of heart failure.

6. Cerebrovascular accident due to thrombosis of left vertebral artery

   I63.012 Cerebral infarction due to thrombosis of left vertebral artery

   Index: Accident, cerebrovascular leads to a generic I63.9 code

   Index: Thrombosis, artery, vertebral—*see Occlusion, artery, vertebral*

   Index: Occlusion, artery, vertebral with infarction, due to thrombosis I63.01-

   In this case, the index sends the coder to several different entries. It might have been best to review the selection in the I63 section and carefully read the choices for an accurate code assignment.

7. Premature ventricular contractions

   I49.3 Ventricular premature depolarization

   Index: Contractions, premature, ventricular

8. Cerebrovascular infarction due to embolism of right middle cerebral artery

   I63.411 Cerebral infarction due to embolism of right middle cerebral artery

   Index: Infarct, Infarction, cerebral, due to embolism, cerebral arteries I63.4-

9. Left bundle branch block

   I44.7 Left bundle branch block, unspecified

   Index: Block, bundle-branch, left

10. Patient treated in the outpatient clinic for dysphagia (pharyngeal phase) as a residual from a previous intracerebral hemorrhage

    I69.191 Dysphagia following nontraumatic intracerebral hemorrhage

    R13.13 Dysphagia pharyngeal phase

    Index: Dysphagia, following, intracerebral hemorrhage

    Note: See the note to guide the coder to use an additional code to identify the type of dysphagia.

Answers for Chapter 8: Diseases of the Respiratory System

Check Your Knowledge of Anatomy

Refer to Figure A-2

1. Pharynx
2. Larynx
3. Trachea
4. Alveoli
5. Bronchiole

6. Bronchus
7. Right Lung
8. Mouth
9. Nasal cavity

Check Your Clinical Knowledge

1. The patient has a piece of candy stuck in his throat that is causing irritation. The physician documents examination of the **pharynx**.
2. The physician documents that the patient has a buildup of fluid in the air sacs of the lungs. This documentation supports the diagnosis of **pulmonary edema.**
3. The physician documents that the patient has wheezing, shortness of breath, and chest tightness. It was noted that the family recently adopted a cat. The documentation supports the diagnosis of **asthma.**
4. The physician notes that there is swelling and mucus buildup in the smallest air passages in the lungs, or the **bronchioles.**
5. The physician documents that the patient has a bacterial pneumonia. The laboratory test revealed **Pseudomonas.**

Coding

1. Hypertrophic adenoids and tonsils

   J35.3 Hypertrophy of tonsils with hypertrophy of adenoids

   Index: Hypertrophy, tonsils with adenoids
2. Chronic pulmonary edema

   J81.1 Chronic pulmonary edema

   Index: Edema, pulmonary—see *Edema, lung*

   Index: Edema, lung, chronic
3. Obstructive rhinitis

   J31.0 Chronic rhinitis

   Index: Rhinitis (obstructive)

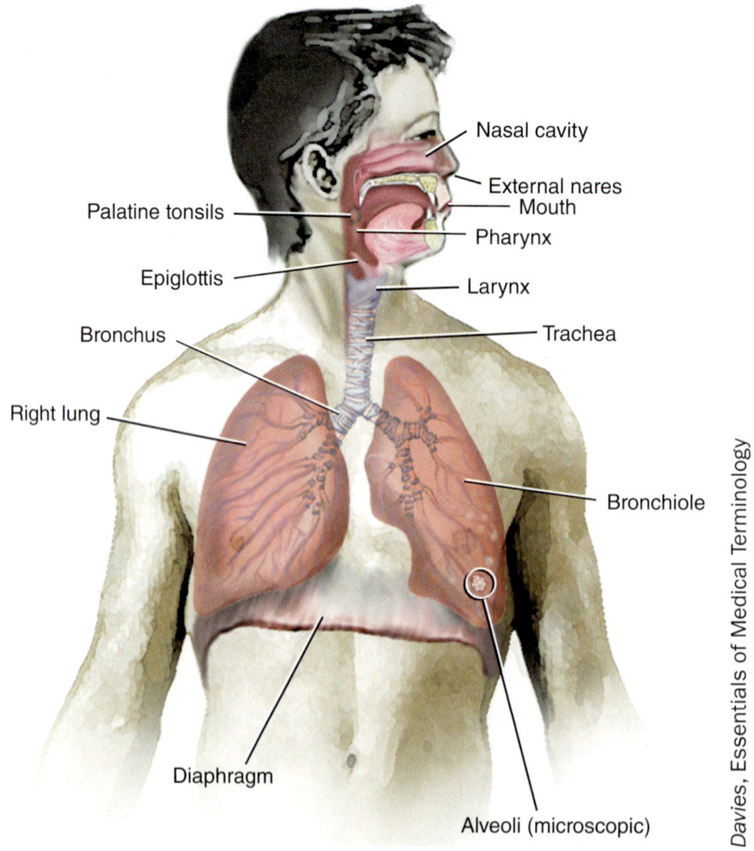

Figure A-2

4. Chronic obstructive pulmonary disease (COPD) with acute bronchitis

   J44.0 Chronic obstructive pulmonary disease with acute lower respiratory infection

   Index: Disease, pulmonary, chronic obstructive, with acute bronchitis

5. Bilateral, complete cleft palate with cleft lip

   Q37.8 Unspecified cleft palate with bilateral cleft lip

   Index: Cleft, lip, bilateral with cleft palate Q37.9

   Note: This condition is classified in the Congenital chapter.

6. Maxillary nasal polyp

   J33.8 Other polyp of sinus

   Index: Polyp, maxillary

7. Severe, persistent asthma with acute exacerbation

   J45.51 Severe persistent with (acute) exacerbation

   Index: Asthma, persistent, severe with exacerbation (acute)

8. Bronchopneumonia due to *staphylococci*

   J15.20 Pneumonia due to *staphylococcus*, unspecified

   Index: Pneumonia, broncho, staphylococcal—*see Pneumonia, staphylococcal*

   Index: Pneumonia, staphylococcal

9. Acute pharyngitis due to the flu

   J10.1 Influenza due to other identified influenza virus with other respiratory manifestations

   Index: Pharyngitis with influenza, flu, or grippe—*see Influenza, with respiratory manifestations*

   Index: Influenza, with respiratory manifestations

10. A 6-year-old child is seen for acute respiratory distress syndrome

    J80 Acute respiratory distress syndrome

    Index: Syndrome, respiratory, distress, acute, child

    Note: Although the Alphabetic Index provides separate entries for child and adult, the code is the same.

Answers for Chapter 9: Diseases of the Digestive System

Check Your Knowledge of Anatomy

Refer to Figure A-3

1. Oral cavity
2. Pharynx
3. Esophagus
4. Ascending colon
5. Descending colon
6. Appendix
7. Anus
8. Rectum
9. Sigmoid colon
10. Ileum
11. Jejunum
12. Duodenum

Check Your Clinical Knowledge

1. The surgeon noted that stones were located in the bile duct and documented the diagnosis of **choledocholithiasis**.
2. The operative report explained that an excessive amount of fluid was located in the peritoneal cavity. This statement was consistent with the postoperative diagnosis of **ascites.**
3. The pathology report revealed that the gallbladder was inflamed, which supported the postoperative diagnosis of **cholecystitis**.
4. The physical examination revealed a protrusion of the intestine through a weakening of the abdominal wall near the groin. This finding supports the diagnosis of a **femoral** hernia**.**
5. The operative report revealed a stricture in the small intestine, supporting documentation of a narrowing of the **ileum.**

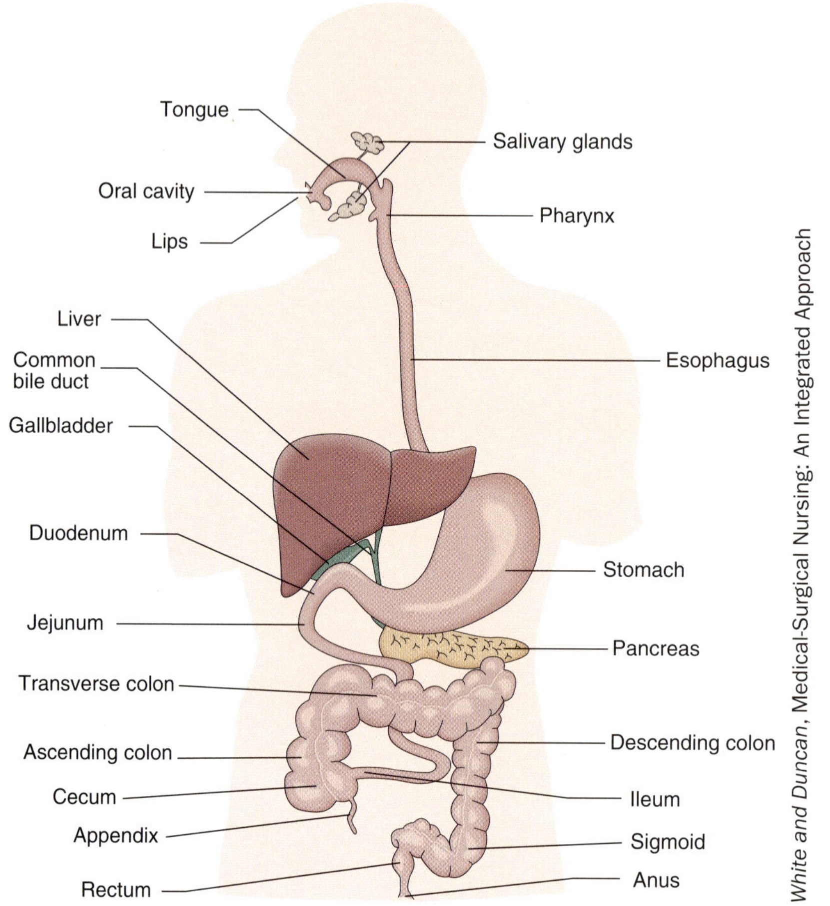

Figure A-3

Coding

1. Recurrent distal esophageal stricture

   K22.2 Esophageal obstruction

   Index: Stricture, esophagus

2. Chronic hepatic failure

   K72.10 Chronic hepatic failure without coma

   Index: Failure, hepatic, chronic

3. Gastrointestinal bleeding (GI) due to angiodysplasia of stomach and duodenum

   K31.811 Angiodysplasia of stomach and duodenum with bleeding

   Index: Angiodysplasia, stomach, with bleeding

4. Alcoholic hepatitis with ascites

   K70.11 Alcoholic hepatitis with ascites

   Index: Hepatitis, alcoholic with ascites

5. Perforated acute duodenal ulcer

   K26.1 Acute duodenal ulcer with perforation

   Index: Ulcer, duodenum, acute, with perforation

6. Preoperative diagnosis: Polyp of the colon.

   Pathology report states adenocarcinoma of the ascending colon

   C18.2 Malignant neoplasm of ascending colon

   Index: Adenocarcinoma—*see Neoplasm, malignant*

   Index: Neoplasm table: Colon—*see Neoplasm, intestine, large*

   Neoplasm, intestine, large, colon, ascending

7. Diverticulosis of ileum with hemorrhaging

   K57.11 Diverticulosis of small intestine without perforation or abscess with bleeding

   Index: Diverticulosis, small intestine with bleeding

8. External hemorrhoids

   K64.4 Residual hemorrhoidal skin tags

   Index: Hemorrhoids, external

9. Acute gastritis with hemorrhaging
   K29.01 Acute gastritis with bleeding
   Index: Gastritis, acute, with bleeding

10. Ulcerated esophageal varices
    I85.00 Esophageal varices without bleeding
    Index: Varices—*see Varix*
    Index: Varix, esophagus
    Note: This code is located in the Circulatory chapter.

Answers for Chapter 10: Diseases of the Skin and Subcutaneous Tissue

Check Your Knowledge of Anatomy

Refer to Figure A-4

1. Sweat pore
2. Epidermis
3. Dermis
4. Subcutaneous fatty tissue
5. Sweat gland
6. Papilla of hair
7. Hair follicle
8. Sebaceous (oil) gland
9. Arrector pili muscle
10. Hair shaft

Check Your Clinical Knowledge

1. **Impetigo** is an extremely contagious skin disease that most commonly affects the face and hands and is caused by streptococcal and staphylococcal bacteria. Plantar warts are a chronic skin condition with a cauliflower-like appearance that are present on the sole of the foot.
2. **Psoriasis**, a noncontagious chronic skin disease, is characterized by a rapid replacement of epidermal cells that appears as red raised lesions with silvery colored scales. Candidiasis is commonly known as thrush and is caused by a fungal infection.
3. Skin redness, also known as **erythema**, is a common sign that occurs for many conditions of the integumentary system. Hematoma is a collection of blood in the tissues of the skin or in an organ, commonly known as a bruise or contusion.
4. Erosion of the skin or mucous membrane that results in tissue loss due to prolonged pressure on the affected area is known as a pressure ulcer or a **decubitus** ulcer. A papule is a small raised lesion.
5. A boil, also known as a **furuncle**, is a small abscess that occurs in the tissues of the skin generally around a hair follicle. A carbuncle is an abscess that involves several furuncles and arises in a cluster of hair follicles.

Coding

1. Acute lymphadenitis of axilla
   L04.2 Acute lymphadentitis of upper limb
   Index: Lymphadentits, acute, axilla
2. Circumscribed neurodermatitis
   L28.0 Lichen simplex chronicus
   Index: Neurodermatitis
3. Yellow nail syndrome
   L60.5 Yellow nail syndrome
   Index: Syndrome, yellow nail
4. Urticaria due to cold
   L50.2 Urticaria due to cold and heat
   Index: Urticaria, due to cold and heat
5. Acute lymphangitis of left arm
   L03.124 Acute lymphangitis of left upper limb
   Index: Lymphagnitis, acute, arm—*see Lymphangitis, acute, upper limb*
6. Dry skin dermatitis
   L85.3 Xerosis cutis
   Index: Dermatitis, dry skin
7. Pressure sore of elbow, stage I
   L89.001 Pressure ulcer of unspecified elbow, stage I
   Index: sore, pressure—*see Ulcer, pressure, by site*

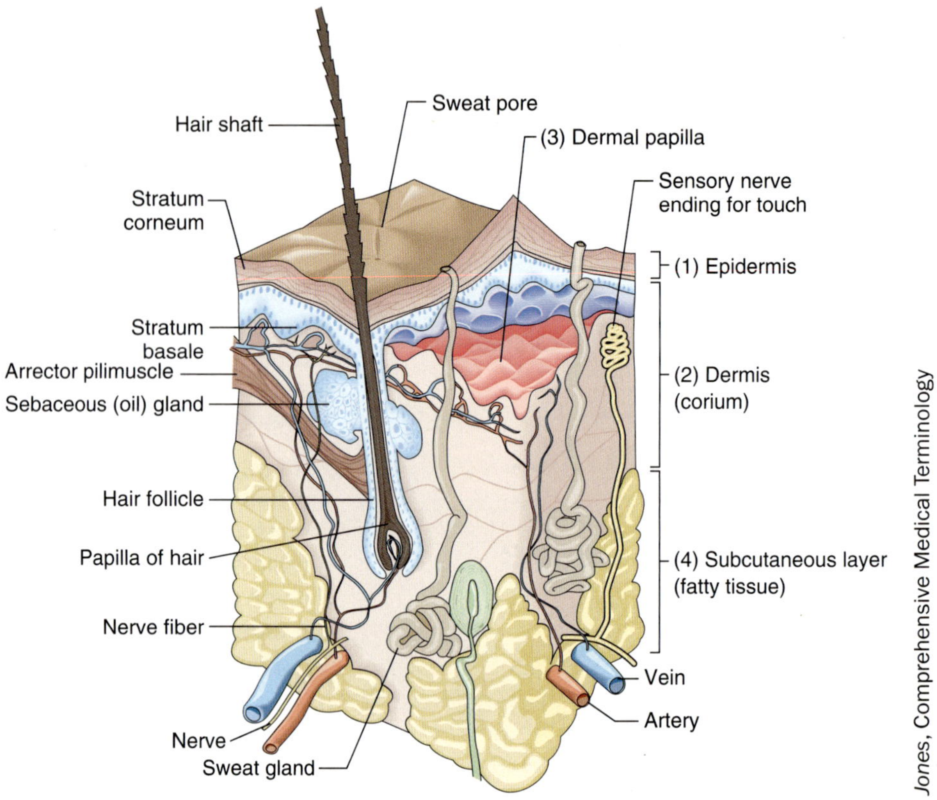

Figure A-4

8. Pilonidal cyst with abscess

   L05.01 Pilondial cyst with abscess

   Index: Cyst, pilondial, with abscess

9. Allergic dermatitis due to contact with chromium, accidental, initial visit

   T56.2x1A Toxic effect of chromium and its compounds, accidental (unintentional), initial visit

   L23.0 Allergic contact dermatitis due to metals

   Index: Dermatitis, contact, allergic, due to chromium

   In the Tabular List an instructional notation appears to "Code first (T36-T65) to identify drug or substance." Reference the Drugs and Chemical table under the term "Chromium." Select the code from the column entitled Poisoning, Accidental (unintentional).

   Under category T56 there is a note to add an appropriate seventh character.

10. Androgenic alopecia

    L64.9 Androgenic alopecia, unspecified

    Index: Alopecia, androgenic

Answers for Chapter 11: Diseases of the Musculoskeletal System and Connective Tissue

Check Your Understanding of Anatomy and Disorders

A. Refer to Figure A-5a

1. Scoliosis

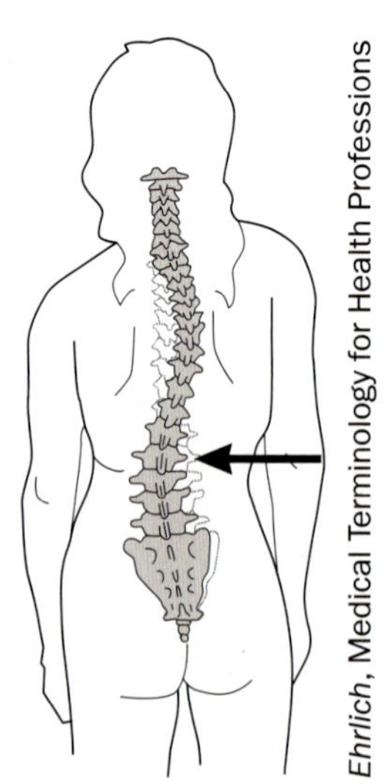

Figure A-5a

A. Refer to Figure A-5b

2. Kyphosis

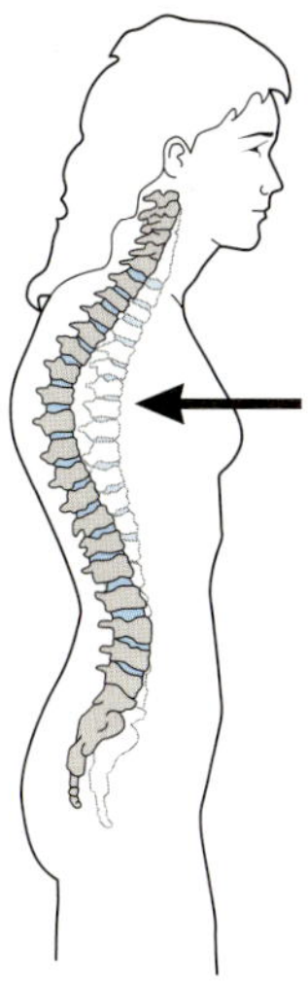

Ehrlich, Medical Terminology for Health Professions

Figure A-5b

A. Refer to Figure A-5c

3. Lordosis

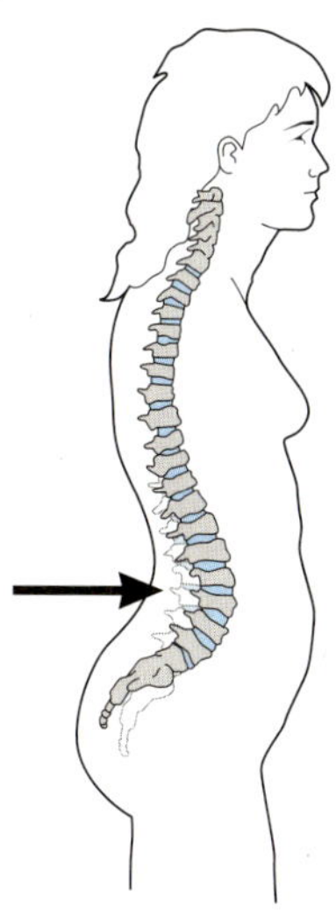

Ehrlich, Medical Terminology for Health Professions

Figure A-5c

3. Refer to Figure A-6

1. Vertebral body

2. Intervertebral disc

3. Cervical vertebrae

4. Thoracic (dorsal) vertebrae

5. Lumbar vertebrae

6. Sacrum

7. Coccyx

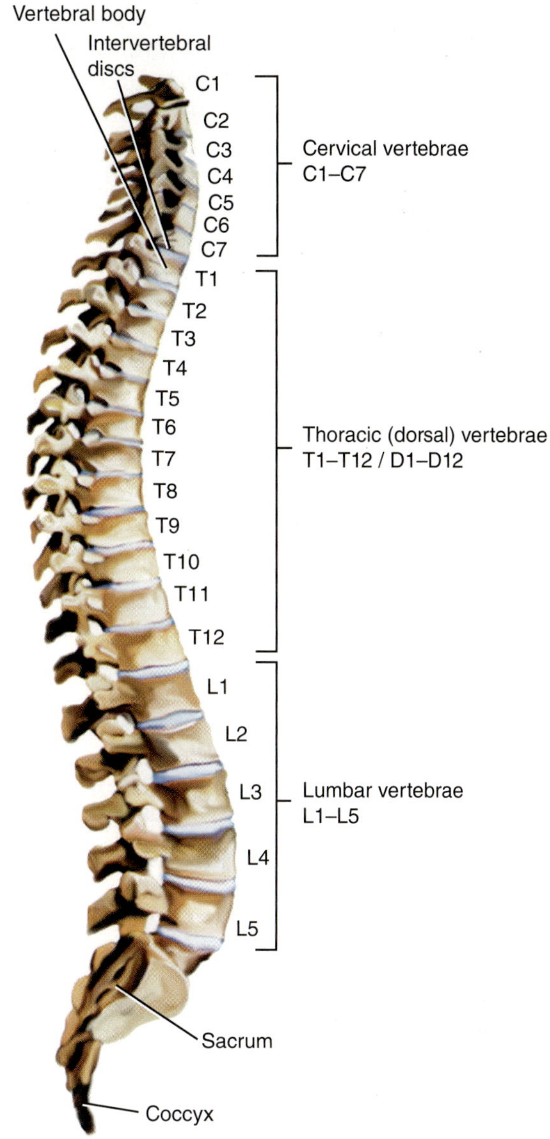

Davies, Essentials of Medical Terminology

Figure A-6

Check Your Clinical Knowledge

1. **Osteoporosis** is a metabolic disease that causes the bone to have a Swiss cheese–like appearance that leads to bone mass loss. Arthritis means an inflammation of a joint.
2. The term "bunion" is commonly used for **hallux valgus**, a deformity that affects the metatarsophalangeal joint of the big toe. Rheumatoid arthritis is an autoimmune disorder that affects the joints and connective tissue of the entire body.

3. The physician documents the following: "In the patient's right hand there is fusion and total loss of joint function." This would suggest that the patient has **ankylosis** of the hand. Bursitis is the inflammation of a bursa which is the fluid-filled sac near a joint.
4. **Osteomalacia** is caused by a deficiency of vitamin D and results in the softening of the bones. Osteomyelitis is an inflammation of the bone that is most commonly caused by the pathogen *Staphylococcus aureus.*
5. An **electromyography** is used to evaluate muscle disorders by inserting a small needle into the muscle tissue and recording the electrical activity. A dual-energy X-ray absorptiometry scan is used to confirm low bone mass.

Coding

1. Juvenile osteochondrosis of pelvis

   M91.0 Juvenile osteochondrosis of pelvis

   Index: Osteochondrosis, juvenile, hip and pelvis, pelvis
2. Rheumatoid vasculitis with rheumatoid arthritis of left shoulder

   M05.212 Rheumatoid vasculitis with rheumatoid arthritis of left shoulder

   Index: Vasculitis, rheumatoid—see *Rheumatoid, vasculitis. Then reference Rheumatoid, vasculitis, shoulder*
3. Rheumatoid bursitis of the right foot and ankle

   M06.271 Rheumatoid bursitis of the right foot and ankle

   Index: Bursitis, rheumatoid, ankle, foot joint
4. Acute gout flare

   M10.9 Gout, unspecified

   Index: Gout, (acute)
5. Left foot, acquired hallux rigidus

   M20.22 Hallux rigidus, left foot

   Index: Hallux, rigidus (acquired)
6. Acquired clubfoot of right foot

   M21.541 Acquired clubfoot, right foot

   Index: Clubfoot, acquired—*see Deformity, limb, clubfoot*
7. Recurrent subluxation of patella, left knee

   M22.12 Recurrent subluxation of patella, left knee

   Index: Subluxation, patella, recurrent (nontraumatic)—*see Dislocation, patella, recurrent, incomplete*
8. Loose body in third left toe joint

   M24.075 Loose body in left toe joint(s)

   Index: Loose, body, joint, toe
9. Myositis ossificans progressiva, left upper arm

   M61.122 Myositis ossificans progressiva, left upper arm

   Index: Myositis, ossificans, progressive, upper arm
10. Right hip abscess of bursa caused by *Staphylococcus aureus*

    M71.051 Abscess of bursa, right hip

    B95.61 *Staphylococcus aureus* as the cause of diseases classified elsewhere

    Index: Abscess, bursa, hip. *Note in Tabular List under M71.0 instructs coder to "Use additional code (B95.-, B96.-) to identify causative organism."*

Answers for Chapter 12: Diseases of the Genitourinary System

Check Your Understanding of Anatomy and Disorders

A. Refer to Figure A-7

1. Left renal artery
2. Adrenal suprarenal glands
3. Left kidney
4. Urinary bladder
5. Prostate gland
6. Urethra
7. Urethral meatus
8. Ureteral orifices
9. Right and left ureters

10. Renal medulla
11. Renal cortex
12. Right kidney

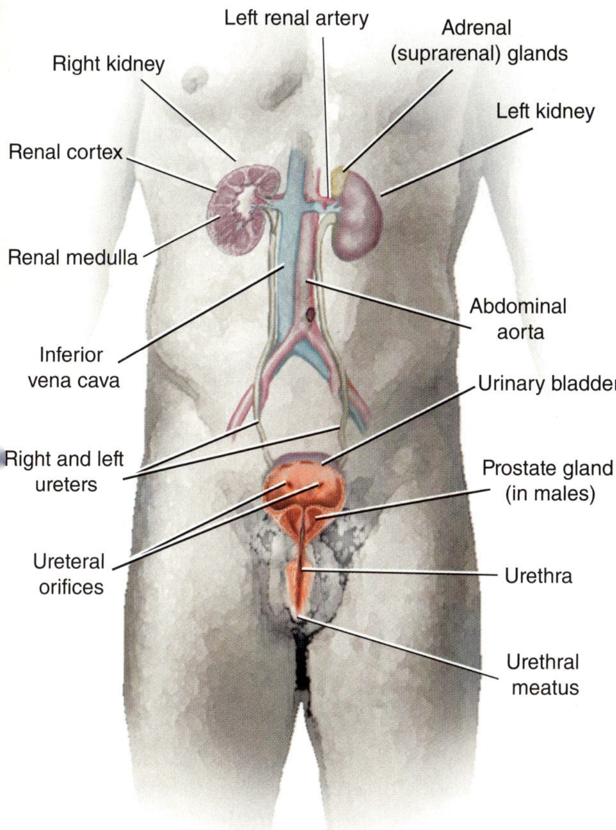

Scott and Fong, Body Structures and Functions

Figure A-7

B. Refer to Figure A-8

1. Ureter
2. Ovary
3. Cervix of uterus
4. Anus
5. Fallopian tube
6. Body of uterus
7. Urinary bladder
8. Clitoris
9. Urethra
10. Vagina

Check Your Clinical Knowledge

1. An inflammation of the fallopian tube is known as **salpingitis.** Oophoritis is an inflammation of the ovaries.
2. Patients with end-stage renal disease require **dialysis.** Insulin is required for patients with some forms of diabetes.
3. A test used to determine the levels of urea nitrogen or waste products in the blood is a **BUN** test. A urine C&S shows the number of white cells or bacteria in the urine, type of bacteria present, and effective antibiotic to prescribe for treatment.
4. **Polycystic disease**, an inherited disease, causes enlargement of both kidneys due to the formation of multiple grape-like cysts. Renal failure occurs when the kidneys fail to cleanse the blood of waste products.
5. **Stress** incontinence occurs when a person is unable to hold urine when he or she coughs, sneezes, or laughs. Overflow incontinence occurs when the bladder is not properly emptying and leaks when overfilled.

Coding

1. Calculus in urethra

   N21.1 Calculus in urethra

   Index: Calculus, urethra

2. Urinary tract obstruction

   N13.9 Obstructive and reflux uropathy, unspecified

   Index: Obstruction, urinary, organ or tract

3. Prostatitis

   N41.9 Prostatitis

   Index: Prostatitis

4. Irregular periods

   N92.6 Irregular menstruation, unspecified

   Index: Periods—*see also Menstruation. Menstruation, irregular*

5. Paravaginal cystocele

   N81.12 Cystocele, lateral

   Index: Cystocele, female, paravaginal

6. Segmental fat necrosis of breast

   N64.1 Fat necrosis of breast

   Index: Necrosis, fat, breast

7. Benign cyst of prepuce

   N47.4 Benign cyst of prepuce

   Index: Cyst, prepuce

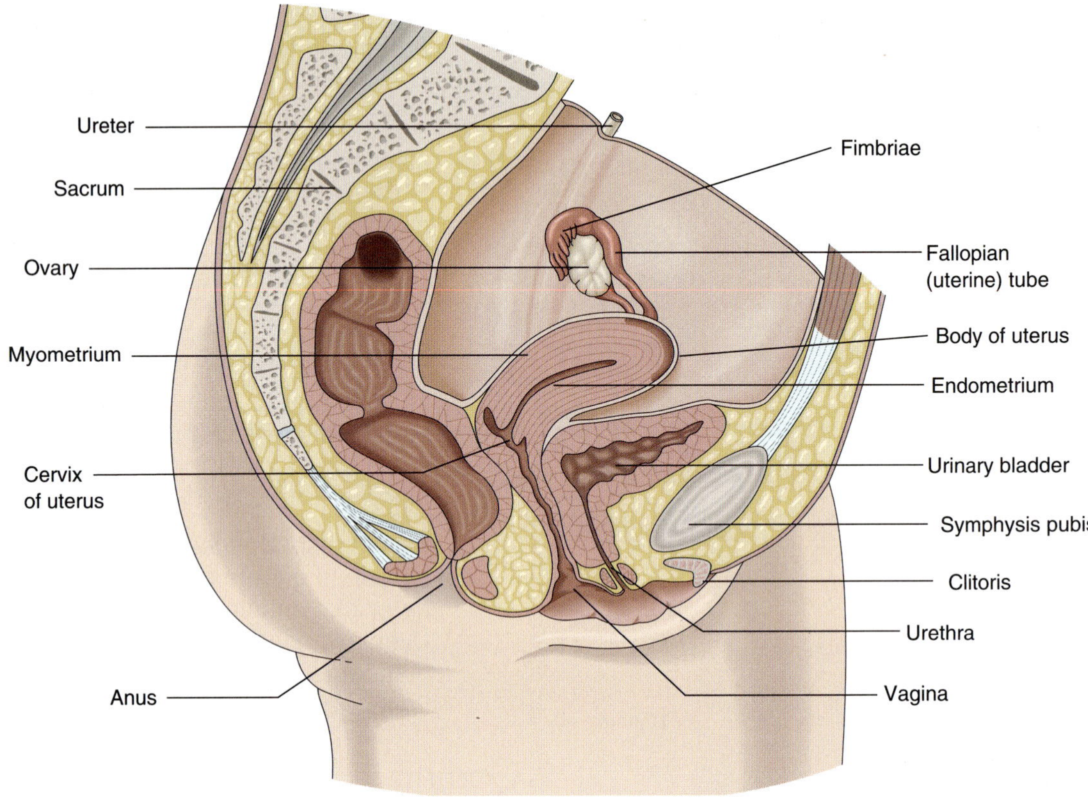

White and Duncan, Medical-Surgical Nursing: An Integrated Approach

Figure A-8

8. Acquired bladder-neck stenosis
N32.0 Bladder-neck obstruction
Index: Stenosis, bladder-neck (acquired)

9. Destrusor muscle hyperactivity
N32.81 Overactive bladder
Index: Hyperactive, hyperactivity, destrusor muscle

10. Acute nephritis
N00.9 Acute nephritic syndrome with unspecified morphologic changes
Index: Nephritis, acute

Answers for Chapter 13: Pregnancy, Childbirth, and the Puerperium

Check Your ICD-10-CM Knowledge

1. ICD-10-CM defines the **second** trimester from 14 weeks 0 days to less than 28 weeks 0 days. ICD-10-CM defines the third trimester from 28 weeks 0 days until delivery.

2. A seventh character of 0 for code O33.5xx0 denotes **single gestation.** A seventh character of 1 for code O33.5xx1 denotes fetus 1.

3. Obstetric **hematoma of vulva** is reported with code O71.7. Obstetric damage to coccyx is reported with code O71.6.

4. **Rupture of fallopian tube** due to pregnancy is classified to code O00.1. Mural pregnancy is classified to code O00.8.

5. A young primigravida, as defined by ICD-10-CM, is a woman who is less than **16** years old at expected date of delivery.

Check Your Clinical Knowledge

1. The most common location of an ectopic pregnancy is the **fallopian tubes.** The cervix is not a common site for an ectopic pregnancy.

2. Excessive vomiting during pregnancy is known as **hyperemesis gravidarum.** A miscarriage is a spontaneous abortion.

3. **Placenta previa** is the abnormal positioning of the placenta in the lower uterus. Aruptio placentae is the sudden separation of the placenta from the uterine wall prior to or at the time of labor.
4. The letters in HELLP syndrome refer to **hemolysis**, elevated liver function, and low platelet level.
5. Pre-eclampsia is a serious condition of pregnancy characterized by hypertension, **edema,** and proteinuria. Coma occurs in eclampsia.

Coding

1. Missed abortion at 17 weeks' gestation with retention of dead fetus

   002.1 Missed abortion

   Index: Abortion, missed

   Z3A.17 17 weeks gestation of pregnancy

   Index: Pregnancy, weeks of gestation
2. 24-week OB visit for 14-year-old primigravida patient

   009.612 Supervision of young primigravida, second trimester

   Index: Pregnancy, supervision, very young mother, primigravida

   Z3A.24 24 weeks gestation of pregnancy

   Index: Pregnancy, weeks of gestation
3. Tubal abortion

   000.1 Tubal pregnancy

   Index: Abortion, tubal

   Z3A.00 Weeks of gestation of pregnancy not specified

   Index: Pregnancy, weeks of gestation
4. Eclampsia during 29th week of pregnancy

   015.03 Eclampsia in pregnancy, third trimester

   Index: Eclampsia, pregnancy

   Z3A.29 29 weeks gestation of pregnancy

   Index: Pregnancy, weeks of gestation
5. Antepartum hemorrhage with coagulation defect at 30 weeks' gestation

   046.003 Antepartum hemorrhage with coagulation defect, unspecified, third trimester

   Index: Hemorrhage, antepartum, with coagulation defect

   Z3A.30 30 weeks gestation of pregnancy

   Index: Pregnancy, weeks of gestation
6. Diabetes mellitus arising during pregnancy controlled by diet

   024.410 Gestational diabetes mellitus in pregnancy, diet-controlled

   Index: Diabetes, gestational, diet-controlled

   Z3A.00 Weeks of gestation of pregnancy not specified

   Index: Pregnancy, weeks of gestation
7. Premature separation of placenta with afibrinogememia, at 31 weeks' gestation

   045.013 Premature separation of placenta with afibrinogenemia, third trimester

   Index: Pregnancy, complicated by, premature separation of placenta 045—*see also Abruptio placentae. Reference Abruptio placentae, with afibrinogememia*

   Z3A.31 31 weeks gestation of pregnancy

   Index: Pregnancy, weeks of gestation
8. *Streptococcus,* group A infection of bladder following delivery

   086.22 Infection of bladder following delivery

   B95.0 *Streptococcus*, group A, as the cause of diseases classified elsewhere

   Index: Puerperal, infection, urinary, bladder

   The Tabular List for code 086.22 instructs the coder to "Use additional code (B95-B97) to identify infectious agent."

   Reference: Infection, as cause of disease classified elsewhere, B95.5.

   Code B95.5 classifies unspecified streptococcus; therefore, code B95.0 should be used to report group A.

9. Cracked nipple due to breast-feeding

   O92.13 Cracked nipple associated with lactation

   Index: Cracked nipple, associated with lactation

10. Cesarean delivery of 7-pound 11-ounce baby girl *(assign an Outcome of Delivery code)*

    O82 Encounter for cesarean delivery without indication

    Z37.0 Single liveborn

    Index: Delivery, cesarean, without indication

    Outcome of delivery, single, liveborn

    Z3A.00 Weeks of gestation of pregnancy not specified

    Index: Pregnancy, weeks of gestation

Answers for Chapter 14: Certain Conditions Originating in the Perinatal Period and Congenital Malformations, Deformations, and Chromosomal Abnormalities

Check Your Knowledge of Conditions

Congenital Conditions

✓ **1.** Pentalogy of Fallot

_____ **2.** Respiratory distress syndrome

_____ **3.** Sepsis of newborn due to *E. coli*

✓ **4.** Cleft palate with bilateral cleft lip

_____ **5.** Neonatal cerebral ischemia

✓ **6.** Transposition of colon

✓ **7.** Complex syndactyly of fingers with synostosis

_____ **8.** Traumatic glaucoma of newborn

_____ **9.** Neonatal melena

✓ **10.** Van der Woude's syndrome

Check Your Clinical Knowledge

1. **Spina bifida** is a congenital disorder in which the posterior portion of the vertebrae of the bony spinal column fails to close over the spinal cord. Cerebral palsy is a paralysis that results from inadequate blood or oxygen supply to the brain during fetal development, the birthing process, or in infancy.
2. **Tetralogy of Fallot** is a combination of four defects of the heart. (Tetralogy of Fallot, hemophilia) Hemophilia is a hereditary X-linked bleeding disorder.
3. **Hirschsprung's disease** typically impacts the sigmoid colon and is due to an absence of nerves therefore causing a lack of peristalsis. Hypospadias is a congenital condition in which there is an abnormal opening of the male urinary meatus on the undersurface of the penis.
4. Congenital varicella is a congenital **viral** disease.
5. **Anencephaly** occurs early in gestation and is a severe form of neural tube deficit with the failure of the cephalic aspect of the neural tube to close. Talipes equinovarus, commonly known as clubfoot, occurs when there is a deformity of the anterior half of the foot and the foot is adducted and inverted.

Coding

1. Lumbar spina bifida with hydrocephalus

   Q05.2 Lumbar spina bifida with hydrocephalus

   Index: Spina bifida, lumbar, with hydrocephalus

2. Rupture of the liver due to birth injury

   P15.0 Birth injury to liver

   Index: Birth, injury, liver

3. Newborn impacted by in utero exposure to tobacco smoke

   P04.2 Newborn (suspected to be) affected by maternal use of tobacco

Index: Tobacco (nicotine), maternal use, affecting newborn

4. Newborn type II, respiratory distress syndrome

   P22.1 Transient tachypnea of newborn

   Index: Syndrome, respiratory, distress, newborn, type II

5. Cephalhematoma due to birth injury

   P12.0 Cephalhematoma due to birth injury

   Index: Cephalhematoma, newborn (birth injury)

6. Congenital funnel chest

   Q67.6 Pectus excavatum

   Index: Funnel, chest, congenital

7. Birth weight of newborn, 525 grams

   P07.02 Extremely low birth weight of newborn, 500–749 grams

   Index: Low, birth weight, extreme, with weight of, 500–749 grams

8. Acidosis of newborn

   P84 Other problems with newborn

   Index: Acidosis, newborn

9. Transient neonatal diabetes mellitus

   P70.2 Neonatal diabetes mellitus

   Index: Diabetes, neonatal (transient)

10. Neonatal rectal hemorrhage

    P54.2 Neonatal rectal hemorrhage

    Index: Hemorrhage, rectum, newborn

Answers for Chapter 15: Symptoms, Signs, and Abnormal Clinical and Laboratory Findings, Not Elsewhere Classified

Check Your Knowledge

1. Circulatory
2. Genitourinary
3. Skin and subcutaneous tissue
4. Respiratory
5. Digestive

Check Your Clinical Knowledge

Clinical Description	Diagnosis
1. C elevated PSA	**A.** seizure activity
2. E abnormal EKG	**B.** visual impairment
3. A abnormal EEG	**C.** prostate cancer
4. B abnormal ERG	**D.** diabetes mellitus
5. D elevated fasting glucose	**E.** myocardial infarction

Coding

1. Elevated CRP

   R79.82 Elevated C-reactive protein (CRP)

   Index: Elevated, C-reactive protein (CRP)

2. Fluid retention

   R60.9 Edema, unspecified

   Index: Retention, fluid

3. Painful urination

   R30.9 Painful micturition, unspecified

   Index: Urination, painful

4. Spastic gait

   R26.1 Paralytic gait

   Index: Gait abnormality, spastic

5. Abnormal bowel sounds

   R19.15 Other abnormal bowel sounds

   Index: Abnormal, bowel sounds

6. Abnormal level of cocaine in the blood

   R78.2 Finding of cocaine in blood

   Index: Findings, abnormal, inconclusive, without diagnosis, in blood (of substance not normally found in blood), cocaine

7. Abnormal liver function study
   R94.5 Abnormal results of liver function studies
   Index: Findings, abnormal, inconclusive, without diagnosis, function study, liver
8. Elevated levels of steroids in urine
   R82.5 Elevated urine levels of drugs, medicaments, and biological substances
   Index: Elevated, elevation, urine level of, steroids
9. Decreased sexual desire
   R68.82 Decreased libido
   Index: Decrease(d), sexual desire
10. Patient is a 10-day-old infant with excessive crying
    R68.11 Excessive crying of infant (baby)
    Index: Excess, excessive, excessively, crying, in infant

Answers for Chapter 16: Injuries, Poisoning, and Certain Other Consequences of External Causes

Check Your Knowledge of Anatomy

Refer to Figure A-9

1. Skull
2. Maxilla
3. Mandible
4. Clavicle
5. Sternum
6. Humerus
7. Ribs
8. Vertebral column
9. Ilium
10. Radius
11. Pubis
12. Ulna
13. Carpals
14. Metacarpals
15. Phalanges of hand
16. Ischium
17. Femur
18. Patella
19. Tibia
20. Fibula
21. Tarsals
22. Metatarsals
23. Phalanges of foot

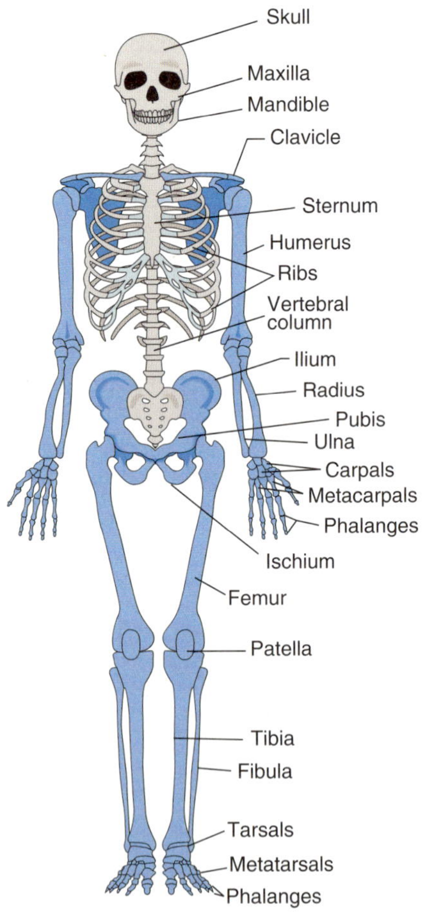

Appendicular skeleton (blue)
Axial skeleton (grey)

Figure A-9

Estes, Health Assessment and Physical Examination

Coding

1. Complete traumatic amputation of left ear

   S08.112A Complete traumatic amputation of left ear

   Index: Amputation, traumatic, ear (complete)

2. Subsequent encounter for puncture wound of the scalp

   S01.03xD Puncture wound without foreign body of scalp

   Index: Puncture, scalp

3. Right eye, penetrating wound of orbit

   S05.41xA Penetrating wound of orbit with or without foreign body, right eye

   Index: Wound, open, orbit—*see Wound, open, ocular, orbit*

4. Posterior displaced Type II dens fracture, subsequent encounter with routine healing

   S12.111D Posterior displaced Type II dens fracture

   Index: Fracture, neck, cervical vertebra, second, dens, posterior

5. Contusion of left front wall of thorax

   S20.212A Contusion of left front wall of thorax

   Index: Contusion, thorax, front

6. Rejection of bone marrow transplant

   T86.01 Bone marrow transplant rejection

   Index: Rejection, bone, marrow

7. Sexual abuse of child

   T74.22xA Child sexual abuse, confirmed

   Index: Abuse, sexual—*see Maltreatment, sexual abuse. Reference Maltreatment, child, sexual abuse, confirmed*

8. Local infection due to port-a-cath

   T80.212A Local infection due to central venous catheter, port or reservior

   Index: Infection, due to, central venous catheter, port or reservior

9. Open transverse fracture of the shaft of the right femur, displaced

   S72.321B Displaced transverse fracture of shaft of right femur

   Index: Fracture, femur, shaft, transverse

10. Sprain in left hip iliofemoral ligament, third follow-up visit

    S73.112D Iliofemoral ligament sprain of left hip

    Index: Sprain, hip, iliofemoral ligament

Answers for Chapter 17: External Causes of Morbidity

Check Your Knowledge of ICD-10-CM

1. aircraft
2. ten
3. nontraffic
4. three-wheeled
5. pedestrian

Coding

1. Tripping over carpet at patient's single family home in bedroom while rough housing *(in addition to an External Cause code, assign a code for both the Place of Occurrence [Y92-] and Activity [Y93-])*

   W22.8xxA Striking against or struck by other objects

   Index to External Cause: Tripping, over, carpet, rug or (small) object

   Y92.013 Bedroom of single family (private) house as the place of occurrence of the external cause

   Index to External Cause: Place of occurrence, residence, house, single family, bedroom

   Y93.83 Rough housing and horseplay

   Index to External Cause: Activity, rough housing and horseplay

2. Bitten by horse

W55.11xA Bitten by horse

Index to External Cause: Bite, horse

3. Fall into hole

   W17.2xxA Fall into hole

   Index to External Cause: Fall, falling, into, hole

4. Gored by goat

   W55.32xA Struck by other hoof stock

   Index to External Cause: Contact with goat, strike

5. Hypodermic needle stick

   W46.0xxA Contact with hypodermic needle

   Index to External Cause: Contract with, needle, hypodermic

6. Subsequent encounter due to helicopter crash causing injury to occupant

   V95.01xD Helicopter crash injuring occupant

   Index to External Cause: Crash, aircraft, helicopter

7. Tree accidentally falling on person

   W20.8xxA Other cause of strike by thrown, projected for falling object

   Index to External Cause: Tree falling on or hitting (accidentally) (person)

8. Injury from walking into lamppost, subsequent encounter

   W22.02xD Walked into lamppost

   Index: Walked into stationary object, lamppost

9. Struck by softball

   W21.07xA Struck by softball

   Index to External Cause: Struck, sport equipment, ball, softball

10. Evaluation of injury to foot by being skated over by sharp skate blades

    W21.32xA Struck by skate blades

    Index to External Causes: Struck, sports equipment, skate blades

    Y92.34 Swimming pool (public) as the place of occurrence of the external cause

Answers for Chapter 18: Factors Influencing Health Status and Contact with Health Services

Check Your Knowledge of ICD-10-CM

1. false
2. false
3. true
4. true
5. false

Coding

1. Carrier of typhoid

   Z22.0 Carrier of typhoid

   Index: Carrier, typhoid

2. Type AB, Rh-negative blood

   Z67.31 Type AB blood, Rh negative

   Index: Blood, type, AB, Rh negative

3. Patient seen in the office for a sports physical

   Z02.5 Encounter for examination for participation in sport

   Index: Examination, medical, sport competition

4. Screening for HPV

   Z11.51 Encounter for screening for human papillomavirus

   Index: Screening, human papillomavirus

5. Occupational exposure to dust

   Z57.2 Occupational exposure to dust

   Index: Exposure, occupational, dust

6. Problems related to child living in a group home

   Z62.22 Institutional upbringing

   Index: Problem (with) (related to), child, living in group home

7. Lack of adequate sleep

   Z72.820 Sleep deprivation

   Index: Lack of, sleep (adequate)

8. Underachievement in school
   Z55.3 Underachievement in school
   Index: Underachievement in school
9. History of estrogen therapy
   Z92.23 Personal history of estrogen therapy
   Index: History, personal, estrogen therapy
10. Encounter for checking of IUD
   Z30.431 Encounter for surveillance of intrauterine contraceptive device
   Index: Contraception, contraceptive, device, checking

Answers for Chapter 19: Transition from ICD-9-CM to ICD-10-CM

Coding

1. Open wound of the nose, initial visit
   ICD-9-CM: 873.20
   ICD-10-CM: S01.20xA
2. Congenital salivary fistula
   ICD-9-CM: 750.24
   ICD-10-CM: Q38.4
3. Acute tonsillitis
   ICD-9-CM: 463
   ICD-10-CM: J03.90
4. Collapsed lung
   ICD-9-CM: 518.0
   ICD-10-CM: J98.19
5. Lung mass
   ICD-9-CM: 786.6
   ICD-10-CM: R91.8
6. Bronchial stenosis
   ICD-9-CM: 519.19
   ICD-10-CM: J98.09
7. Chronic hepatitis C
   ICD-9-CM: 070.54
   ICD-10-CM: B18.2
8. Alcohol withdrawal
   ICD-9-CM: 291.81
   ICD-10-CM: F10.239
9. Panic disorder
   ICD-9-CM: 300.01
   ICD-10-CM: F41.0
10. Obsessive-compulsive disorder
   ICD-9-CM: 300.3
   ICD-10-CM: F42

Answers for Chapter 20: Coding with ICD-10-PCS

Alphabetic Index Exercise

1. See Drainage
2. See Dilation, Heart, and Great Vessels
3. See Excision
4. See Omentum, lesser
5. See Nerve, Facial

PCS Table Exercise

1. 0NH00NZ (craniotomy is an open procedure)
2. 0NH03MZ

Section Exercise

1. **6** Extracorporeal Therapies
2. **0** Reduction, fracture states to reference Root Operation Reposition
3. **2** Placement
4. **G** Mental Health
5. **H** Substance Abuse Treatment

Body System Exercise

1. **D** Right hemicolectomy
2. **P** Scapulectomy
3. **8** Dilation of left lacrimal duct
4. **6** Percutaneous mechanical thrombectomy-femoral vein
5. **F** Laparoscopic cholecystectomy

Root Operation Exercise 1

1. Fragmentation
2. Extirpation

3. Drainage
4. Fragmentation
5. Extirpation

Root Operation Exercise 2

1. Alphabetic Index provides two Root Operations under cholecystectomy: Excision and Resection. This indicates that the coder should review the documentation. In this case the entire gallbladder was removed; therefore, the correct character selection to review in the Tables would be 0FT4.
2. Alphabetic Index provides an entry under Resection for the lingula of the bronchus; therefore, the correct four characters of the code are 0BT9.
3. There is no entry for Resection of the tail of the pancreas. This meets the definition of Excision (portion of body part)—there is no subdivision classification for resection of tail of pancreas. Refer to Excision in the Alphabetic Index for 0FBG.

Root Operation Exercise 3

1. Revision
2. Replacement
3. Dilation
4. Reposition
5. Drainage

Body Part Exercise 1

1. *use* Muscle, Foot, Left. Transfer, Muscle, Foot, Left—0KXW
2. *use* Nerve, Tibial. Excision, Nerve, Tibia—01BG
3. *use* Artery, Femoral, Left. Repair, Artery, Femoral, Left—04QL

Body Part Exercise 2

1. __8__ The surgeon excised a polyp from the first portion of the small intestine.
2. __6__ A biopsy was performed from the region of the stomach where it connects to the small intestine.
3. __C__ The surgeon states that there is a lesion located on the sphincter muscle that connects the small intestine to the large intestine.

Approach Exercise 1

1. Via natural or artificial opening endoscopic
2. Percutaneous
3. Open
4. Percutaneous endoscopic
5. Percutaneous

Approach Exercise 2

1. Via natural or artificial opening endoscopic
2. Open
3. External
4. Open
5. Via natural or artificial opening endoscopic

Approach Exercise 3

1. Percutaneous (right femoral artery was accessed). Further web research will reveal that the Seldinger technique uses a needle to access the artery.
2. Open (incision was opened over the patella)
3. Percutaneous endoscopic (umbilical incision made and Visiport introduced). Perform a web search on Visiport and it will reveal that it is an instrument used in laparoscopic procedures.

Device Exercise 1

1. Use Intraluminal Device
2. Use Synthetic Substitute
3. Use Intraluminal Device
4. Use Synthetic Substitute

Device Exercise 2

1. Autologous tissue substitute
2. Synthetic substitute
3. Zooplastic tissue

Qualifier Case Study

Case Study

Answer: 0SRB02A Metal (titanium) on Plastic (Polyethylene). The Press Fit method is uncemented. Perform a web search for hip replacement methods for a full explanation of the types displayed in the PCS table.

Building an ICD-10-PCS Code

1. Bilateral liposuction of upper arms (elective procedure)

   0X083ZZ

   0X093ZZ

Character	Description
Section	Medical and Surgical
Body System	Anatomical Regions, Upper Extremities
Operation	Alteration
Body Part	Upper Arms (right-character 8) (left-character 9)
Approach	Percutaneous
Device	No Device
Qualifier	No Qualifier

   Index: No entry for Liposuction, apply definitions of Root Operation.

   Root Operation: Alteration

   Perform web research to determine how the procedure is performed: Percutaneous approach.

   Index: Alternation, Arm, Upper, Left 0X09 and Right 0X08

2. Laparoscopic-assisted total vaginal hysterectomy (LAVH)

   0UT9FZZ

Character	Description
Section	Medical and Surgical
Body System	Female Reproductive System
Operation	Resection
Body Part	Uterus
Approach	Via Natural or Artificial Opening with Percutaneous Endoscopic Assistance
Device	No Device
Qualifier	No Qualifier

   Index: Hysterectomy provides two choices: Excision and Resection

   Root Operation: Resection, Uterus 0UT9

   This is the most common use of this type of approach. Review the documentation to determine if the cervix and/or tubes and ovaries were also removed.

3. Advancement flap skin graft covering left forearm

   0HXEXZZ

Character	Description
Section	Medical and Surgical
Body System	Skin and Breast
Operation	Transfer
Body Part	Skin, Left Lower Arm
Approach	External
Device	No Device
Qualifier	No Qualifier

   Index: Advancement—*see Reposition or see Transfer (advancement flap is a transfer since the original blood source is left intact)*

   Index: Transfer, skin, Lower Arm, Left 0HXEXZZ

4. Open reduction with internal fixation, displaced left lateral ankle fracture

0SSG04Z

Character	Description
Section	Medical and Surgical
Body System	Lower Joints
Operation	Reposition
Body Part	Ankle Joint, Left
Approach	Open
Device	Internal Fixation Device
Qualifier	No Qualifier

Index: Reduction, Fracture—*see Reposition*

Index: Reposition, Joint, Ankle, Leg 0SSG

5. ERCP with balloon dilation of common bile duct

0F798ZZ

Character	Description
Section	Medical and Surgical
Body System	Hepatobiliary System and Pancreas
Operation	Dilation
Body Part	Common Bile Duct
Approach	Via Natural or Artificial Opening Endoscopic
Device	No Device
Qualifier	No Qualifier

Index: Dilation, Duct, Common Bile 0F79

Note that the use of the balloon (device) is not assigned a character value. Official coding guideline (B6.1a.) states that a device is coded only if a device remains after the procedure is completed. ERCP is the approach (endoscopic).

Operative Report 1

PROCEDURE PERFORMED: Right breast lumpectomy.

ICD-10-PCS Code(s)

0HBT0ZX Medical/Surgical, Skin and Breast, Excision, Breast (right), Open, No Device, Diagnostic

Coding Notes: Search for lumpectomy in the index for a reference to either "see Excision" or "see Resection." Apply definitions from the Root Operations. *Resection* is removal of ALL of a body part and *Excision* is cutting out a PORTION of a body part.

Index: Excision, breast, right 0HBT

Reference the table to build the remainder of the characters.

Operative Report 2

PROCEDURE PERFORMED: Open reduction and internal fixation of left distal radius.

ICD-10-PCS Code(s):

0PSJ04Z Medical/Surgical, Upper Bones, Reposition, Radius (left), Open, Internal Fixation Device, No Qualifier

Index: Reduction, fracture—*see Reposition. Reposition, radius, left 0PSJ*

Reference the table to build the remainder of the characters.

Operative Report 3

PROCEDURE PERFORMED: Esophagogastroduodenoscopy with cautery.

POSTOPERATIVE DIAGNOSES: Gastrointestinal (GI) bleed and angiodysplasia of the stomach.

ICD-10-PCS Code(s):

0D568ZZ Medical/Surgical, Gastrointestinal, Destruction, Stomach, Via Natural or Artificial Opening Endoscopic, No Device, No Qualifier

Coding Notes: Use of cautery supports the definition of the Root Operation *Destruction*. Destruction is the physical eradication of all or a portion of a body part by the direct use of energy, force, or a destructive agent.

Index: Destruction, stomach 0D56

Reference the table to build the remainder of the characters.

Operative Report 4

PROCEDURE: Colonoscopy.

ICD-10-PCS Code(s):

0DJD8ZZ Medical/Surgical, Gastrointestinal System, Inspection, Lower Intestinal Tract, Via Natural or Artificial Opening Endoscopic, No Device, No Qualifier

Index: Colonoscopy 0DJD8ZZ

Coding Notes: In this case, the entire code is provided from the Index. Note that the Root Operation is *Inspection*.

Operative Report 5

POSTOPERATIVE DIAGNOSIS: Right nasal foreign body.

His nose was examined and a small cotton foreign body was removed from the anterior aspect of the nose.

ICD-10-PCS Code(s):

09CKXZZ Medical/Surgical, Nose, Extirpation, Nose, External, (No Device, No Qualifier)

Coding Notes: In this case, coders must apply definitions for Root Operations to successfully use the Index. There is no entry for "removal of foreign body." *Extirpation* is the Root Operation. The definition is "taking or cutting out solid matter from a body part."

Index: *Extirpation, Nose 09CK*

Reference the table to build the remainder of the characters.

Answers for Chapter 21: Application of Coding Guidelines

1. A

   Guideline Section: I.C.19.e.5.b

2. B

   Guideline Section: I.C.19.e.5.a

3. B

   Guideline Section: II.I.1

4. D

   Guideline Section: II, A

5. A

   Guideline Section: III.A

6. B

   Guideline Section: I.C.19.b.1

7. C

   Guideline Section: I.C.19.e.5

8. B

   Guideline Section: I.C.15.n

9. A

   Guideline Section: I.C.19.c.

10. B

    Guideline Section: I.C.1.a.b

Answers for Chapter 22: Coding Case Studies

1. ICD-10-CM code(s): N85.8, D62

   ICD-10-PCS code(s): 0UDB8ZX

2. ICD-10-CM code(s): Z51.11, C50.911, Z90.11

3. ICD-10-CM code(s): K29.00, R03.0

4. ICD-10-CM code(s): K80.20

   ICD-10-PCS code(s): 0FT40ZZ, 0FJ44ZZ

5. ICD-10-CM code(s): R10.9

6. ICD-10-CM code(s): F10.231

7. ICD-10-CM code(s): J44.1

8. ICD-10-CM code(s): I20.0

9. ICD-10-CM code(s): S82.252A

   ICD-10-PCS code(s): 0QSH0ZZ

10. ICD-10-CM code(s): Z38.00, Q86.0

Answers for Chapter 23: Decision-Based Coding

Case Study 1

Coding Assignment	Rationale
ICD-10-CM Code(s): D18.01 Hemangioma of skin and subcutaneous tissue (correct)	Correct assignment
ICD-10-PCS Code(s): 0JBL0ZZ (incorrect)	The body part character should be M for left upper leg, not L for right upper leg Correct code assignment: **0JBM0ZZ**

Case Study 2

Coding Assignment	Rationale
ICD-10-CM Code(s): K80.50 Calculus of bile duct without cholangitis or cholecystitis without obstruction (correct)	Correct assignment
ICD-10-PCS Code(s): 0FT44ZZ (correct)	Correct assignment

Case Study 3

Coding Assignment	Rationale
ICD-10-CM Code(s): S82.201A Unspecified fracture of shaft of right tibia (incorrect)	The code is correct but the extension D should be assigned for subsequent encounter for closed fracture with routine healing. Correct code: **S82.201D**
ICD-10-PCS Code(s): 0QPGX4Z (incorrect)	The approach character X is incorrect; it is an open approach. Correct code: **0QPG04Z**

Case Study 4

Coding Assignment	Rationale
ICD-10-CM Code(s): R13.10 Dysphagia, unspecified (correct) K21.9 Gastro-esophageal reflux disease without esophagitis (correct) K22.70 Barrett's esophagus without dysplasia (do not report)	The code selection for Dysphagia and GERD is correct. The code for Barrett's esophagus should not be reported according to coding guidelines. In an outpatient setting, a "rule out" diagnosis is not assigned a code. In this case, "rule out" means that the physician is considering the diagnosis but has not been confirmed.
ICD-10-PCS Code(s): 0DB38ZZ (incorrect)	Biopsies were taken for diagnostic purposes. The last character should be "X." Correct code: **0DB38ZX**

Case Study 5

Coding Assignment	Rationale
ICD-10-CM Code(s): Z45.09 Encounter for adjustment and management of other cardiac device (correct) I49.9 Cardiac arrhythmia, unspecified (correct)	Correct assignment
ICD-10-PCS Code(s): 0WP80YZ (incorrect)	Cardiac recorder lies directly under the skin. Index: Removal of device from—Subcutaneous Tissue and Fascia, Trunk Correct code assignment Medical/Surgical, Subcutaneous Tissue and Fascia, Open, Cardiac Rhythm Related Device **0JPT0PZ**

Appendix B: Anatomical Diagrams

This appendix can be used by the student as a reference tool. A comprehensive understanding of human anatomy is essential for correct code assignment.

Lymphatic Circulation and Major Lymph Node Locations

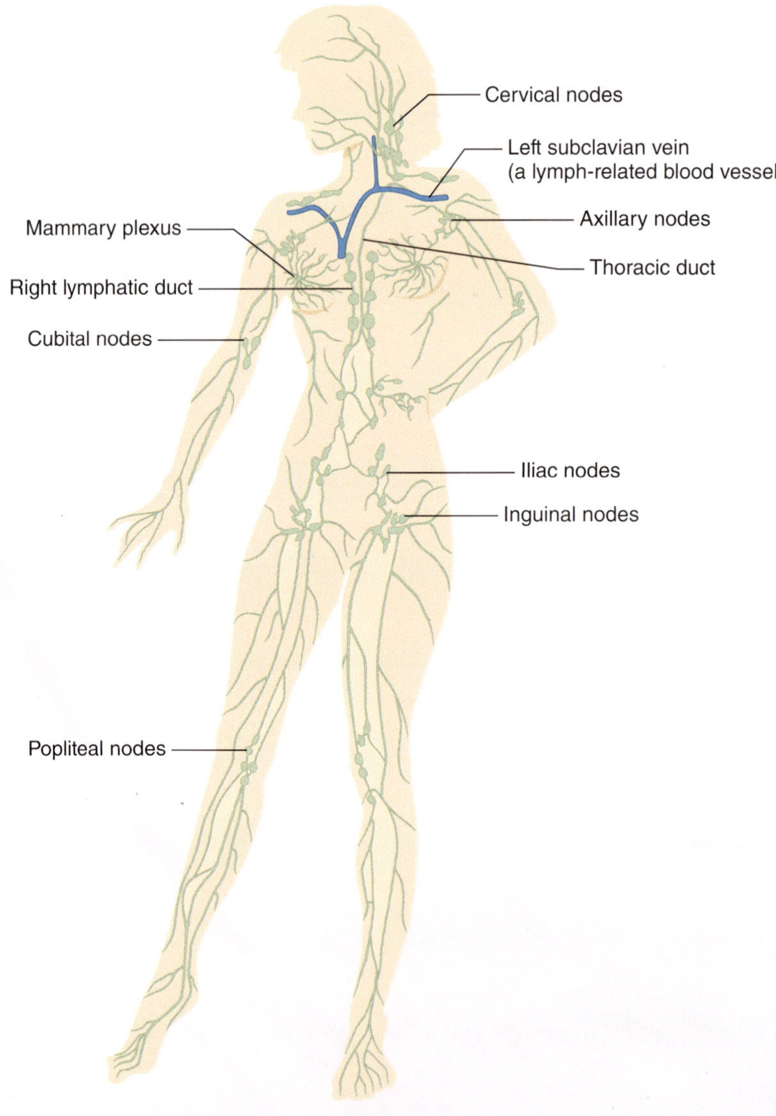

Dennerll, Medical Terminology: A Programmed Systems Approach

External View of the Heart

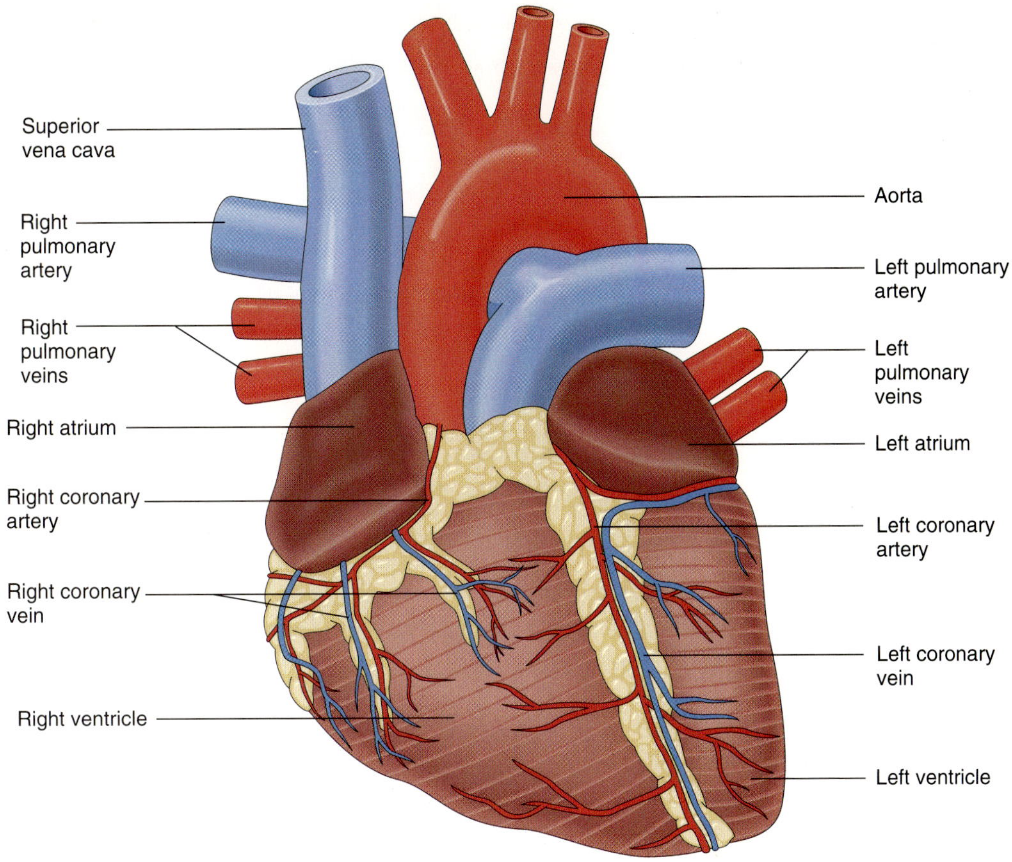

Ehrlich, Medical Terminology for Health Professions

Structures of the Gastrointestinal System

A.

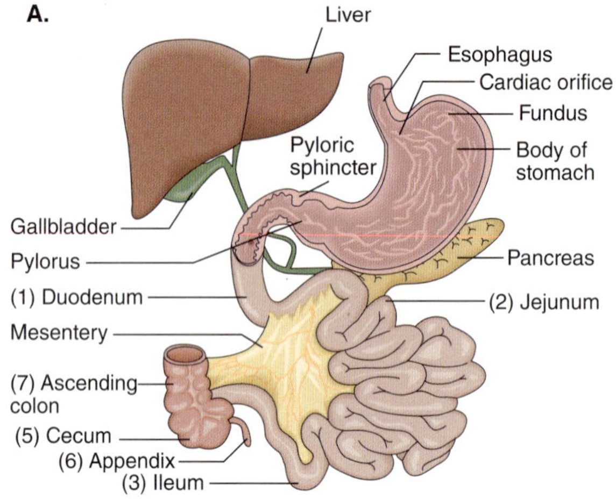

B.

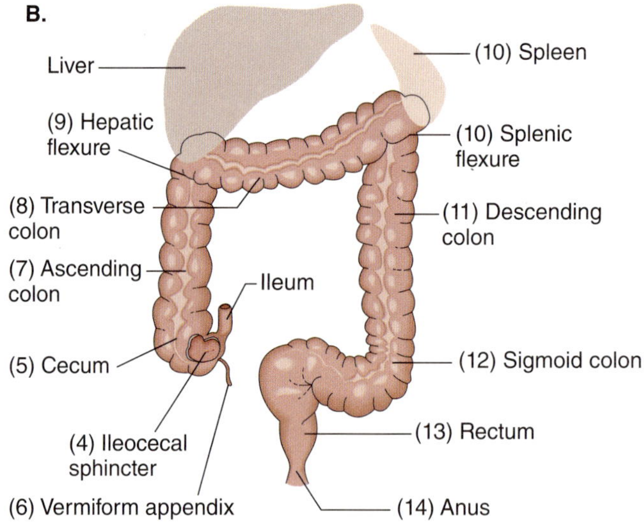

Jones, Comprehensive Medical Terminology

Endocrine Glands

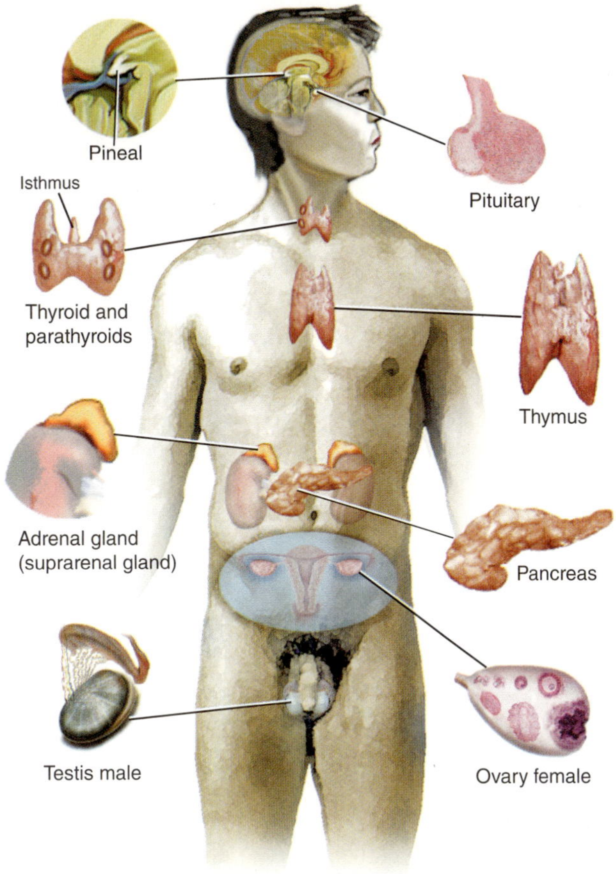

Davies, Essentials of Medical Terminology

Structures of the Eyeball Shown in Cross-Section

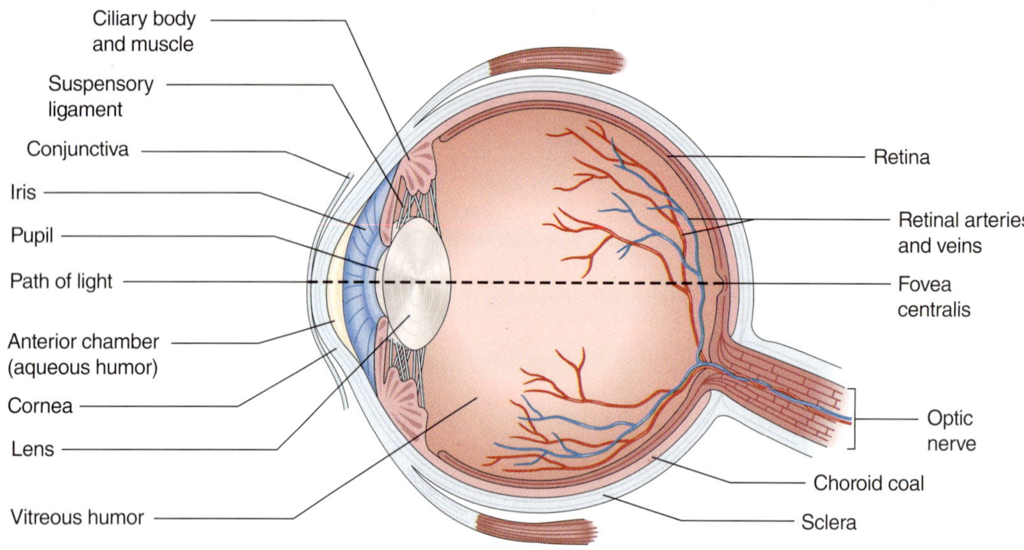

Ehrlich, Medical Terminology for Health Professions

Structures of the Ears Shown in Cross-Section

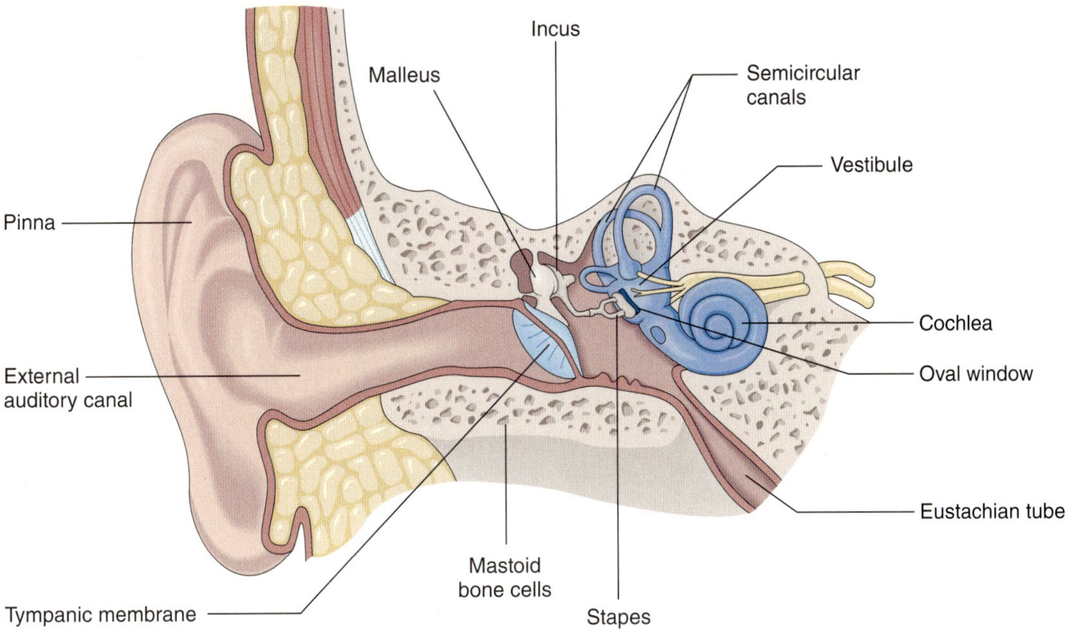

The Skin

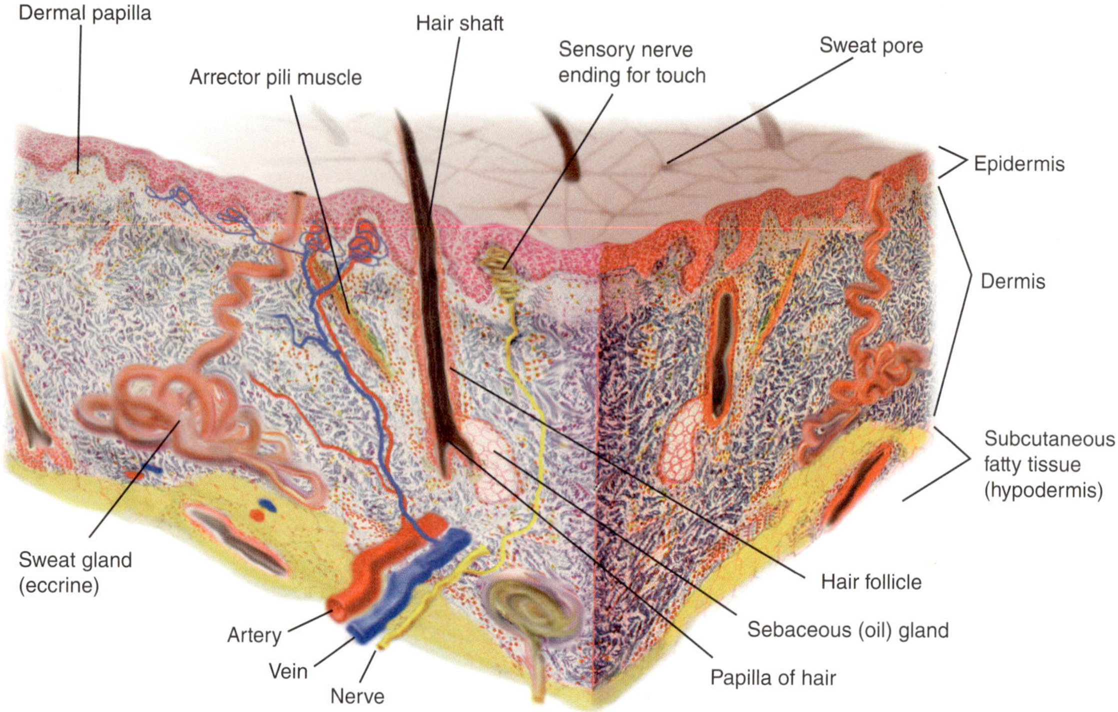

Estes, Health Assessment and Physical Examination

Major Superficial Muscles of the Body: Anterior View

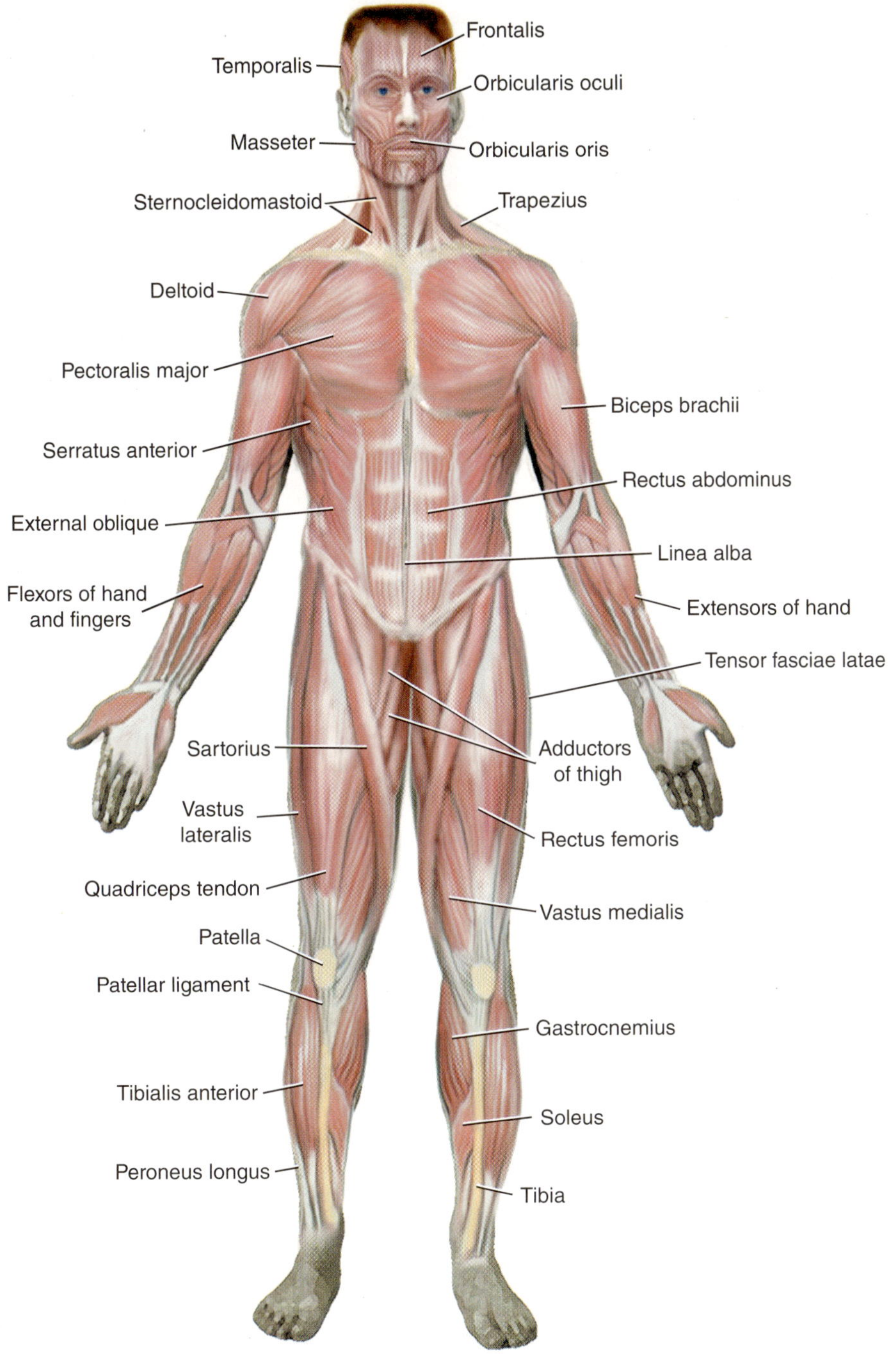

Scott and Fong, Body Structures and Functions

Major Superficial Muscles of the Body: Posterior View

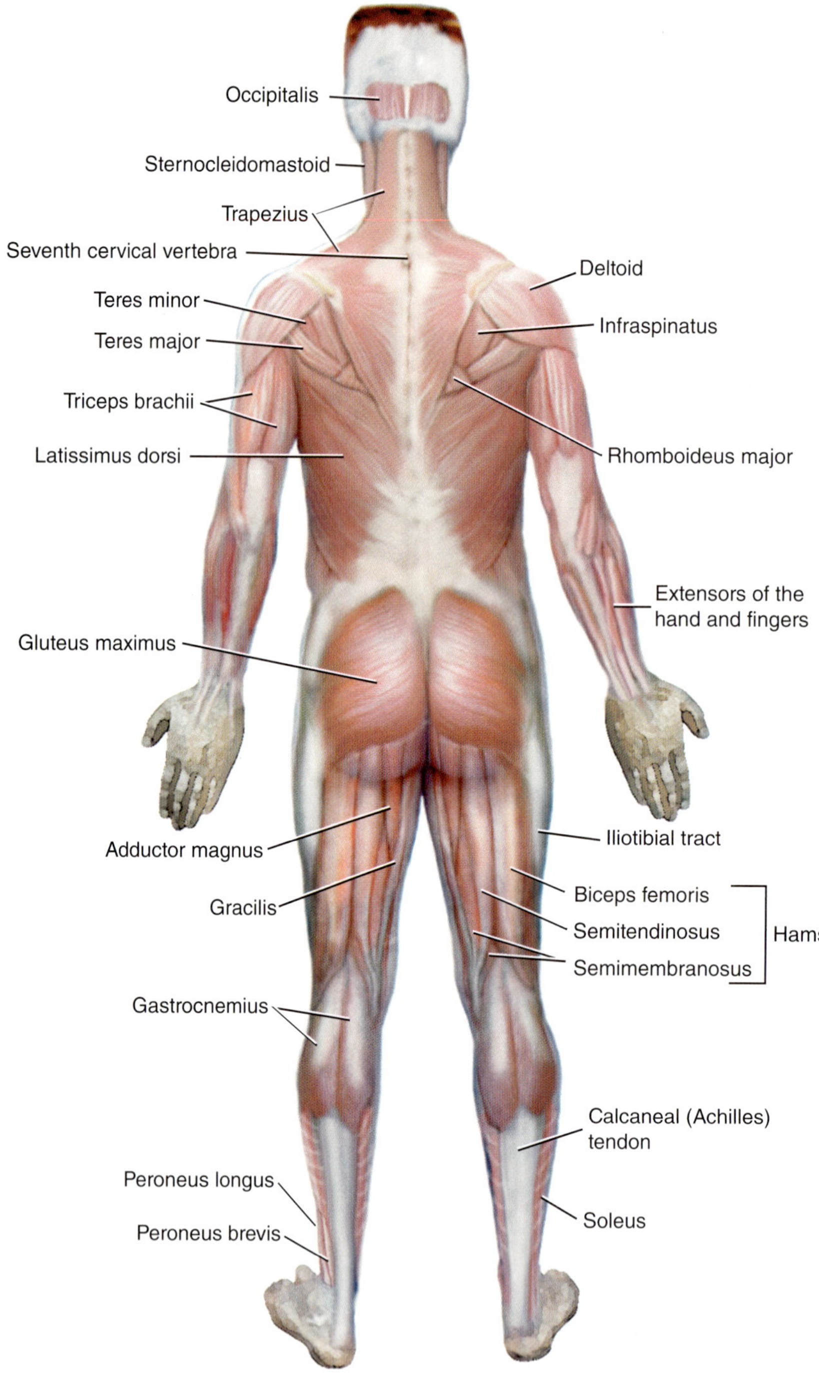

Scott and Fong, Body Structures and Functions

Lateral View of the Brain

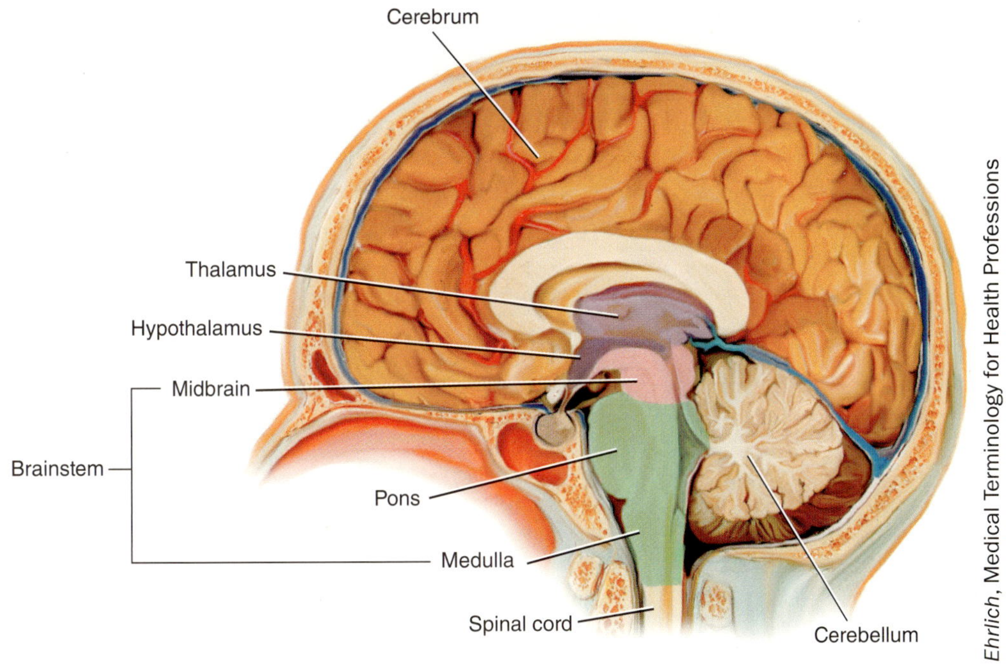

(A) internal brain structure

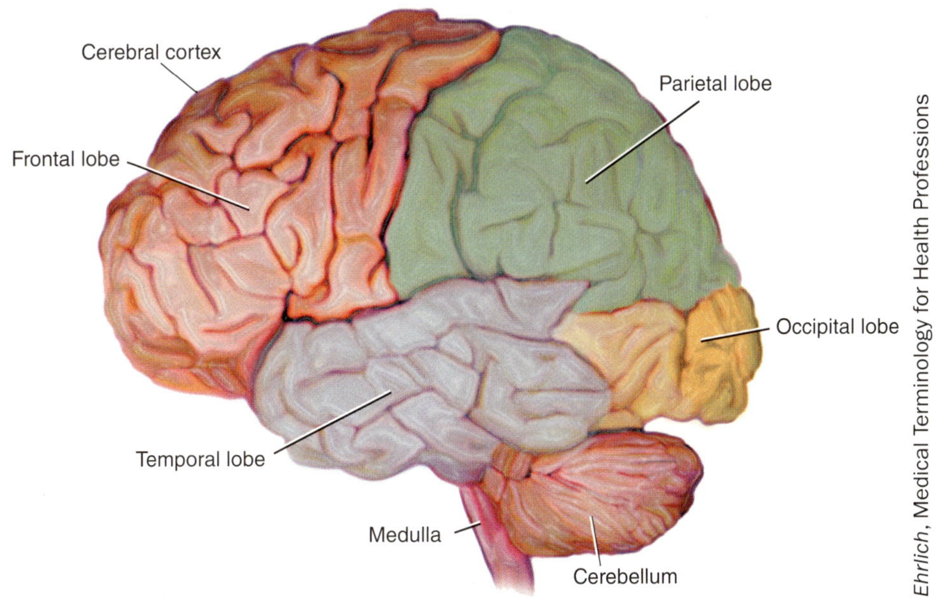

(B) external brain structure

Fetus in Position at Term

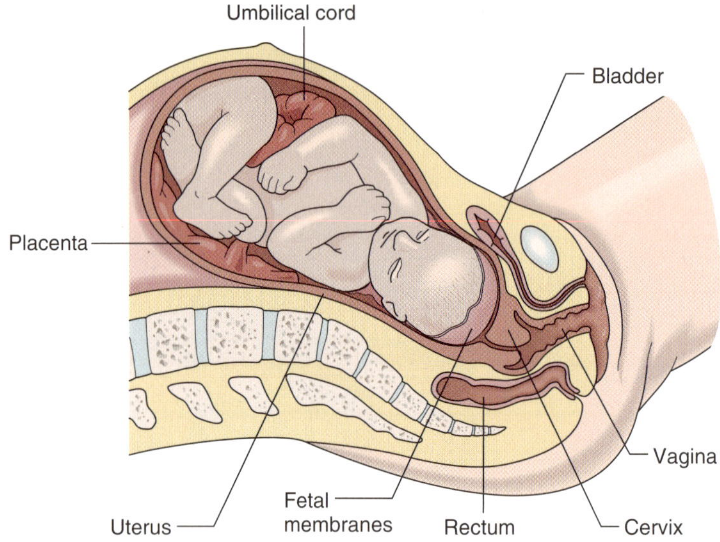

Ehrlich, Medical Terminology for Health Professionals

External Female Genitalia

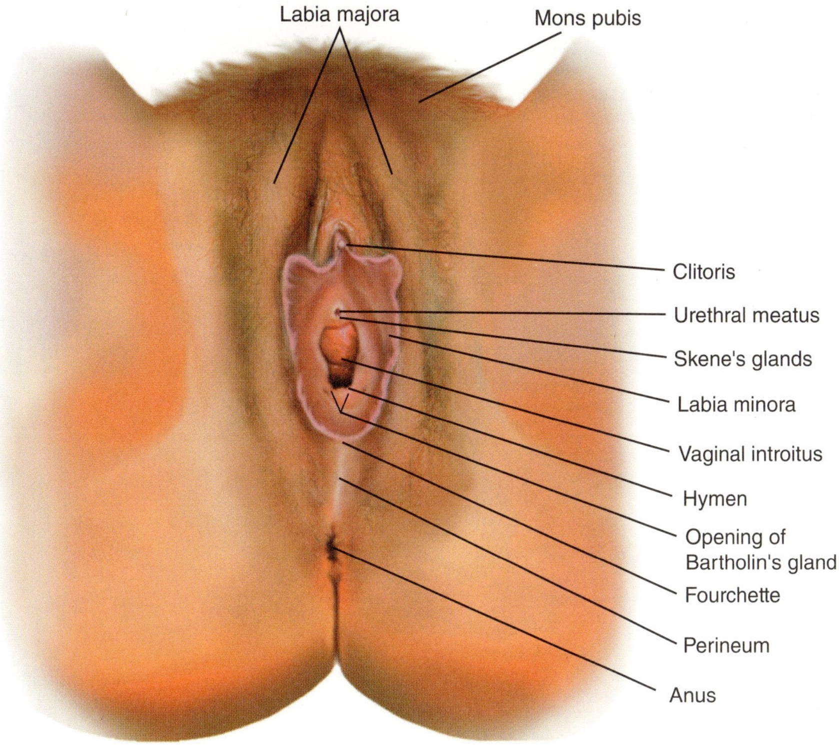

Estes, Health Assessment and Physical Examination

Cross Section of the Female Breast

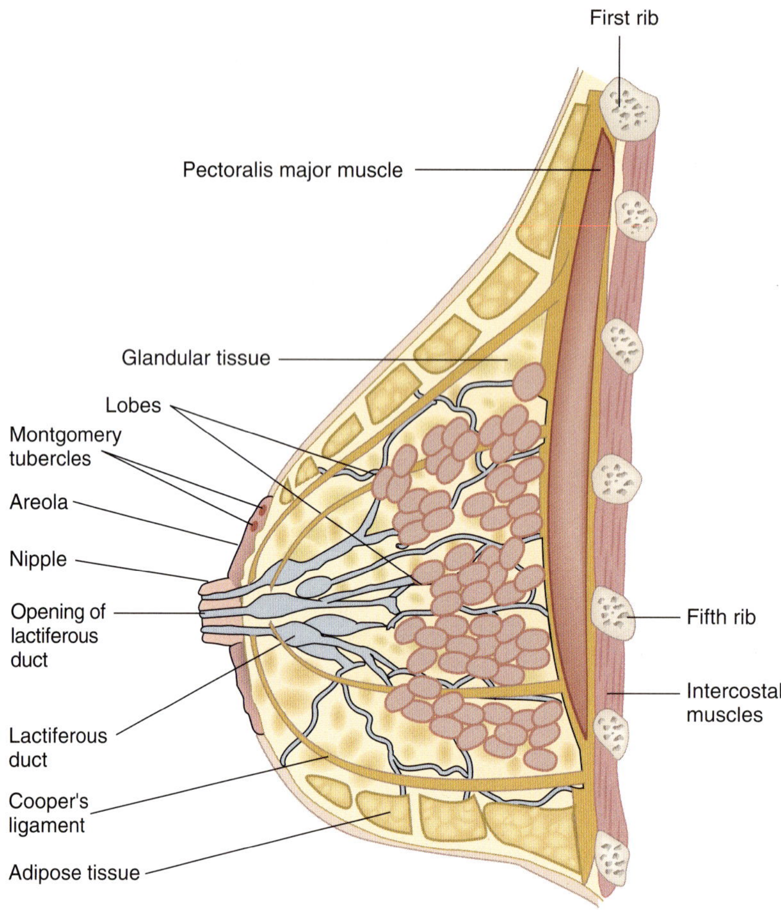

White and Duncan, Medical-Surgical Nursing: An Integrated Approach

Male Reproductive System

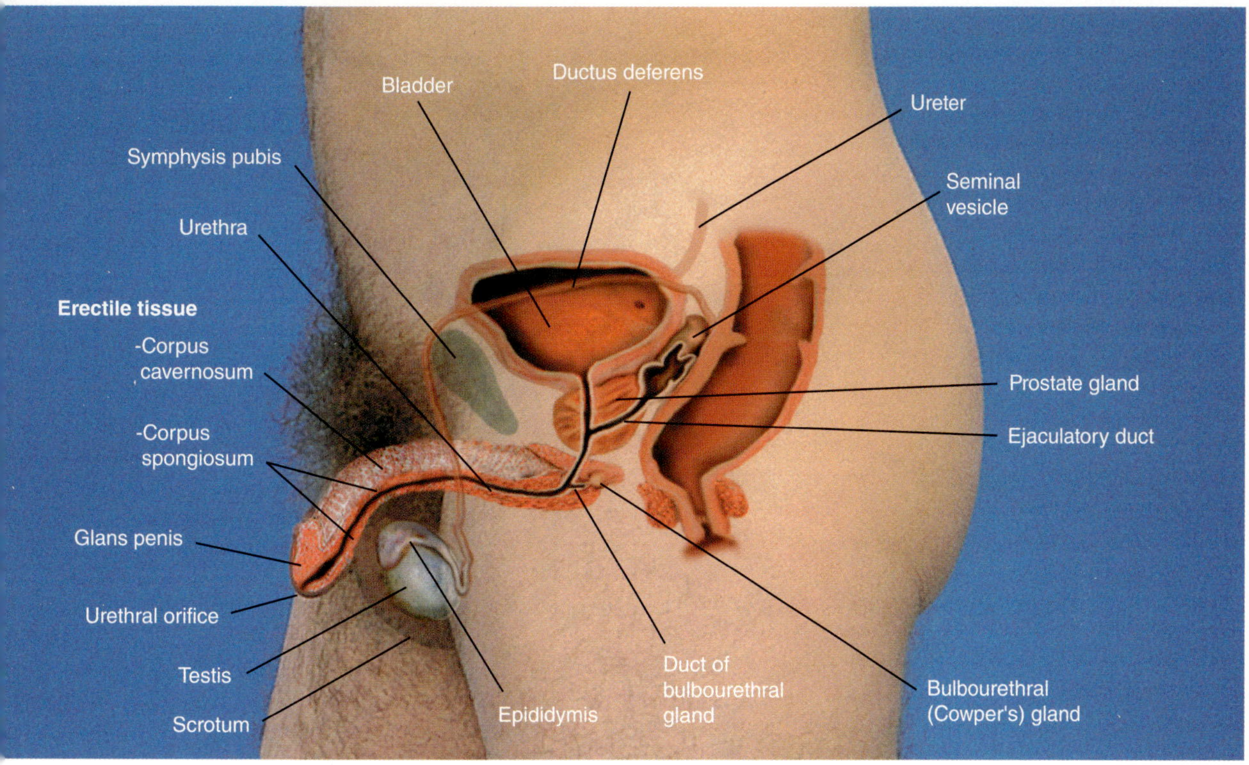

Estes, Health Assessment and Physical Examination

Structures of the Respiratory System

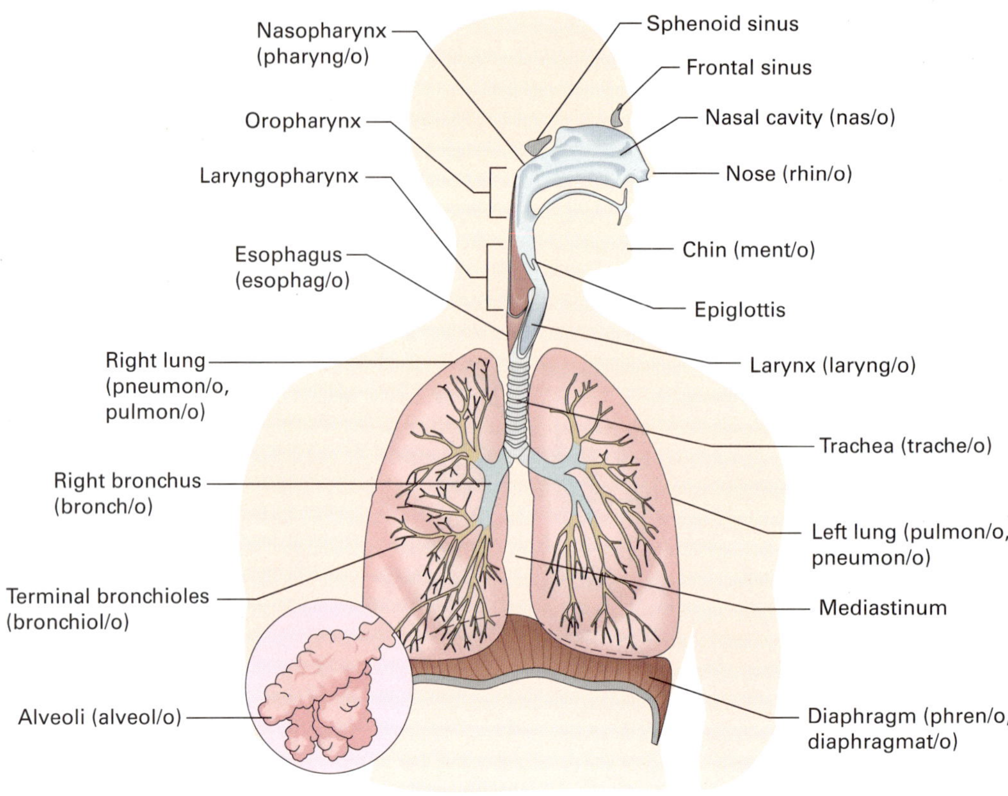

Lateral View of the Adult Human Skeleton

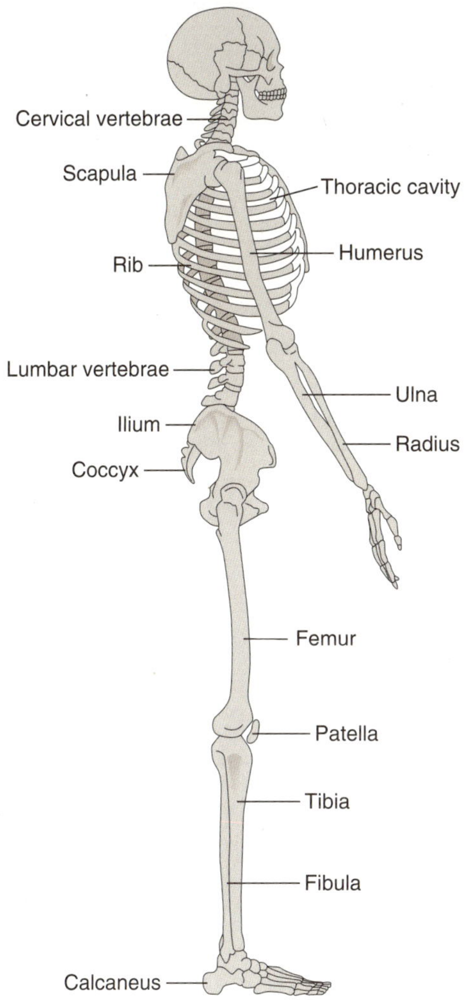

Ehrlich, Medical Terminology for Health Professionals

Posterior View of the Human Skeleton

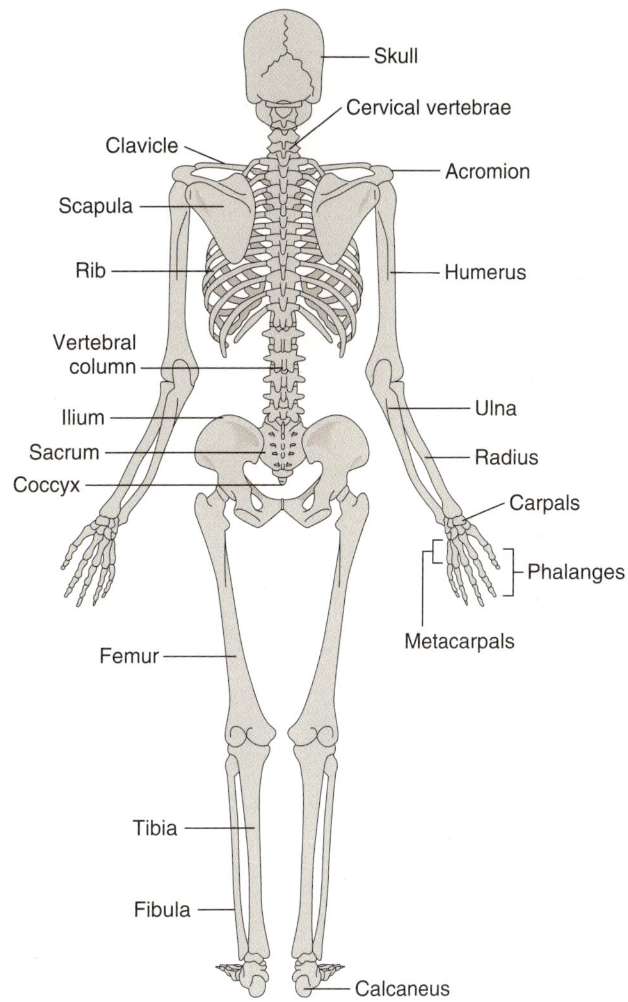

Ehrlich, Medical Terminology for Health Professionals

Urinary System

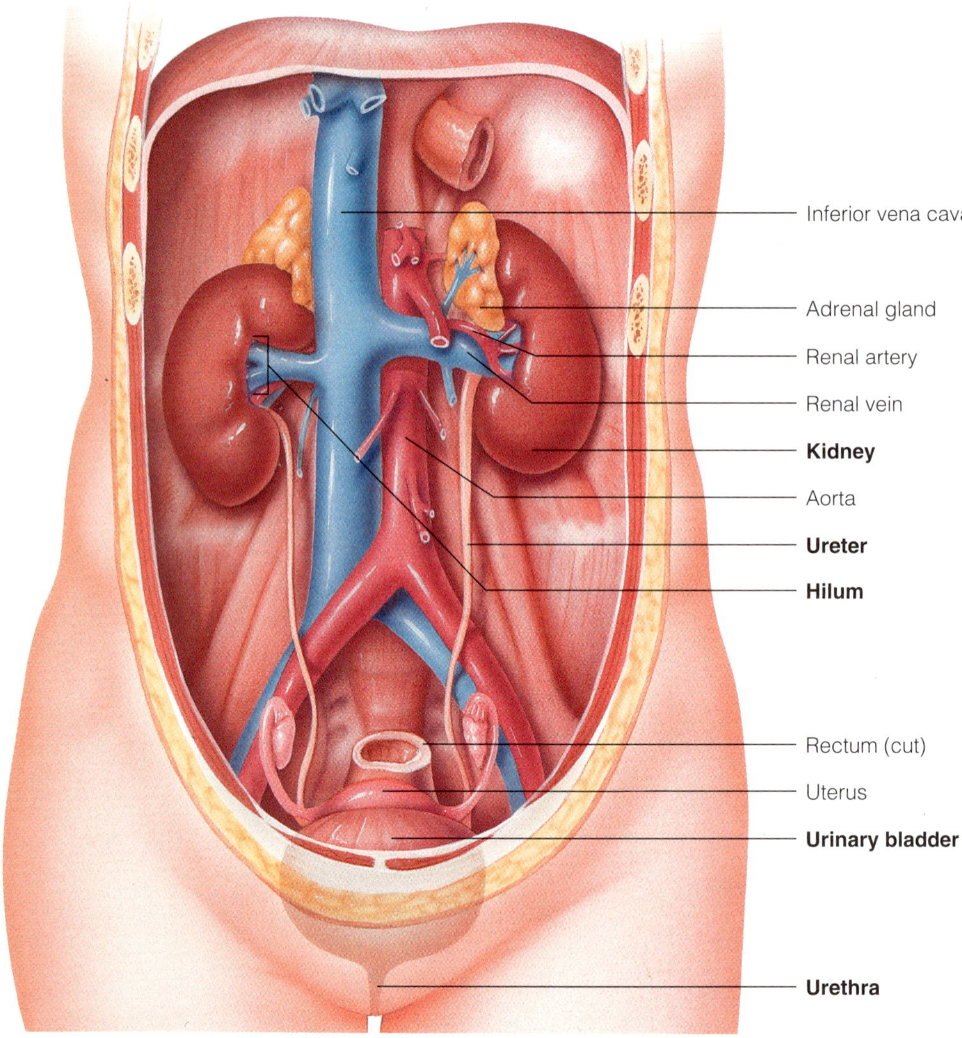

Davies, Essentials of Medical Terminology

Division of the Abdomen into Quadrants

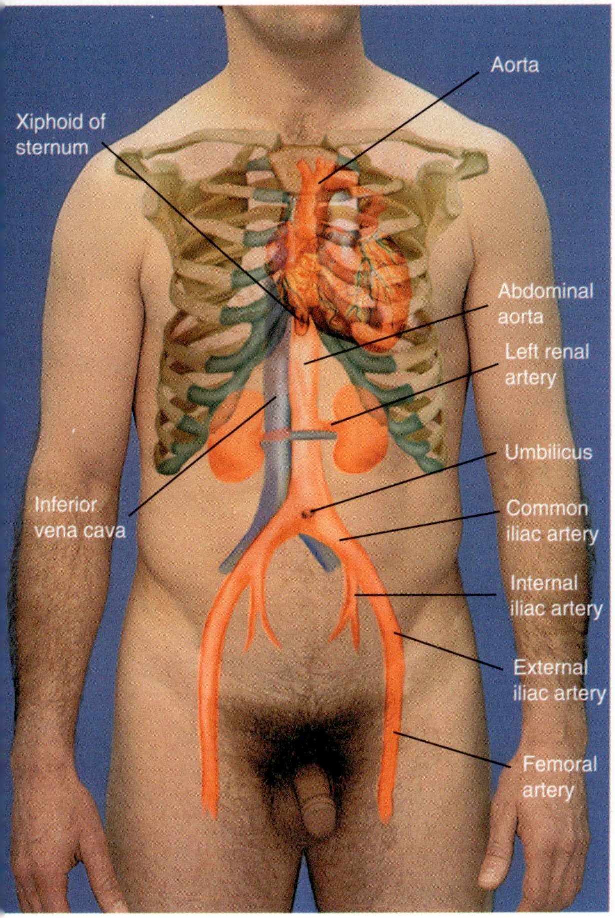

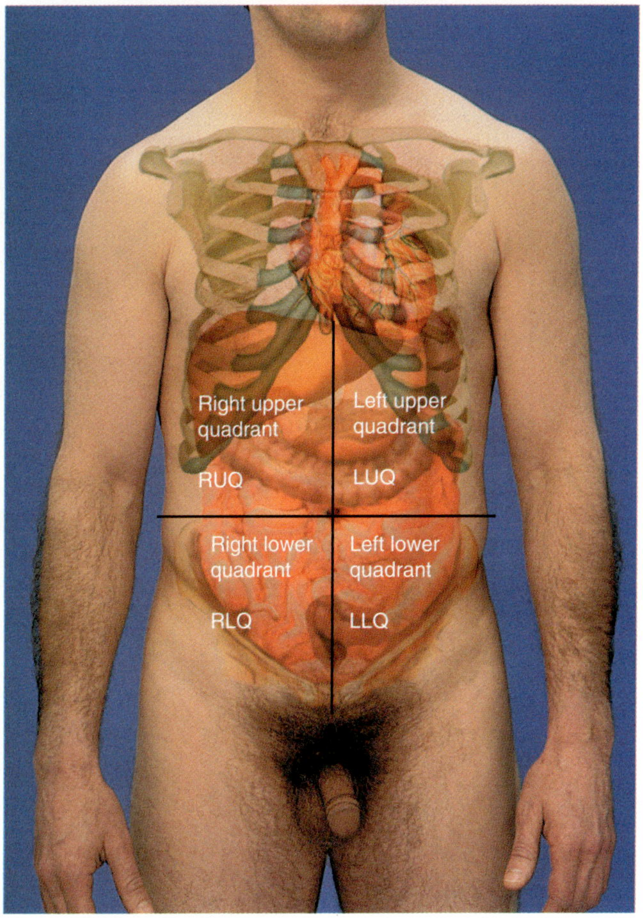

Directional Terms Relating to the Anatomical Position

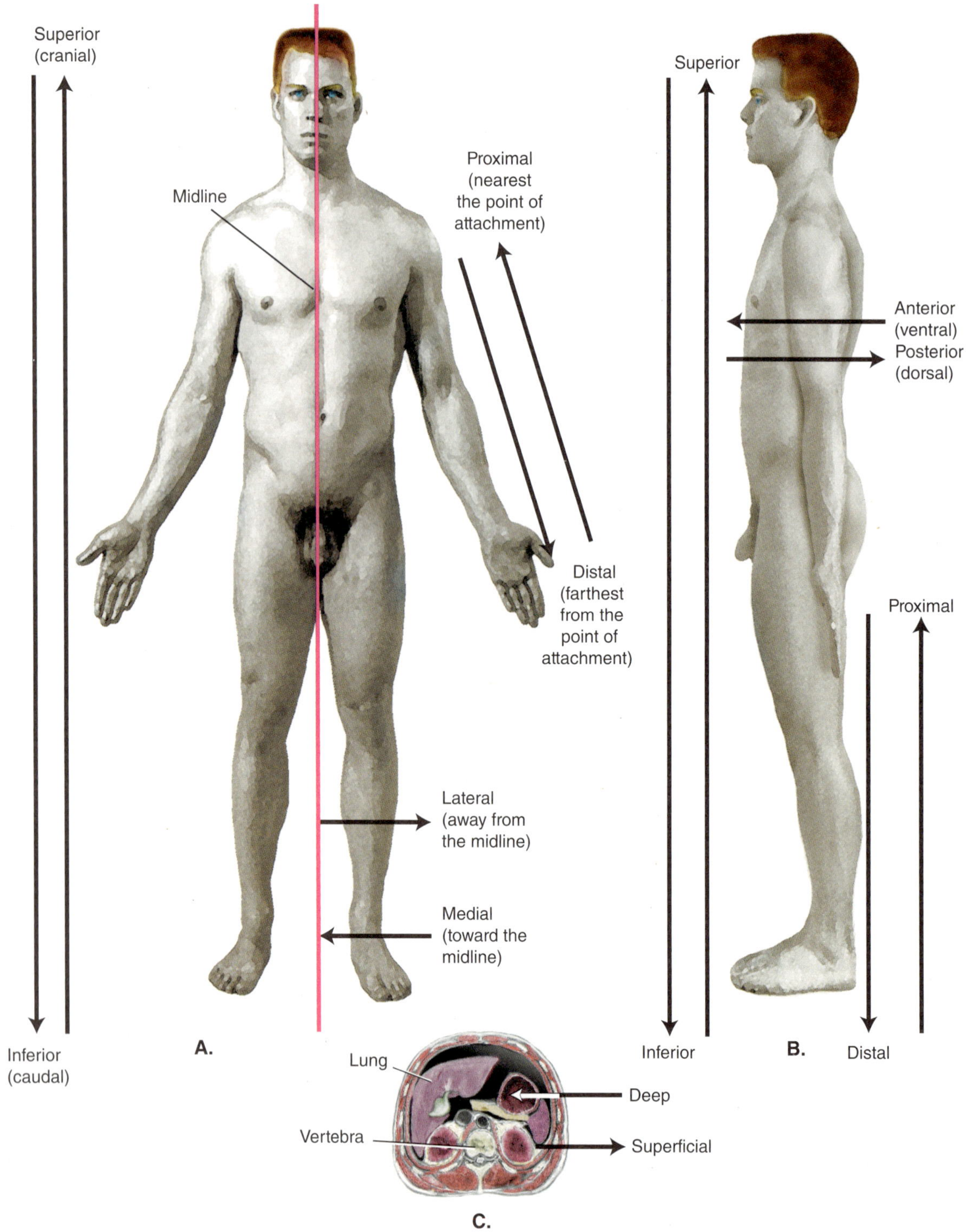

(A) anatomical position,
(B) lateral view of the body,
(C) directional terms deep and superficial

Appendix C: Definitions for Root Operations

Section 0—Medical and Surgical

Character 3 - Operation	
Alteration	**Definition:** Modifying the anatomic structure of a body part without affecting the function of the body part **Explanation:** Principal purpose is to improve appearance **Includes/Examples:** Face lift, breast augmentation
Bypass	**Definition:** Altering the route of passage of the contents of a tubular body part **Explanation:** Rerouting contents of a body part to a downstream area of the normal route, to a similar route and body part, or to an abnormal route and dissimilar body part. Includes one or more anastomoses, with or without the use of a device **Includes/Examples:** Coronary artery bypass, colostomy formation
Change	**Definition:** Taking out or off a device from a body part and putting back an identical or similar device in or on the same body part without cutting or puncturing the skin or a mucous membrane **Explanation:** All CHANGE procedures are coded using the approach EXTERNAL **Includes/Examples:** Urinary catheter change, gastrostomy tube change
Control	**Definition:** Stopping, or attempting to stop, postprocedural bleeding **Explanation:** The site of the bleeding is coded as an anatomical region and not to a specific body part **Includes/Examples:** Control of post-prostatectomy hemorrhage, control of post-tonsillectomy hemorrhage
Creation	**Definition:** Making a new genital structure that does not take over the function of a body part **Explanation:** Used only for sex change operations **Includes/Examples:** Creation of vagina in a male, creation of penis in a female
Destruction	**Definition:** Physical eradication of all or a portion of a body part by the direct use of energy, force, or a destructive agent **Explanation:** None of the body part is physically taken out **Includes/Examples:** Fulguration of rectal polyp, cautery of skin lesion

(*Continues*)

Character 3 - Operation (*Continued*)

Detachment	**Definition:** Cutting off all or a portion of the upper or lower extremities **Explanation:** The body part value is the site of the detachment, with a qualifier if applicable to further specify the level where the extremity was detached **Includes/Examples:** Below knee amputation, disarticulation of shoulder
Dilation	**Definition:** Expanding an orifice or the lumen of a tubular body part **Explanation:** The orifice can be a natural orifice or an artificially created orifice. Accomplished by stretching a tubular body part using intraluminal pressure or by cutting part of the orifice or wall of the tubular body part **Includes/Examples:** Percutaneous transluminal angioplasty, pyloromyotomy
Division	**Definition:** Cutting into a body part, without draining fluids and/or gases from the body part, in order to separate or transect a body part **Explanation:** All or a portion of the body part is separated into two or more portions **Includes/Examples:** Spinal cordotomy, osteotomy
Drainage	**Definition:** Taking or letting out fluids and/or gases from a body part **Explanation:** The qualifier DIAGNOSTIC is used to identify drainage procedures that are biopsies **Includes/Examples:** Thoracentesis, incision and drainage
Excision	**Definition:** Cutting out or off, without replacement, a portion of a body part **Explanation:** The qualifier DIAGNOSTIC is used to identify excision procedures that are biopsies **Includes/Examples:** Partial nephrectomy, liver biopsy
Extirpation	**Definition:** Taking or cutting out solid matter from a body part **Explanation:** The solid matter may be an abnormal by-product of a biological function or a foreign body; it may be imbedded in a body part or in the lumen of a tubular body part. The solid matter may or may not have been previously broken into pieces **Includes/Examples:** Thrombectomy, choledocholithotomy
Extraction	**Definition:** Pulling or stripping out or off all or a portion of a body part by the use of force **Explanation:** The qualifier DIAGNOSTIC is used to identify extraction procedures that are biopsies **Includes/Examples:** Dilation and curettage, vein stripping

(*Continues*)

Character 3 - Operation (*Continued*)

Fragmentation	**Definition:** Breaking solid matter in a body part into pieces **Explanation:** Physical force (e.g., manual, ultrasonic) applied directly or indirectly is used to break the solid matter into pieces. The solid matter may be an abnormal by-product of a biological function or a foreign body. The pieces of solid matter are not taken out **Includes/Examples:** Extracorporeal shockwave lithotripsy, transurethral lithotripsy
Fusion	**Definition:** Joining together portions of an articular body part rendering the articular body part immobile **Explanation:** The body part is joined together by fixation device, bone graft, or other means **Includes/Examples:** Spinal fusion, ankle arthrodesis
Insertion	**Definition:** Putting in a nonbiological appliance that monitors, assists, performs, or prevents a physiological function but does not physically take the place of a body part **Includes/Examples:** Insertion of radioactive implant, insertion of central venous catheter
Inspection	**Definition:** Visually and/or manually exploring a body part **Explanation:** Visual exploration may be performed with or without optical instrumentation. Manual exploration may be performed directly or through intervening body layers **Includes/Examples:** Diagnostic arthroscopy, exploratory laparotomy
Map	**Definition:** Locating the route of passage of electrical impulses and/or locating functional areas in a body part **Explanation:** Applicable only to the cardiac conduction mechanism and the central nervous system **Includes/Examples:** Cardiac mapping, cortical mapping
Occlusion	**Definition:** Completely closing an orifice or the lumen of a tubular body part **Explanation:** The orifice can be a natural orifice or an artificially created orifice **Includes/Examples:** Fallopian tube ligation, ligation of inferior vena cava
Reattachment	**Definition:** Putting back in or on all or a portion of a separated body part to its normal location or other suitable location **Explanation:** Vascular circulation and nervous pathways may or may not be reestablished **Includes/Examples:** Reattachment of hand, reattachment of avulsed kidney

(*Continues*)

Character 3 - Operation (*Continued*)

Release	**Definition:** Freeing a body part from an abnormal physical constraint **Explanation:** Some of the restraining tissue may be taken out but none of the body part is taken out **Includes/Examples:** Adhesiolysis, carpal tunnel release
Removal	**Definition:** Taking out or off a device from a body part **Explanation:** If a device is taken out and a similar device put in without cutting or puncturing the skin or mucous membrane, the procedure is coded to the root operation CHANGE. Otherwise, the procedure for taking out a device is coded to the root operation REMOVAL **Includes/Examples:** Drainage tube removal, cardiac pacemaker removal
Repair	**Definition:** Restoring, to the extent possible, a body part to its normal anatomic structure and function **Explanation:** Used only when the method to accomplish the repair is not one of the other root operations **Includes/Examples:** Colostomy takedown, suture of laceration
Replacement	**Definition:** Putting in or on biological or synthetic material that physically takes the place and/or function of all or a portion of a body part **Explanation:** The body part may have been taken out or replaced, or may be taken out, physically eradicated, or rendered nonfunctional during the Replacement procedure. A Removal procedure is coded for taking out the device used in a previous replacement procedure **Includes/Examples:** Total hip replacement, bone graft, free skin graft
Reposition	**Definition:** Moving to its normal location, or other suitable location, all or a portion of a body part **Explanation:** The body part is moved to a new location from an abnormal location, or from a normal location where it is not functioning correctly. The body part may or may not be cut out or off to be moved to the new location **Includes/Examples:** Reposition of undescended testicle, fracture reduction
Resection	**Definition:** Cutting out or off, without replacement, all of a body part **Includes/Examples:** Total nephrectomy, total lobectomy of lung
Restriction	**Definition:** Partially closing an orifice or the lumen of a tubular body part **Explanation:** The orifice can be a natural orifice or an artificially created orifice **Includes/Examples:** Esophagogastric fundoplication, cervical cerclage

(*Continue*

Character 3 - Operation (*Continued*)

Revision	**Definition:** Correcting, to the extent possible, a portion of a malfunctioning device or the position of a displaced device **Explanation:** Revision can include correcting a malfunctioning or displaced device by taking out and/or putting in part of the device **Includes/Examples:** Adjustment of position of pacemaker lead, recementing of hip prosthesis
Supplement	**Definition:** Putting in or on biological or synthetic material that physically reinforces and/or augments the function of a portion of a body part **Explanation:** The biological material is nonliving, or is living and from the same individual. The body part may have been previously replaced, and the Supplement procedure is performed to physically reinforce and/or augment the function of the replaced body part **Includes/Examples:** Herniorrhaphy using mesh, free nerve graft, mitral valve ring annuloplasty put a new acetabular liner in a previous hip replacement
Transfer	**Definition:** Moving, without taking out, all or a portion of a body part to another location to take over the function of all or a portion of a body part **Explanation:** The body part transferred remains connected to its vascular and nervous supply **Includes/Examples:** Tendon transfer, skin pedicle flap transfer
Transplantation	**Definition:** Putting in or on all or a portion of a living body part taken from another individual or animal to physically take the place and/or function of all or a portion of a similar body part **Explanation:** The native body part may or may not be taken out, and the transplanted body part may take over all or a portion of its function **Includes/Examples:** Kidney transplant, heart transplant

Appendix D: Body Parts

Section 0—Medical and Surgical

Character 4 - Body Part

1st Toe, Left 1st Toe, Right	**Includes:** Hallux
Abdomen Muscle, Left Abdomen Muscle, Right	**Includes:** External oblique muscle Internal oblique muscle Pyramidalis muscle Rectus abdominis muscle Transversus abdominis muscle
Abdominal Aorta	**Includes:** Inferior phrenic artery Lumbar artery Median sacral artery Middle suprarenal artery Ovarian artery Testicular artery
Abdominal Sympathetic Nerve	**Includes:** Abdominal aortic plexus Auerbach's (myenteric) plexus Celiac (solar) plexus Celiac ganglion Gastric plexus Hepatic plexus Inferior hypogastric plexus Inferior mesenteric ganglion Inferior mesenteric plexus Meissner's (submucous) plexus Myenteric (Auerbach's) plexus

(*Continues*

Character 4 - Body Part (*Continued*)

	Pancreatic plexus Pelvic splanchnic nerve Renal plexus Solar (celiac) plexus Splenic plexus Submucous (Meissner's) plexus Superior hypogastric plexus Superior mesenteric ganglion Superior mesenteric plexus Suprarenal plexus
Abducens Nerve	**Includes:** Sixth cranial nerve
Accessory Nerve	**Includes:** Eleventh cranial nerve
Acoustic Nerve	**Includes:** Cochlear nerve Eighth cranial nerve Scarpa's (vestibular) ganglion Spiral ganglion Vestibular (Scarpa's) ganglion Vestibular nerve Vestibulocochlear nerve
Adenoids	**Includes:** Pharyngeal tonsil
Adrenal Gland Adrenal Gland, Left Adrenal Gland, Right Adrenal Glands, Bilateral	**Includes:** Suprarenal gland
Ampulla of Vater	**Includes:** Duodenal ampulla Hepatopancreatic ampulla

(*Continues*)

Character 4 - Body Part (*Continued*)

Anal Sphincter	**Includes:** External anal sphincter Internal anal sphincter
Ankle Bursa and Ligament, Left Ankle Bursa and Ligament, Right	**Includes:** Calcaneofibular ligament Deltoid ligament Ligament of the lateral malleolus Talofibular ligament
Ankle Joint, Left Ankle Joint, Right	**Includes:** Inferior tibiofibular joint Talocrural joint
Anterior Chamber, Left Anterior Chamber, Right	**Includes:** Aqueous humour
Anterior Tibial Artery, Left Anterior Tibial Artery, Right	**Includes:** Anterior lateral malleolar artery Anterior medial malleolar artery Anterior tibial recurrent artery Dorsalis pedis artery Posterior tibial recurrent artery
Anus	**Includes:** Anal orifice
Aortic Valve	**Includes:** Aortic annulus
Appendix	**Includes:** Vermiform appendix
Ascending Colon	**Includes:** Hepatic flexure
Atrial Septum	**Includes:** Interatrial septum

(*Continues*

Character 4 - Body Part (*Continued*)

Atrium, Left	**Includes:** Atrium pulmonale Left auricular appendix
Atrium, Right	**Includes:** Atrium dextrum cordis Right auricular appendix Sinus venosus
Auditory Ossicle, Left Auditory Ossicle, Right	**Includes:** Incus Malleus Ossicular chain Stapes
Axillary Artery, Left Axillary Artery, Right	**Includes:** Anterior circumflex humeral artery Lateral thoracic artery Posterior circumflex humeral artery Subscapular artery Superior thoracic artery Thoracoacromial artery
Azygos Vein	**Includes:** Right ascending lumbar vein Right subcostal vein
Basal Ganglia	**Includes:** Basal nuclei Claustrum Corpus striatum Globus pallidus Substantia nigra Subthalamic nucleus
Basilic Vein, Left Basilic Vein, Right	**Includes:** Median antebrachial vein Median cubital vein

(*Continues*)

Character 4 - Body Part (*Continued*)

Bladder	**Includes:** Trigone of bladder
Brachial Artery, Left Brachial Artery, Right	**Includes:** Inferior ulnar collateral artery Profunda brachii Superior ulnar collateral artery
Brachial Plexus	**Includes:** Axillary nerve Dorsal scapular nerve First intercostal nerve Long thoracic nerve Musculocutaneous nerve Subclavius nerve Suprascapular nerve
Brachial Vein, Left Brachial Vein, Right	**Includes:** Radial vein Ulnar vein
Brain	**Includes:** Cerebrum Corpus callosum Encephalon
Breast, Bilateral Breast, Left Breast, Right	**Includes:** Mammary duct Mammary gland
Buccal Mucosa	**Includes:** Buccal gland Labial gland Molar gland Palatine gland
Carotid Bodies, Bilateral Carotid Body, Left Carotid Body, Right	**Includes:** Carotid glomus

(*Continues*

Character 4 - Body Part (*Continued*)

Carpal Joint, Left Carpal Joint, Right	**Includes:** Intercarpal joint Midcarpal joint
Carpal, Left Carpal, Right	**Includes:** Capitate bone Hamate bone Lunate bone Pisiform bone Scaphoid bone Trapezium bone Trapezoid bone Triquetral bone
Celiac Artery	**Includes:** Celiac trunk
Cephalic Vein, Left Cephalic Vein, Right	**Includes:** Accessory cephalic vein
Cerebellum	**Includes:** Culmen
Cerebral Hemisphere	**Includes:** Frontal lobe Occipital lobe Parietal lobe Temporal lobe
Cerebral Meninges	**Includes:** Arachnoid mater Leptomeninges Pia mater
Cerebral Ventricle	**Includes:** Aqueduct of Sylvius Cerebral aqueduct (Sylvius) Choroid plexus Ependyma

(*Continues*)

Character 4 - Body Part (*Continued*)

	Foramen of Monro (intraventricular) Fourth ventricle Interventricular foramen (Monro) Left lateral ventricle Right lateral ventricle Third ventricle
Cervical Nerve	**Includes:** Greater occipital nerve Suboccipital nerve Third occipital nerve
Cervical Plexus	**Includes:** Ansa cervicalis Cutaneous (transverse) cervical nerve Great auricular nerve Lesser occipital nerve Supraclavicular nerve Transverse (cutaneous) cervical nerve
Cervical Vertebra	**Includes:** Spinous process Vertebral arch Vertebral foramen Vertebral lamina Vertebral pedicle
Cervical Vertebral Joint	**Includes:** Atlantoaxial joint Cervical facet joint
Cervical Vertebral Joints, two or more	**Includes:** Cervical facet joint
Cervicothoracic Vertebral Joint	**Includes:** Cervicothoracic facet joint

(*Continues*)

Character 4 - Body Part (*Continued*)

Cisterna Chyli	**Includes:** Intestinal lymphatic trunk Lumbar lymphatic trunk
Coccygeal Glomus	**Includes:** Coccygeal body
Colic Vein	**Includes:** Ileocolic vein Left colic vein Middle colic vein Right colic vein
Conduction Mechanism	**Includes:** Atrioventricular node Bundle of His Bundle of Kent Sinoatrial node
Conjunctiva, Left Conjunctiva, Right	**Includes:** Plica semilunaris
Dura Mater	**Includes:** Cranial dura mater Dentate ligament Diaphragma sellae Falx cerebri Spinal dura mater Tentorium cerebelli
Elbow Bursa and Ligament, Left Elbow Bursa and Ligament, Right	**Includes:** Annular ligament Olecranon bursa Radial collateral ligament Ulnar collateral ligament
Elbow Joint, Left Elbow Joint, Right	**Includes:** Humeroradial joint Humeroulnar joint Proximal radioulnar joint

(*Continues*)

Character 4 - Body Part (*Continued*)

Epidural Space	**Includes:** Cranial epidural space Extradural space Spinal epidural space
Epiglottis	**Includes:** Glossoepiglottic fold
Esophagogastric Junction	**Includes:** Cardia Cardioesophageal junction Gastroesophageal (GE) junction
Esophagus, Lower	**Includes:** Abdominal esophagus
Esophagus, Middle	**Includes:** Thoracic esophagus
Esophagus, Upper	**Includes:** Cervical esophagus
Ethmoid Bone, Left Ethmoid Bone, Right	**Includes:** Cribriform plate
Ethmoid Sinus, Left Ethmoid Sinus, Right	**Includes:** Ethmoidal air cell
Eustachian Tube, Left Eustachian Tube, Right	**Includes:** Auditory tube Pharyngotympanic tube
External Auditory Canal, Left External Auditory Canal, Right	**Includes:** External auditory meatus
External Carotid Artery, Left External Carotid Artery, Right	**Includes:** Ascending pharyngeal artery Internal maxillary artery Lingual artery Maxillary artery Occipital artery

(*Continues*

Character 4 - Body Part (*Continued*)

	Posterior auricular artery Superior thyroid artery
External Ear, Bilateral External Ear, Left External Ear, Right	**Includes:** Antihelix Antitragus Auricle Earlobe Helix Pinna Tragus
External Iliac Artery, Left External Iliac Artery, Right	**Includes:** Deep circumflex iliac artery Inferior epigastric artery
External Jugular Vein, Left External Jugular Vein, Right	**Includes:** Posterior auricular vein
Extraocular Muscle, Left Extraocular Muscle, Right	**Includes:** Inferior oblique muscle Inferior rectus muscle Lateral rectus muscle Medial rectus muscle Superior oblique muscle Superior rectus muscle
Eye, Left Eye, Right	**Includes:** Ciliary body Posterior chamber
Face Artery	**Includes:** Angular artery Ascending palatine artery External maxillary artery Facial artery Inferior labial artery Submental artery Superior labial artery

(*Continues*)

Character 4 - Body Part (*Continued*)

Face Vein, Left Face Vein, Right	**Includes:** Angular vein Anterior facial vein Common facial vein Deep facial vein Frontal vein Posterior facial (retromandibular) vein Supraorbital vein
Facial Muscle	**Includes:** Buccinator muscle Corrugator supercilii muscle Depressor anguli oris muscle Depressor labii inferioris muscle Depressor septi nasi muscle Depressor supercilii muscle Levator anguli oris muscle Levator labii superioris alaeque nasi muscle Levator labii superioris muscle Mentalis muscle Nasalis muscle Occipitofrontalis muscle Orbicularis oris muscle Procerus muscle Risorius muscle Zygomaticus muscle
Facial Nerve	**Includes:** Chorda tympani Geniculate ganglion Greater superficial petrosal nerve Nerve to the stapedius Parotid plexus Posterior auricular nerve Seventh cranial nerve Submandibular ganglion

(*Continues*)

Character 4 - Body Part (*Continued*)

Fallopian Tube, Left Fallopian Tube, Right	**Includes:** Oviduct Salpinx Uterine tube
Femoral Artery, Left Femoral Artery, Right	**Includes:** Circumflex iliac artery Deep femoral artery Descending genicular artery External pudendal artery Superficial epigastric artery
Femoral Nerve	**Includes:** Anterior crural nerve Saphenous nerve
Femoral Shaft, Left Femoral Shaft, Right	**Includes:** Body of femur
Femoral Vein, Left Femoral Vein, Right	**Includes:** Deep femoral (profunda femoris) vein Popliteal vein Profunda femoris (deep femoral) vein
Fibula, Left Fibula, Right	**Includes:** Body of fibula Head of fibula Lateral malleolus
Finger Nail	**Includes:** Nail bed Nail plate
Finger Phalangeal Joint, Left Finger Phalangeal Joint, Right	**Includes:** Interphalangeal (IP) joint

(*Continues*)

Character 4 - Body Part (*Continued*)

Foot Artery, Left Foot Artery, Right	**Includes:** Arcuate artery Dorsal metatarsal artery Lateral plantar artery Lateral tarsal artery Medial plantar artery
Foot Bursa and Ligament, Left Foot Bursa and Ligament, Right	**Includes:** Calcaneocuboid ligament Cuneonavicular ligament Intercuneiform ligament Interphalangeal ligament Metatarsal ligament Metatarsophalangeal ligament Subtalar ligament Talocalcaneal ligament Talocalcaneonavicular ligament Tarsometatarsal ligament
Foot Muscle, Left Foot Muscle, Right	**Includes:** Abductor hallucis muscle Adductor hallucis muscle Extensor digitorum brevis muscle Extensor hallucis brevis muscle Flexor digitorum brevis muscle Flexor hallucis brevis muscle Quadratus plantae muscle
Foot Vein, Left Foot Vein, Right	**Includes:** Common digital vein Dorsal metatarsal vein Dorsal venous arch Plantar digital vein Plantar metatarsal vein Plantar venous arch
Frontal Bone, Left Frontal Bone, Right	**Includes:** Zygomatic process of frontal bone

(*Continues*

Character 4 - Body Part (*Continued*)

Gastric Artery	**Includes:** Left gastric artery Right gastric artery
Glenoid Cavity, Left Glenoid Cavity, Right	**Includes:** Glenoid fossa (of scapula)
Glomus Jugulare	**Includes:** Jugular body
Glossopharyngeal Nerve	**Includes:** Carotid sinus nerve Ninth cranial nerve Tympanic nerve
Greater Omentum	**Includes:** Gastrocolic ligament Gastrocolic omentum Gastrophrenic ligament Gastrosplenic ligament
Greater Saphenous Vein, Left Greater Saphenous Vein, Right	**Includes:** External pudendal vein Great saphenous vein Superficial circumflex iliac vein Superficial epigastric vein
Hand Artery, Left Hand Artery, Right	**Includes:** Deep palmar arch Princeps pollicis artery Radialis indicis Superficial palmar arch
Hand Bursa and Ligament, Left Hand Bursa and Ligament, Right	**Includes:** Carpometacarpal ligament Intercarpal ligament Interphalangeal ligament Lunotriquetral ligament Metacarpal ligament

(*Continues*)

Character 4 - Body Part (*Continued*)

	Metacarpophalangeal ligament Pisohamate ligament Pisometacarpal ligament Scapholunate ligament Scaphotrapezium ligament
Hand Muscle, Left Hand Muscle, Right	**Includes:** Hypothenar muscle Palmar interosseous muscle Thenar muscle
Hand Vein, Left Hand Vein, Right	**Includes:** Dorsal metacarpal vein Palmar (volar) digital vein Palmar (volar) metacarpal vein Superficial palmar venous arch Volar (palmar) digital vein Volar (palmar) metacarpal vein
Head and Neck Bursa and Ligament	**Includes:** Alar ligament of axis Cervical interspinous ligament Cervical intertransverse ligament Cervical ligamentum flavum Lateral temporomandibular ligament Sphenomandibular ligament Stylomandibular ligament Transverse ligament of atlas
Head and Neck Sympathetic Nerve	**Includes:** Cavernous plexus Cervical ganglion Ciliary ganglion Internal carotid plexus Otic ganglion

(*Continues*)

Character 4 - Body Part (*Continued*)

	Pterygopalatine (sphenopalatine) ganglion Sphenopalatine (pterygopalatine) ganglion Stellate ganglion Submandibular ganglion Submaxillary ganglion
Head Muscle	**Includes:** Auricularis muscle Masseter muscle Pterygoid muscle Splenius capitis muscle Temporalis muscle Temporoparietalis muscle
Heart, Left	**Includes:** Left coronary sulcus Obtuse margin
Heart, Right	**Includes:** Right coronary sulcus
Hemiazygos Vein	**Includes:** Left ascending lumbar vein Left subcostal vein
Hepatic Artery	**Includes:** Common hepatic artery Gastroduodenal artery Hepatic artery proper
Hip Bursa and Ligament, Left Hip Bursa and Ligament, Right	**Includes:** Iliofemoral ligament Ischiofemoral ligament Pubofemoral ligament Transverse acetabular ligament Trochanteric bursa
Hip Joint, Left Hip Joint, Right	**Includes:** Acetabulofemoral joint

(*Continues*)

Character 4 - Body Part (*Continued*)

Hip Muscle, Left Hip Muscle, Right	**Includes:** Gemellus muscle Gluteus maximus muscle Gluteus medius muscle Gluteus minimus muscle Iliacus muscle Obturator muscle Piriformis muscle Psoas muscle Quadratus femoris muscle Tensor fasciae latae muscle
Humeral Head, Left Humeral Head, Right	**Includes:** Greater tuberosity Lesser tuberosity Neck of humerus (anatomical)(surgical)
Humeral Shaft, Left Humeral Shaft, Right	**Includes:** Lateral epicondyle of humerus Medial epicondyle of humerus
Hypogastric Vein, Left Hypogastric Vein, Right	**Includes:** Gluteal vein Internal iliac vein Internal pudendal vein Lateral sacral vein Middle hemorrhoidal vein Obturator vein Uterine vein Vaginal vein Vesical vein
Hypoglossal Nerve	**Includes:** Twelfth cranial nerve
Hypothalamus	**Includes:** Mammillary body

(*Continues*)

Character 4 - Body Part (*Continued*)

Inferior Mesenteric Artery	**Includes:** Sigmoid artery Superior rectal artery
Inferior Mesenteric Vein	**Includes:** Sigmoid vein Superior rectal vein
Inferior Vena Cava	**Includes:** Postcava Right inferior phrenic vein Right ovarian vein Right second lumbar vein Right suprarenal vein Right testicular vein
Inguinal Region, Bilateral Inguinal Region, Left Inguinal Region, Right	**Includes:** Inguinal canal Inguinal triangle
Inner Ear, Left Inner Ear, Right	**Includes:** Bony labyrinth Bony vestibule Cochlea Oval window Round window Semicircular canal
Innominate Artery	**Includes:** Brachiocephalic artery Brachiocephalic trunk
Innominate Vein, Left Innominate Vein, Right	**Includes:** Brachiocephalic vein Inferior thyroid vein
Internal Carotid Artery, Left Internal Carotid Artery, Right	**Includes:** Caroticotympanic artery Carotid sinus Ophthalmic artery

(*Continues*)

Character 4 - Body Part (*Continued*)

Internal Iliac Artery, Left Internal Iliac Artery, Right	**Includes:** Deferential artery Hypogastric artery Iliolumbar artery Inferior gluteal artery Inferior vesical artery Internal pudendal artery Lateral sacral artery Middle rectal artery Obturator artery Superior gluteal artery Umbilical artery Uterine artery Vaginal artery
Internal Mammary Artery, Left Internal Mammary Artery, Right	**Includes:** Anterior intercostal artery Internal thoracic artery Musculophrenic artery Pericardiophrenic artery Superior epigastric artery
Intracranial Artery	**Includes:** Anterior cerebral artery Anterior choroidal artery Anterior communicating artery Basilar artery Circle of Willis Middle cerebral artery Posterior cerebral artery Posterior communicating artery Posterior inferior cerebellar artery (PICA)
Intracranial Vein	**Includes:** Anterior cerebral vein Basal (internal) cerebral vein Dural venous sinus

(*Continues*)

Character 4 - Body Part (*Continued*)

	Great cerebral vein Inferior cerebellar vein Inferior cerebral vein Internal (basal) cerebral vein Middle cerebral vein Ophthalmic vein Superior cerebellar vein Superior cerebral vein
Jejunum	**Includes:** Duodenojejunal flexure
Kidney	**Includes:** Renal calyx Renal capsule Renal cortex Renal segment
Kidney Pelvis, Left Kidney Pelvis, Right	**Includes:** Ureteropelvic junction (UPJ)
Kidney, Left Kidney, Right Kidneys, Bilateral	**Includes:** Renal calyx Renal capsule Renal cortex Renal segment
Knee Bursa and Ligament, Left Knee Bursa and Ligament, Right	**Includes:** Anterior cruciate ligament (ACL) Lateral collateral ligament (LCL) Ligament of head of fibula Medial collateral ligament (MCL) Patellar ligament Popliteal ligament Posterior cruciate ligament (PCL) Prepatellar bursa

(*Continues*)

Character 4 - Body Part (*Continued*)

Knee Joint, Left Knee Joint, Right	**Includes:** Femoropatellar joint Femorotibial joint Lateral meniscus Medial meniscus
Knee Tendon, Left Knee Tendon, Right	**Includes:** Patellar tendon
Lacrimal Duct, Left Lacrimal Duct, Right	**Includes:** Lacrimal canaliculus Lacrimal punctum Lacrimal sac Nasolacrimal duct
Larynx	**Includes:** Aryepiglottic fold Arytenoid cartilage Corniculate cartilage Cricoid cartilage Cuneiform cartilage False vocal cord Glottis Rima glottidis Thyroid cartilage Ventricular fold
Lens, Left Lens, Right	**Includes:** Zonule of Zinn
Lesser Omentum	**Includes:** Gastrohepatic omentum Hepatogastric ligament
Lesser Saphenous Vein, Left Lesser Saphenous Vein, Right	**Includes:** Small saphenous vein
Liver	**Includes:** Quadrate lobe

(*Continues*)

Character 4 - Body Part (*Continued*)

Lower Arm and Wrist Muscle, Left Lower Arm and Wrist Muscle, Right	**Includes:** Anatomical snuffbox Brachioradialis muscle Extensor carpi radialis muscle Extensor carpi ulnaris muscle Flexor carpi radialis muscle Flexor carpi ulnaris muscle Flexor pollicis longus muscle Palmaris longus muscle Pronator quadratus muscle Pronator teres muscle
Lower Eyelid, Left Lower Eyelid, Right	**Includes:** Inferior tarsal plate Medial canthus
Lower Femur, Left Lower Femur, Right	**Includes:** Lateral condyle of femur Lateral epicondyle of femur Medial condyle of femur Medial epicondyle of femur
Lower Leg Muscle, Left Lower Leg Muscle, Right	**Includes:** Extensor digitorum longus muscle Extensor hallucis longus muscle Fibularis brevis muscle Fibularis longus muscle Flexor digitorum longus muscle Flexor hallucis longus muscle Gastrocnemius muscle Peroneus brevis muscle Peroneus longus muscle Popliteus muscle Soleus muscle Tibialis anterior muscle Tibialis posterior muscle

(*Continues*)

Character 4 - Body Part (*Continued*)

Lower Leg Tendon, Left Lower Leg Tendon, Right	**Includes:** Achilles tendon
Lower Lip	**Includes:** Frenulum labii inferioris Vermilion border
Lumbar Nerve	**Includes:** Lumbosacral trunk Superior clunic (cluneal) nerve
Lumbar Plexus	**Includes:** Accessory obturator nerve Genitofemoral nerve Iliohypogastric nerve Ilioinguinal nerve Lateral femoral cutaneous nerve Obturator nerve Superior gluteal nerve
Lumbar Spinal Cord	**Includes:** Cauda equina Conus medullaris
Lumbar Sympathetic Nerve	**Includes:** Lumbar ganglion Lumbar splanchnic nerve
Lumbar Vertebra	**Includes:** Spinous process Vertebral arch Vertebral foramen Vertebral lamina Vertebral pedicle
Lumbar Vertebral Joint Lumbar Vertebral Joints, two or more Lumbosacral Joint	**Includes:** Lumbar facet joint **Includes:** Lumbosacral facet joint

(*Continues*

Character 4 - Body Part (*Continued*)

Lymphatic, Aortic	**Includes:** Celiac lymph node Gastric lymph node Hepatic lymph node Lumbar lymph node Pancreaticosplenic lymph node Paraaortic lymph node Retroperitoneal lymph node
Lymphatic, Head	**Includes:** Buccinator lymph node Infraauricular lymph node Infraparotid lymph node Parotid lymph node Preauricular lymph node Submandibular lymph node Submaxillary lymph node Submental lymph node Subparotid lymph node Suprahyoid lymph node
Lymphatic, Left Axillary	**Includes:** Anterior (pectoral) lymph node Apical (subclavicular) lymph node Brachial (lateral) lymph node Central axillary lymph node Lateral (brachial) lymph node Pectoral (anterior) lymph node Posterior (subscapular) lymph node Subclavicular (apical) lymph node Subscapular (posterior) lymph node
Lymphatic, Left Lower Extremity	**Includes:** Femoral lymph node Popliteal lymph node

(*Continues*)

Character 4 - Body Part (*Continued*)

Lymphatic, Left Neck	**Includes:** Cervical lymph node Jugular lymph node Mastoid (postauricular) lymph node Occipital lymph node Postauricular (mastoid) lymph node Retropharyngeal lymph node Supraclavicular (Virchow's) lymph node Virchow's (supraclavicular) lymph node
Lymphatic, Left Upper Extremity	**Includes:** Cubital lymph node Deltopectoral (infraclavicular) lymph node Epitrochlear lymph node Infraclavicular (deltopectoral) lymph node Supratrochlear lymph node
Lymphatic, Mesenteric	**Includes:** Inferior mesenteric lymph node Pararectal lymph node Superior mesenteric lymph node
Lymphatic, Pelvis	**Includes:** Common iliac (subaortic) lymph node Gluteal lymph node Iliac lymph node Inferior epigastric lymph node Obturator lymph node Sacral lymph node Subaortic (common iliac) lymph node Suprainguinal lymph node
Lymphatic, Right Axillary	**Includes:** Anterior (pectoral) lymph node Apical (subclavicular) lymph node Brachial (lateral) lymph node

(*Continues*

Character 4 - Body Part (*Continued*)

	Central axillary lymph node Lateral (brachial) lymph node Pectoral (anterior) lymph node Posterior (subscapular) lymph node Subclavicular (apical) lymph node Subscapular (posterior) lymph node
Lymphatic, Right Lower Extremity	**Includes:** Femoral lymph node Popliteal lymph node
Lymphatic, Right Neck	**Includes:** Cervical lymph node Jugular lymph node Mastoid (postauricular) lymph node Occipital lymph node Postauricular (mastoid) lymph node Retropharyngeal lymph node Right jugular trunk Right lymphatic duct Right subclavian trunk Supraclavicular (Virchow's) lymph node Virchow's (supraclavicular) lymph node
Lymphatic, Right Upper Extremity	**Includes:** Cubital lymph node Deltopectoral (infraclavicular) lymph node Epitrochlear lymph node Infraclavicular (deltopectoral) lymph node Supratrochlear lymph node
Lymphatic, Thorax	**Includes:** Intercostal lymph node Mediastinal lymph node Parasternal lymph node Paratracheal lymph node Tracheobronchial lymph node

(*Continues*)

Character 4 - Body Part (*Continued*)

Mandible, Left Mandible, Right	**Includes:** Alveolar process of mandible Condyloid process Mandibular notch Mental foramen
Mastoid Sinus, Left Mastoid Sinus, Right	**Includes:** Mastoid air cells
Maxilla, Left Maxilla, Right	**Includes:** Alveolar process of maxilla
Maxillary Sinus, Left Maxillary Sinus, Right	**Includes:** Antrum of Highmore
Median Nerve	**Includes:** Anterior interosseous nerve Palmar cutaneous nerve
Medulla Oblongata	**Includes:** Myelencephalon
Mesentery	**Includes:** Mesoappendix Mesocolon
Metacarpocarpal Joint, Left Metacarpocarpal Joint, Right	**Includes:** Carpometacarpal (CMC) joint
Metatarsal-Phalangeal Joint, Left Metatarsal-Phalangeal Joint, Right	**Includes:** Metatarsophalangeal (MTP) joint
Metatarsal-Tarsal Joint, Left Metatarsal-Tarsal Joint, Right	**Includes:** Tarsometatarsal joint
Middle Ear, Left Middle Ear, Right	**Includes:** Tympanic cavity
Minor Salivary Gland	**Includes:** Anterior lingual gland

(*Continues*)

Character 4 - Body Part (*Continued*)

Mitral Valve	**Includes:** Bicuspid valve Left atrioventricular valve Mitral annulus
Nasal Bone	**Includes:** Vomer of nasal septum
Nasal Septum	**Includes:** Quadrangular cartilage Septal cartilage Vomer bone
Nasal Turbinate	**Includes:** Inferior turbinate Middle turbinate Nasal concha Superior turbinate
Nasopharynx	**Includes:** Choana Fossa of Rosenmuller Pharyngeal recess Rhinopharynx
Neck Muscle, Left Neck Muscle, Right	**Includes:** Anterior vertebral muscle Arytenoid muscle Cricothyroid muscle Infrahyoid muscle Levator scapulae muscle Platysma muscle Scalene muscle Splenius cervicis muscle Sternocleidomastoid muscle Suprahyoid muscle Thyroarytenoid muscle

(*Continues*)

Character 4 - Body Part (*Continued*)

Nipple, Left Nipple, Right	**Includes:** Areola
Nose	**Includes:** Columella External naris Greater alar cartilage Internal naris Lateral nasal cartilage Lesser alar cartilage Nasal cavity Nostril
Occipital Bone, Left Occipital Bone, Right	**Includes:** Foramen magnum
Oculomotor Nerve	**Includes:** Third cranial nerve
Olfactory Nerve	**Includes:** First cranial nerve Olfactory bulb
Optic Nerve	**Includes:** Optic chiasma Second cranial nerve
Orbit, Left Orbit, Right	**Includes:** Bony orbit Orbital portion of ethmoid bone Orbital portion of frontal bone Orbital portion of lacrimal bone Orbital portion of maxilla Orbital portion of palatine bone Orbital portion of sphenoid bone Orbital portion of zygomatic bone
Pancreatic Duct	**Includes:** Duct of Wirsung

(*Continues*

Character 4 - Body Part (*Continued*)

Pancreatic Duct, Accessory	**Includes:** Duct of Santorini
Parotid Duct, Left Parotid Duct, Right	**Includes:** Stensen's duct
Pelvic Bone, Left Pelvic Bone, Right	**Includes:** Iliac crest Ilium Ischium Pubis
Pelvic Cavity	**Includes:** Retropubic space
Penis	**Includes:** Corpus cavernosum Corpus spongiosum
Perineum Muscle	**Includes:** Bulbospongiosus muscle Cremaster muscle Deep transverse perineal muscle Ischiocavernosus muscle Superficial transverse perineal muscle
Peritoneum	**Includes:** Epiploic foramen
Peroneal Artery, Left Peroneal Artery, Right	**Includes:** Fibular artery
Peroneal Nerve	**Includes:** Common fibular nerve Common peroneal nerve External popliteal nerve Lateral sural cutaneous nerve

(*Continues*)

Character 4 - Body Part (*Continued*)

Pharynx	**Includes:** Hypopharynx Laryngopharynx Oropharynx Piriform recess (sinus)
Phrenic Nerve	**Includes:** Accessory phrenic nerve
Pituitary Gland	**Includes:** Adenohypophysis Hypophysis Neurohypophysis
Pons	**Includes:** Apneustic center Basis pontis Locus ceruleus Pneumotaxic center Pontine tegmentum Superior olivary nucleus
Popliteal Artery, Left Popliteal Artery, Right	**Includes:** Inferior genicular artery Middle genicular artery Superior genicular artery Sural artery
Portal Vein	**Includes:** Hepatic portal vein
Prepuce	**Includes:** Foreskin Glans penis
Pudendal Nerve	**Includes:** Posterior labial nerve Posterior scrotal nerve

(Continues

Character 4 - Body Part (*Continued*)

Pulmonary Artery, Left	**Includes:** Arterial canal (duct) Botallo's duct Pulmoaortic canal
Pulmonary Valve	**Includes:** Pulmonary annulus Pulmonic valve
Pulmonary Vein, Left	**Includes:** Left inferior pulmonary vein Left superior pulmonary vein
Pulmonary Vein, Right	**Includes:** Right inferior pulmonary vein Right superior pulmonary vein
Radial Artery, Left Radial Artery, Right	**Includes:** Radial recurrent artery
Radial Nerve	**Includes:** Dorsal digital nerve Musculospiral nerve Palmar cutaneous nerve Posterior interosseous nerve
Radius, Left Radius, Right	**Includes:** Ulnar notch
Rectum	**Includes:** Anorectal junction
Renal Artery, Left Renal Artery, Right	**Includes:** Inferior suprarenal artery Renal segmental artery
Renal Vein, Left	**Includes:** Left inferior phrenic vein Left ovarian vein Left second lumbar vein

(*Continues*)

Character 4 - Body Part (*Continued*)

	Left suprarenal vein Left testicular vein
Retina, Left Retina, Right	**Includes:** Fovea Macula Optic disc
Retroperitoneum	**Includes:** Retroperitoneal space
Sacral Plexus	**Includes:** Inferior gluteal nerve Posterior femoral cutaneous nerve Pudendal nerve
Sacral Sympathetic Nerve	**Includes:** Ganglion impar (ganglion of Walther) Pelvic splanchnic nerve Sacral ganglion Sacral splanchnic nerve
Sacrococcygeal Joint	**Includes:** Sacrococcygeal symphysis
Scapula, Left Scapula, Right	**Includes:** Acromion (process) Coracoid process
Sciatic Nerve	**Includes:** Ischiatic nerve
Shoulder Bursa and Ligament, Left Shoulder Bursa and Ligament, Right	**Includes:** Acromioclavicular ligament Coracoacromial ligament Coracoclavicular ligament Coracohumeral ligament Costoclavicular ligament Glenohumeral ligament

(*Continues*)

Character 4 - Body Part (*Continued*)

	Glenoid ligament (labrum) Interclavicular ligament Sternoclavicular ligament Subacromial bursa Transverse humeral ligament Transverse scapular ligament
Shoulder Joint, Left Shoulder Joint, Right	**Includes:** Glenohumeral joint
Shoulder Muscle, Left Shoulder Muscle, Right	**Includes:** Deltoid muscle Infraspinatus muscle Subscapularis muscle Supraspinatus muscle Teres major muscle Teres minor muscle
Sigmoid Colon	**Includes:** Rectosigmoid junction Sigmoid flexure
Skin	**Includes:** Dermis Epidermis Sebaceous gland Sweat gland
Sphenoid Bone, Left Sphenoid Bone, Right	**Includes:** Greater wing Lesser wing Optic foramen Pterygoid process Sella turcica
Spinal Canal	**Includes:** Vertebral canal
Spinal Cord	**Includes:** Denticulate ligament

(*Continues*)

Character 4 - Body Part (*Continued*)

Spinal Meninges	**Includes:** Arachnoid mater Leptomeninges Pia mater
Spleen	**Includes:** Accessory spleen
Splenic Artery	**Includes:** Left gastroepiploic artery Pancreatic artery Short gastric artery
Splenic Vein	**Includes:** Left gastroepiploic vein Pancreatic vein
Sternum	**Includes:** Manubrium Suprasternal notch Xiphoid process
Stomach, Pylorus	**Includes:** Pyloric antrum Pyloric canal Pyloric sphincter
Subarachnoid Space	**Includes:** Cranial subarachnoid space Spinal subarachnoid space
Subclavian Artery, Left Subclavian Artery, Right	**Includes:** Costocervical trunk Dorsal scapular artery Internal thoracic artery
Subcutaneous Tissue and Fascia, Scalp	**Includes:** Galea aponeurotica

(Continues)

Character 4 - Body Part (*Continued*)

Subcutaneous Tissue and Fascia, Face	**Includes:** Masseteric fascia Orbital fascia
Subcutaneous Tissue and Fascia, Anterior Neck	**Includes:** Deep cervical fascia Pretracheal fascia
Subcutaneous Tissue and Fascia, Posterior Neck	**Includes:** Prevertebral fascia
Subcutaneous Tissue and Fascia, Chest	**Includes:** Pectoral fascia
Subcutaneous Tissue and Fascia, Right Upper Arm Subcutaneous Tissue and Fascia, Left Upper Arm	**Includes:** Axillary fascia Deltoid fascia Infraspinatus fascia Subscapular aponeurosis Supraspinatus fascia
Subcutaneous Tissue and Fascia, Right Lower Arm Subcutaneous Tissue and Fascia, Left Lower Arm	**Includes:** Antebrachial fascia Bicipital aponeurosis
Subcutaneous Tissue and Fascia, Right Hand Subcutaneous Tissue and Fascia, Left Hand	**Includes:** Palmar fascia (aponeurosis)
Subcutaneous Tissue and Fascia, Right Upper Leg Subcutaneous Tissue and Fascia, Left Upper Leg	**Includes:** Crural fascia Fascia lata Iliac fascia Iliotibial tract (band)
Subcutaneous Tissue and Fascia, Right Foot Subcutaneous Tissue and Fascia, Left Foot	**Includes:** Plantar fascia (aponeurosis)

(*Continues*)

Character 4 - Body Part (*Continued*)

Subcutaneous Tissue and Fascia, Trunk	**Includes:** External oblique aponeurosis Transversalis fascia
Subdural Space	**Includes:** Cranial subdural space Spinal subdural space
Submaxillary Gland, Left Submaxillary Gland, Right	**Includes:** Submandibular gland
Superior Mesenteric Artery	**Includes:** Ileal artery Ileocolic artery Inferior pancreaticoduodenal artery Jejunal artery
Superior Mesenteric Vein	**Includes:** Right gastroepiploic vein
Superior Vena Cava	**Includes:** Precava
Tarsal Joint, Left Tarsal Joint, Right	**Includes:** Calcaneocuboid joint Cuboideonavicular joint Cuneonavicular joint Intercuneiform joint Subtalar (talocalcaneal) joint Talocalcaneal (subtalar) joint Talocalcaneonavicular joint
Tarsal, Left Tarsal, Right	**Includes:** Calcaneus Cuboid bone

(*Continues*

Character 4 - Body Part (*Continued*)

	Intermediate cuneiform bone Lateral cuneiform bone Medial cuneiform bone Navicular bone Talus bone
Temporal Artery, Left Temporal Artery, Right	**Includes:** Middle temporal artery Superficial temporal artery Transverse facial artery
Temporal Bone, Left Temporal Bone, Right	**Includes:** Mastoid process Petrous part of temoporal bone Tympanic part of temoporal bone Zygomatic process of temporal bone
Thalamus	**Includes:** Epithalamus Geniculate nucleus Metathalamus Pulvinar
Thoracic Aorta	**Includes:** Aortic arch Aortic intercostal artery Ascending aorta Bronchial artery Esophageal artery Subcostal artery
Thoracic Duct	**Includes:** Left jugular trunk Left subclavian trunk
Thoracic Nerve	**Includes:** Intercostal nerve Intercostobrachial nerve Subcostal nerve

(*Continues*)

Character 4 - Body Part (*Continued*)

Thoracic Sympathetic Nerve	**Includes:** Cardiac plexus Esophageal plexus Greater splanchnic nerve Inferior cardiac nerve Least splanchnic nerve Lesser splanchnic nerve Middle cardiac nerve Pulmonary plexus Superior cardiac nerve Thoracic aortic plexus Thoracic ganglion
Thoracic Vertebra	**Includes:** Spinous process Vertebral arch Vertebral foramen Vertebral lamina Vertebral pedicle
Thoracic Vertebral Joint Thoracic Vertebral Joints, 2 to 7 Thoracic Vertebral Joints, eight or more	**Includes:** Costotransverse joint Costovertebral joint Thoracic facet joint
Thoracolumbar Vertebral Joint	**Includes:** Thoracolumbar facet joint
Thorax Bursa and Ligament, Left Thorax Bursa and Ligament, Right	**Includes:** Costotransverse ligament Costoxiphoid ligament Sternocostal ligament
Thorax Muscle, Left Thorax Muscle, Right	**Includes:** Intercostal muscle Levatores costarum muscle

(*Continues*

Character 4 - Body Part (*Continued*)

	Pectoralis major muscle Pectoralis minor muscle Serratus anterior muscle Subclavius muscle Subcostal muscle Transverse thoracis muscle
Thymus	**Includes:** Thymus gland
Thyroid Artery, Left Thyroid Artery, Right	**Includes:** Cricothyroid artery Hyoid artery Sternocleidomastoid artery Superior laryngeal artery Superior thyroid artery Thyrocervical trunk
Tibia, Left Tibia, Right	**Includes:** Lateral condyle of tibia Medial condyle of tibia Medial malleolus
Tibial Nerve	**Includes:** Lateral plantar nerve Medial plantar nerve Medial popliteal nerve Medial sural cutaneous nerve
Toe Nail	**Includes:** Nail bed Nail plate
Toe Phalangeal Joint, Left Toe Phalangeal Joint, Right	**Includes:** Interphalangeal (IP) joint
Tongue	**Includes:** Frenulum linguae Lingual tonsil

(*Continues*)

Character 4 - Body Part (*Continued*)

Tongue, Palate, Pharynx Muscle	**Includes:** Chondroglossus muscle Genioglossus muscle Hyoglossus muscle Inferior longitudinal muscle Levator veli palatini muscle Palatoglossal muscle Palatopharyngeal muscle Pharyngeal constrictor muscle Salpingopharyngeus muscle Styloglossus muscle Stylopharyngeus muscle Superior longitudinal muscle Tensor veli palatini muscle
Tonsils	**Includes:** Palatine tonsil
Transverse Colon	**Includes:** Splenic flexure
Tricuspid Valve	**Includes:** Right atrioventricular valve Tricuspid annulus
Trigeminal Nerve	**Includes:** Fifth cranial nerve Gasserian ganglion Mandibular nerve Maxillary nerve Ophthalmic nerve Trifacial nerve
Trochlear Nerve	**Includes:** Fourth cranial nerve

(*Continues*

Character 4 - Body Part (*Continued*)

Trunk Bursa and Ligament, Left Trunk Bursa and Ligament, Right	**Includes:** Iliolumbar ligament Interspinous ligament Intertransverse ligament Ligamentum flavum Pubic ligament Sacrococcygeal ligament Sacroiliac ligament Sacrospinous ligament Sacrotuberous ligament Supraspinous ligament
Trunk Muscle, Left Trunk Muscle, Right	**Includes:** Coccygeus muscle Erector spinae muscle Interspinalis muscle Intertransversarius muscle Latissimus dorsi muscle Levator ani muscle Quadratus lumborum muscle Rhomboid major muscle Rhomboid minor muscle Serratus posterior muscle Transversospinalis muscle Trapezius muscle
Tympanic Membrane, Left Tympanic Membrane, Right	**Includes:** Pars flaccida
Ulna, Left Ulna, Right	**Includes:** Olecranon process Radial notch
Ulnar Artery, Left Ulnar Artery, Right	**Includes:** Anterior ulnar recurrent artery Common interosseous artery Posterior ulnar recurrent artery

(*Continues*)

Character 4 - Body Part (*Continued*)

Ulnar Nerve	**Includes:** Cubital nerve
Upper Arm Muscle, Left Upper Arm Muscle, Right	**Includes:** Biceps brachii muscle Brachialis muscle Coracobrachialis muscle Triceps brachii muscle
Upper Eyelid, Left Upper Eyelid, Right	**Includes:** Lateral canthus Levator palpebrae superioris muscle Orbicularis oculi muscle Superior tarsal plate
Upper Femur, Left Upper Femur, Right	**Includes:** Femoral head Greater trochanter Lesser trochanter Neck of femur
Upper Leg Muscle, Left Upper Leg Muscle, Right	**Includes:** Adductor brevis muscle Adductor longus muscle Adductor magnus muscle Biceps femoris muscle Gracilis muscle Pectineus muscle Quadriceps (femoris) Rectus femoris muscle Sartorius muscle Semimembranosus muscle Semitendinosus muscle Vastus intermedius muscle Vastus lateralis muscle Vastus medialis muscle

(*Continues*)

Character 4 - Body Part (*Continued*)

Upper Lip	**Includes:** Frenulum labii superioris Vermilion border
Ureter Ureter, Left Ureter, Right Ureters, Bilateral	**Includes:** Ureteral orifice Ureterovesical orifice
Urethra	**Includes:** Bulbourethral (Cowper's) gland Cowper's (bulbourethral) gland External urethral sphincter Internal urethral sphincter Membranous urethra Penile urethra Prostatic urethra
Uterine Supporting Structure	**Includes:** Broad ligament Infundibulopelvic ligament Ovarian ligament Round ligament of uterus
Uterus	**Includes:** Fundus uteri Myometrium Perimetrium Uterine cornu
Uvula	**Includes:** Palatine uvula
Vagus Nerve	**Includes:** Anterior vagal trunk Pharyngeal plexus Pneumogastric nerve Posterior vagal trunk

(*Continues*)

Character 4 - Body Part (*Continued*)

	Pulmonary plexus Recurrent laryngeal nerve Superior laryngeal nerve Tenth cranial nerve
Vas Deferens Vas Deferens, Bilateral Vas Deferens, Left Vas Deferens, Right	**Includes:** Ductus deferens Ejaculatory duct
Ventricle, Right	**Includes:** Conus arteriosus
Ventricular Septum	**Includes:** Interventricular septum
Vertebral Artery, Left Vertebral Artery, Right	**Includes:** Anterior spinal artery Posterior spinal artery
Vertebral Vein, Left Vertebral Vein, Right	**Includes:** Deep cervical vein Suboccipital venous plexus
Vestibular Gland	**Includes:** Bartholin's (greater vestibular) gland Greater vestibular (Bartholin's) gland Paraurethral (Skene's) gland Skene's (paraurethral) gland
Vitreous, Left Vitreous, Right	**Includes:** Vitreous body
Vocal Cord, Left Vocal Cord, Right	**Includes:** Vocal fold
Vulva	**Includes:** Labia majora Labia minora

(*Continues*)

Character 4 - Body Part (*Continued*)

Wrist Bursa and Ligament, Left Wrist Bursa and Ligament, Right	**Includes:** Palmar ulnocarpal ligament Radial collateral carpal ligament Radiocarpal ligament Radioulnar ligament Ulnar collateral carpal ligament
Wrist Joint, Left Wrist Joint, Right	**Includes:** Distal radioulnar joint Radiocarpal joint

Appendix E: ICD-10-PCS Coding Guidelines

ICD-10-PCS Coding Guidelines

Table of Contents

Conventions

A1
ICD-10-PCS codes are composed of seven characters. Each character is an axis of classification that specifies information about the procedure performed. Within a defined code range, a character specifies the same type of information in that axis of classification.
Example: The fifth axis of classification specifies the approach in sections 0 through 4 and 7 through 9 of the system.

A2
One of 34 possible values can be assigned to each axis of classification in the seven-character code: they are the numbers 0 through 9 and the alphabet (except I and O because they are easily confused with the numbers 1 and 0). The number of unique values used in an axis of classification differs as needed.
Example: Where the fifth axis of classification specifies the approach, seven different approach values are currently used to specify the approach.

A3
The valid values for an axis of classification can be added to as needed.
Example: If a significantly distinct type of device is used in a new procedure, a new device value can be added to the system.

A4
As with words in their context, the meaning of any single value is a combination of its axis of classification and any preceding values on which it may be dependent.
Example: The meaning of a body part value in the Medical and Surgical section is always dependent on the body system value. The body part value 0 in the Central Nervous body system specifies Brain and the body part value 0 in the Peripheral Nervous body system specifies Cervical Plexus.

A5
As the system is expanded to become increasingly detailed, over time more values will depend on preceding values for their meaning.
Example: In the Lower Joints body system, the device value 3 in the root operation Insertion specifies Infusion Device and the device value 3 in the root operation Fusion specifies Interbody Fusion Device.

A6
The purpose of the alphabetic index is to locate the appropriate table that contains all information necessary to construct a procedure code. The PCS Tables should always be consulted to find the most appropriate valid code.

A7
It is not required to consult the index first before proceeding to the tables to complete the code. A valid code may be chosen directly from the tables.

A8
All seven characters must be specified to be a valid code. If the documentation is incomplete for coding purposes, the physician should be queried for the necessary information.

A9
Within a PCS table, valid codes include all combinations of choices in characters 4 through 7 contained in the same row of the table. In the example below, 0JHT3VZ is a valid code, and 0JHW3VZ is *not* a valid code.

Section: 0 Medical and Surgical
Body System: J Subcutaneous Tissue and Fascia
Operation: H Insertion: Putting in a nonbiological appliance that monitors, assists, performs, or prevents a physiological function but does not physically take the place of a body part

Body Part	Approach	Device	Qualifier
S Subcutaneous Tissue and Fascia, Head and Neck V Subcutaneous Tissue and Fascia, Upper Extremity W Subcutaneous Tissue and Fascia, Lower Extremity	0 Open 3 Percutaneous	1 Radioactive Element 3 Infusion Device	Z No Qualifier
T Subcutaneous Tissue and Fascia, Trunk	0 Open 3 Percutaneous	1 Radioactive Element 3 Infusion Device V Infusion Pump	Z No Qualifier

A10
"And," when used in a code description, means "and/or."
Example: Lower Arm and Wrist Muscle means lower arm and/or wrist muscle.

A11
Many of the terms used to construct PCS codes are defined within the system. It is the coder's responsibility to determine what the documentation in the medical record equates to in the PCS definitions. The physician is not expected to use the terms used in PCS

code descriptions, nor is the coder required to query the physician when the correlation between the documentation and the defined PCS terms is clear.

Example: When the physician documents "partial resection" the coder can independently correlate "partial resection" to the root operation Excision without querying the physician for clarification.

Medical and Surgical Section Guidelines (section 0)

B2. Body System

General guidelines
B2.1a
The procedure codes in the general anatomical regions body systems should only be used when the procedure is performed on an anatomical region rather than a specific body part (e.g., root operations Control and Detachment, drainage of a body cavity) or on the rare occasion when no information is available to support assignment of a code to a specific body part.
Example: Control of postoperative hemorrhage is coded to the root operation Control found in the general anatomical regions body systems.

B2.1b
Body systems designated as upper or lower contain body parts located above or below the diaphragm respectively.
Example: Vein body parts above the diaphragm are found in the Upper Veins body system; vein body parts below the diaphragm are found in the Lower Veins body system.

B3. Root Operation

General guidelines
B3.1a
In order to determine the appropriate root operation, the full definition of the root operation as contained in the PCS Tables must be applied.

B3.1b
Components of a procedure specified in the root operation definition and explanation are not coded separately. Procedural steps necessary to reach the operative site and close the operative site are also not coded separately.
Example: Resection of a joint as part of a joint replacement procedure is included in the root operation definition of Replacement and is not coded separately. Laparotomy performed to reach the site of an open liver biopsy is not coded separately.

Multiple procedures
B3.2
During the same operative episode, multiple procedures are coded if:
a. The same root operation is performed on different body parts as defined by distinct values of the body part character.
Example: Diagnostic excision of liver and pancreas are coded separately.
b. The same root operation is repeated at different body sites that are included in the same body part value.
Example: Excision of the sartorius muscle and excision of the gracilis muscle are both included in the upper leg muscle body part value, and multiple procedures are coded.
c. Multiple root operations with distinct objectives are performed on the same body part.
Example: Destruction of sigmoid lesion and bypass of sigmoid colon are coded separately.
d. The intended root operation is attempted using one approach, but is converted to a different approach.
Example: Laparoscopic cholecystectomy converted to an open cholecystectomy is coded as percutaneous endoscopic Inspection and open Resection.

Discontinued procedures
B3.3
If the intended procedure is discontinued, code the procedure to the root operation performed. If a procedure is discontinued before any other root operation is performed, code the root operation Inspection of the body part or anatomical region inspected.
Example: A planned aortic valve replacement procedure is discontinued after the initial thoracotomy and before any incision is made in the heart muscle, when the patient becomes hemodynamically unstable. This procedure is coded as an open Inspection of the mediastinum.

Biopsy followed by more definitive treatment
B3.4
If a diagnostic Excision, Extraction, or Drainage procedure (biopsy) is followed by a more definitive procedure, such as Destruction, Excision or Resection at the same procedure site, both the biopsy and the more definitive treatment are coded.
Example: Biopsy of breast followed by partial mastectomy at the same procedure site, both the biopsy and the partial mastectomy procedure are coded.

Overlapping body layers
B3.5
If the root operations Excision, Repair or Inspection are performed on overlapping layers of the musculoskeletal system, the body part specifying the deepest layer is coded.
Example: Excisional debridement that includes skin and subcutaneous tissue and muscle is coded to the muscle body part.

Bypass procedures
B3.6a
Bypass procedures are coded by identifying the body part bypassed "from" and the body part bypassed "to." The fourth character body part specifies the body part bypassed from, and the qualifier specifies the body part bypassed to.
Example: Bypass from stomach to jejunum, stomach is the body part and jejunum is the qualifier.

B3.6b
Coronary arteries are classified by number of distinct sites treated, rather than number of coronary arteries or anatomic name of a coronary artery (e.g., left anterior descending). Coronary artery bypass procedures are coded differently than other bypass procedures as described in the previous guideline. Rather than identifying the body part bypassed from, the body part identifies the number of coronary artery sites bypassed to, and the qualifier specifies the vessel bypassed from.
Example: Aortocoronary artery bypass of one site on the left anterior descending coronary artery and one site on the obtuse marginal coronary artery is classified in the body part axis of classification as two coronary artery sites and the qualifier specifies the aorta as the body part bypassed from.

B3.6c
If multiple coronary artery sites are bypassed, a separate procedure is coded for each coronary artery site that uses a different device and/or qualifier.
Example: Aortocoronary artery bypass and internal mammary coronary artery bypass are coded separately.

Control vs. more definitive root operations
B3.7
The root operation Control is defined as, "Stopping, or attempting to stop, postprocedural bleeding." If an attempt to stop postprocedural bleeding is initially unsuccessful, and to stop the bleeding requires performing any of the definitive root operations Bypass,

Detachment, Excision, Extraction, Reposition, Replacement, or Resection, then that root operation is coded instead of Control.
Example: Resection of spleen to stop postprocedural bleeding is coded to Resection instead of Control.

Excision vs. Resection
B3.8
PCS contains specific body parts for anatomical subdivisions of a body part, such as lobes of the lungs or liver and regions of the intestine. Resection of the specific body part is coded whenever all of the body part is cut out or off, rather than coding Excision of a less specific body part.
Example: Left upper lung lobectomy is coded to Resection of Upper Lung Lobe, Left rather than Excision of Lung, Left.

Excision for graft
B3.9
If an autograft is obtained from a different body part in order to complete the objective of the procedure, a separate procedure is coded.
Example: Coronary bypass with excision of saphenous vein graft, excision of saphenous vein is coded separately.

Fusion procedures of the spine
B3.10a
The body part coded for a spinal vertebral joint(s) rendered immobile by a spinal fusion procedure is classified by the level of the spine (e.g. thoracic). There are distinct body part values for a single vertebral joint and for multiple vertebral joints at each spinal level.
Example: Body part values specify Lumbar Vertebral Joint, Lumbar Vertebral Joints, 2 or More and Lumbosacral Vertebral Joint.

B3.10b
If multiple vertebral joints are fused, a separate procedure is coded for each vertebral joint that uses a different device and/or qualifier.
Example: Fusion of lumbar vertebral joint, posterior approach, anterior column and fusion of lumbar vertebral joint, posterior approach, posterior column are coded separately.

B3.10c
Combinations of devices and materials are often used on a vertebral joint to render the joint immobile. When combinations of devices are used on the same vertebral joint, the device value coded for the procedure is as follows:

- If an interbody fusion device is used to render the joint immobile (alone or containing other material like bone graft), the procedure is coded with the device value Interbody Fusion Device

- If bone graft is the *only* device used to render the joint immobile, the procedure is coded with the device value Nonautologous Tissue Substitute or Autologous Tissue Substitute
- If a mixture of autologous and nonautologous bone graft (with or without biological or synthetic extenders or binders) is used to render the joint immobile, code the procedure with the device value Autologous Tissue Substitute

Examples: Fusion of a vertebral joint using a cage style interbody fusion device containing morsellized bone graft is coded to the device Interbody Fusion Device.
Fusion of a vertebral joint using a bone dowel interbody fusion device made of cadaver bone and packed with a mixture of local morsellized bone and demineralized bone matrix is coded to the device Interbody Fusion Device.
Fusion of a vertebral joint using both autologous bone graft and bone bank bone graft is coded to the device Autologous Tissue Substitute.

Inspection procedures

B3.11a
Inspection of a body part(s) performed in order to achieve the objective of a procedure is not coded separately.
Example: Fiberoptic bronchoscopy performed for irrigation of bronchus, only the irrigation procedure is coded.

B3.11b
If multiple tubular body parts are inspected, the most distal body part inspected is coded. If multiple non-tubular body parts in a region are inspected, the body part that specifies the entire area inspected is coded.
Examples: Cystoureteroscopy with inspection of bladder and ureters is coded to the ureter body part value.
Exploratory laparotomy with general inspection of abdominal contents is coded to the peritoneal cavity body part value.

B3.11c
When both an Inspection procedure and another procedure are performed on the same body part during the same episode, if the Inspection procedure is performed using a different approach than the other procedure, the Inspection procedure is coded separately.
Example: Endoscopic Inspection of the duodenum is coded separately when open Excision of the duodenum is performed during the same procedural episode.

Occlusion vs. Restriction for vessel embolization procedures

B3.12
If the objective of an embolization procedure is to completely close a vessel, the root operation Occlusion is coded. If the objective of an embolization procedure is to narrow the lumen of a vessel, the root operation Restriction is coded.
Examples: Tumor embolization is coded to the root operation Occlusion, because the objective of the procedure is to cut off the blood supply to the vessel.

Embolization of a cerebral aneurysm is coded to the root operation Restriction, because the objective of the procedure is not to close off the vessel entirely, but to narrow the lumen of the vessel at the site of the aneurysm where it is abnormally wide.

Release procedures
B3.13
In the root operation Release, the body part value coded is the body part being freed and not the tissue being manipulated or cut to free the body part.
Example: Lysis of intestinal adhesions is coded to the specific intestine body part value.

Release vs. Division
B3.14
If the sole objective of the procedure is freeing a body part without cutting the body part, the root operation is Release. If the sole objective of the procedure is separating or transecting a body part, the root operation is Division.
Examples: Freeing a nerve root from surrounding scar tissue to relieve pain is coded to the root operation Release. Severing a nerve root to relieve pain is coded to the root operation Division.

Reposition for fracture treatment
B3.15
Reduction of a displaced fracture is coded to the root operation Reposition and the application of a cast or splint in conjunction with the Reposition procedure is not coded separately. Treatment of a nondisplaced fracture is coded to the procedure performed.
Examples: Putting a pin in a nondisplaced fracture is coded to the root operation Insertion.
Casting of a nondisplaced fracture is coded to the root operation Immobilization in the Placement section.

Transplantation vs. Administration
B3.16
Putting in a mature and functioning living body part taken from another individual or animal is coded to the root operation Transplantation. Putting in autologous or nonautologous cells is coded to the Administration section.
Example: Putting in autologous or nonautologous bone marrow,
pancreatic islet cells or stem cells is coded to the Administration section.

B4. Body Part

General guidelines
B4.1a
If a procedure is performed on a portion of a body part that does not have a separate body part value, code the body part value corresponding to the whole body part.
Example: A procedure performed on the alveolar process of the mandible is coded to the mandible body part.

B4.1b
If the prefix "peri" is combined with a body part to identify the site of the procedure, the procedure is coded to the body part named.
Example: A procedure site identified as perirenal is coded to the kidney body part.

Branches of body parts
B4.2
Where a specific branch of a body part does not have its own body part value in PCS, the body part is coded to the closest proximal branch that has a specific body part value.
Example: A procedure performed on the mandibular branch of the trigeminal nerve is coded to the trigeminal nerve body part value

Bilateral body part values
B4.3
Bilateral body part values are available for a limited number of body parts. If the identical procedure is performed on contralateral body parts, and a bilateral body part value exists for that body part, a single procedure is coded using the bilateral body part value. If no bilateral body part value exists, each procedure is coded separately using the appropriate body part value.
Example: The identical procedure performed on both fallopian tubes is coded once using the body part value Fallopian Tube, Bilateral. The identical procedure performed on both knee joints is coded twice using the body part values Knee Joint, Right and Knee Joint, Left.

Coronary arteries
B4.4
The coronary arteries are classified as a single body part that is further specified by number of sites treated and not by name or number of arteries. Separate body part values are used to specify the number of sites treated when the same procedure is performed on multiple sites in the coronary arteries.
Examples: Angioplasty of two distinct sites in the left anterior descending coronary artery with placement of two stents is coded as Dilation of Coronary Arteries, Two Sites, with Intraluminal Device.
Angioplasty of two distinct sites in the left anterior descending coronary artery, one with stent placed and one without, is coded separately as Dilation of Coronary Artery, One Site with Intraluminal Device, and Dilation of Coronary Artery, One Site with no device.

Tendons, ligaments, bursae and fascia near a joint

B4.5

Procedures performed on tendons, ligaments, bursae and fascia supporting a joint are coded to the body part in the respective body system that is the focus of the procedure. Procedures performed on joint structures themselves are coded to the body part in the joint body systems.

Example: Repair of the anterior cruciate ligament of the knee is coded to the knee bursae and ligament body part in the bursae and ligaments body system. Knee arthroscopy with shaving of articular cartilage is coded to the knee joint body part in the Lower Joints body system.

Skin, subcutaneous tissue and fascia overlying a joint

B4.6

If a procedure is performed on the skin, subcutaneous tissue or fascia overlying a joint, the procedure is coded to the following body part:

- Shoulder is coded to Upper Arm
- Elbow is coded to Lower Arm
- Wrist is coded to Lower Arm
- Hip is coded to Upper Leg
- Knee is coded to Lower Leg
- Ankle is coded to Foot

Fingers and toes

B4.7

If a body system does not contain a separate body part value for fingers, procedures performed on the fingers are coded to the body part value for the hand. If a body system does not contain a separate body part value for toes, procedures performed on the toes are coded to the body part value for the foot.

Example: Excision of finger muscle is coded to one of the hand muscle body part values in the Muscles body system.

B5. Approach

Open approach with percutaneous endoscopic assistance
B5.2
Procedures performed using the open approach with percutaneous endoscopic assistance are coded to the approach Open.
Example: Laparoscopic-assisted sigmoidectomy is coded to the approach Open.

External approach
B5.3a
Procedures performed within an orifice on structures that are visible without the aid of any instrumentation are coded to the approach External.
Example: Resection of tonsils is coded to the approach External.

B5.3b
Procedures performed indirectly by the application of external force through the intervening body layers are coded to the approach External.
Example: Closed reduction of fracture is coded to the approach External.

Percutaneous procedure via device
B5.4
Procedures performed percutaneously via a device placed for the procedure are coded to the approach Percutaneous.
Example: Fragmentation of kidney stone performed via percutaneous nephrostomy is coded to the approach Percutaneous.

B6. Device

General guidelines

B6.1a

A device is coded only if a device remains after the procedure is completed. If no device remains, the device value No Device is coded.

B6.1b

Materials such as sutures, ligatures, radiological markers and temporary post-operative wound drains are considered integral to the performance of a procedure and are not coded as devices.

B6.1c

Procedures performed on a device only and not on a body part are specified in the root operations Change, Irrigation, Removal and Revision, and are coded to the procedure performed.

Example: Irrigation of percutaneous nephrostomy tube is coded to the root operation Irrigation of indwelling device in the Administration section.

Drainage device

B6.2

A separate procedure to put in a drainage device is coded to the root operation Drainage with the device value Drainage Device.

Obstetric Section Guidelines (section 1)

C. Obstetrics Section

Products of conception

C1

Procedures performed on the products of conception are coded to the Obstetrics section. Procedures performed on the pregnant female other than the products of conception are coded to the appropriate root operation in the Medical and Surgical section.

Example: Amniocentesis is coded to the products of conception body part in the Obstetrics section. Repair of obstetric urethral laceration is coded to the urethra body part in the Medical and Surgical section.

Procedures following delivery or abortion

C2

Procedures performed following a delivery or abortion for curettage of the endometrium or evacuation of retained products of conception are all coded in the Obstetrics section, to the root operation Extraction and the body part Products of Conception, Retained. Diagnostic or therapeutic dilation and curettage performed during times other than the postpartum or post-abortion period are all coded in the Medical and Surgical section, to the root operation Extraction and the body part Endometrium.